Horse Racing & Rock 'N' Roll

How America's Live Music Capital

Tripped Out, Cowboyed Up and Shook the World

A Backstage Memoir by

Woody Roberts

PRESS

709

with

TREATY OAK PUBLISHERS

Published by
PRESS
709

Produced by
TREATY OAK PUBLISHERS
www.treatyoakpublishers.com
ISBN: 978-1-943658-40-4

TO

Doug Sahm, the man who introduced me to San Antonio.

Eddie Wilson, the man who introduced me to Austin... and became my brother.

Each generation creates new heroes. Therefore, the chronicler, passing one account to another, changes characters and narrative.

Anatoly T. Fomenko,

HISTORY: FICTION OR SCIENCE?

CONTENTS

The Armadillo and Willie Nelson

Snapshots of a Music Capital

Movies and Games Austin Style

Manor Downs and Stevie Ray Vaughan

FOREWORD

Thinking of who might write the foreword to *HORSE RACING &
ROCK 'N' ROLL*, I put Margaret Moser at the head of my shortlist. Queen
of the Austin music writers. Different from all the others, Margaret
was not another chronicler writing reports from the outside. She was
a part of the scene and writing from the inside. I've not known anyone
who loved the music and those who make it more than Margaret. She
hung with the bands and befriended musicians young and old.

Margaret had once asked to interview me so I thought possibly
she would consent. Not realizing how terribly far her cancer had
progressed, I sent my request off in an email. Under hospice care she
replied right away:

> *YES. I have been trying to formulate the same thing, asking
> you to talk to me so. Yes. Yes yes yes. I have limited time and
> will happily give it all to you. I live off Kings Court on
> Valentino Place or over at Tex Pop nearby. I am thrilled you
> are doing this. Looking forward to this much needed effort.*
>
> *Send away!*
>
> > *xxx*
> > *Margaret*

Her time indeed was limited. Strength soon faded and within a
week Margaret died.

MARGARET MOSER

1954-2017

South Texas Museum of Popular Culture,
Founder and Curator 2011-2017

Austin Music Awards, Director 1983-2014

The Austin Chronicle, Music Writer 1981-2014

San Marcos Record, Music Reporter 1979-1980

The Austin Sun, Music Reviewer 1976-1978

INTRODUCTION

Q: What do you call a Renaissance Man in Texas?

A: Woody Roberts

As a top-rated deejay who'd graduated to become a national award-winning radio executive, a 30-year-old Woody Roberts threw it all away. He hitched across America in search of rediscovering his joy. And he located it back where his journey began, in Texas country and blues music and in the all-embracing new-old Texas culture that spawned that music.

Woody Roberts wanted Austin to comprehend its hippie-but-homespun soul and he wanted that spirit to spread from Central Texas through the world. The wide-eyed projects Woody chronicles in this colorful, often hilarious backstage memoir sometimes succeeded giddily against all odds, sometimes stalled and failed, but all in all he got his wish.

Woody became part of a highly disorganized, lovable pack of freaks sans business suits who helped make Austin into a music powerhouse. His pals knew that Woody, with his myriad loves of all kinds of music, psychology, futurists like Bucky Fuller and Marshall McLuhan, and the worlds-elsewhere of science fiction, could think beyond any box and help them make their wild ideals sustainable. Whether it meant populating Willie Nelson's first annual music picnic which had threatened to be a bust and ended up clogging traffic for Woodstock-like miles or whether it meant attempting and finally, sadly, not quite being able to create an Austin progressive version of Nashville's Grand Ole Opry, Woody was there.

Now we can be with him in these episodes from a generous, spirited life—the life of a man of many parts and the life of a city that became a scene.

Robert Weisbuch
former president of the Woodrow Wilson Foundation
and Drew University, a Professor Emeritus of English at the
University of Michigan who was raised on rock-and-roll radio.

This memoir is based on my memories with situational reconstructions. From my perspective, it accurately recreates the period covered.

Woody Roberts

Horse Racing
&
Rock 'N' Roll

THE ARMADILLO AND WILLIE NELSON

No one ever made a difference by being like everyone else.

P. T. Barnum

1

Willie Has a Picnic

On a hot June day in the San Antonio of 1973, I was about to walk out the door when my desk phone rang. I grabbed the handset. "Woody here."

"Woody Roberts, this is Eddie Wilson."

"Hey, Eddie, great to hear from ya. How's your world at the Armadillo?"

"We're havin' more fun than most folks can even imagine."

"Super. I'm on my way out the door and heading down to HemisFair Plaza for a deejay meeting. Can I call you back?"

"Wondering if you'll come to Austin for a planning session at my house tonight, seven o'clock. We need some help. Armadillo Productions signed on to produce the Willie Nelson Fourth of July Picnic in Dripping Springs. We're two weeks out, tickets aren't selling, and Willie's team is running scared."

I had never heard of Dripping Springs.

"How do I find your house?"

Eddie Wilson represented Armadillo World Headquarters, a unique Austin concert facility getting top-notch music press and gaining recognition from fans and the industry for its tasteful shows. I was starting up my new career as a media consultant specializing in strategy and marketing for the entertainment industry.

At a very young age, I'd become a junkie for music and media. My mother had once been a teenaged singer for an orchestra and owned a collection of big band 78 rpm records. Ten-inch shellacs are known as the birthplace of three-minute songs because they didn't have room for a longer groove. Mom claimed before I learned to read I could pick up a record and tell her the song title. My dad worked at a newspaper connected to a radio station and television station.

So I grew up walking from the pressroom past the reporters' desks to look through a window at a deejay taking listener requests, while on down the hall, a TV newscaster rehearsed his stories for the day. That was in Johnstown, Pennsylvania. The same town where Moondog Alen Freed, the deejay credited with coining the phrase "rock 'n' roll," was born.

Maybe pop music was in my blood.

While attending Bellaire High School in Houston, Texas, I filed records at the local hit music station, KNUZ 1230-AM. This was 1956. During that summer's vacation, I volunteered to be the go-fer of a late-night TV show hosted by talented funny man Jim Ross on channel 11 KGUL.

My big thrill came when I became his show's on-camera hands; the job was lifting various items like kitchen knives and silver platters during his live commercials. Entering the University of Houston, age seventeen, my freshman college majors were Radio-TV-Film and Psychology.

By age nineteen, I was program director of a radio

station in Fort Lauderdale. Before I knew it, the year was 1967 and at twenty-six years old I had just become the nation's youngest general manager in a big market at KTSA 550-AM, San Antonio. Age thirty is when I resigned, and four months later departed to reboot my life. I would start over as a media consultant. The only one in Texas. That was 1972.

"What's a media consultant?" said my future partner, attorney Mike Tolleson.

It was a gutsy midlife attempt to broaden my experiences and work for myself. And now, KEXL 104.5-FM, owned by Doubleday Broadcasting, was my client.

* * *

SINCE ITS EARLY DAYS, the medium of radio was critical to success in the music business. You could say this star-making machinery was first turned on when Bing Crosby left Paul Whiteman's jazz orchestra to go solo. In September of 1931, American listeners heard the first CBS broadcast of *15 Minutes with Bing Crosby*. It was musically historic. Two months later he signed with Brunswick Records.

By the time KITE FM, with its 100,000 watts of stereo, changed its call letters to KEXL, the station had secured its own place in history. It was the first station in Central and South Texas to broadcast album rock music full-time when maybe fifteen such outlets existed worldwide. And its late night deejay Allen Grimm was the state's first full-time progressive rock jock. Here was a deejay who had never played 45s or worked in Top 40 radio. Grimm went straight into album tracks.

However, it was in Austin two years earlier, 1965,

where Bill Josey and his son Bill, Jr.—aka deejay Rim Kelley—became the first in the world to regularly broadcast progressive rock shows. They did it with an 850-watt monaural FM signal at 95.5 called KAZZ.

The new sounds were played late night, and a few college audiophiles, ones who owned appropriate radios, primarily comprised its audience. Students hung reception antennas from their dorm windows. Though FM was introduced as an expensive option for cars in 1952, the units were not yet stock accessories, and the first stereo dashboard receivers weren't offered until 1969. In fact, it was 1978 before FM radio had more listeners than AM.

At KAZZ, the elder Josey handled sales and his son programmed. These two radio innovators played a key role in jumpstarting Austin's live music scene by featuring local musicians performing original songs. They started up Sonobeat Records and recorded in nightclubs; KAZZ would broadcast these performances.

To me, it's uber cool that Bill and Jr. Josey cut their baby teeth in the same place I did, in Galveston at KILE 1400-AM. K-Isle was a hot little Top 40 station used by many deejays as their steppingstone into Houston.

In the late 1960s, San Antonio listeners tuned in KEXL not just for rock music, but also for alternative journalism updates from Earth News instead of Associated Press. And you could find out about sharing car rides to other cities or listen to Dr. Tom Payte's advice on how to treat herpes and handle a drug problem or where to get free flu shots and birth control pills. Local activist Tom Flowers reported on Vietnam War draft resistance and gave locations for pacifist meetings.

KEXL is where you got the latest concert info

and received warnings if bad acid was on the streets. Underground newspapers, such as *The Rag* in Austin, along with FM rockers such as KEXL, spread the new counterculture lifestyle across the U.S.

* * *

ON THAT SUNNY June morning, I walked into KEXL and found RCA's record promotion man from Houston standing in the lobby. Al Mathias. We had been friends since the mid-'60s. I told him I was off to a meeting with Willie Nelson. "He's having an outdoor concert at Dripping Springs."

"Another one? Wonder who put up the money?"

"Huh? It's been done before?"

"Last year, March. There was a country music show called the Dripping Springs Reunion. Promoter lost money."

"Never heard about it."

"Hardly anybody came. Maybe three thousand people when I was there, maybe."

"Did Willie play?"

"Don't know. He was there, hanging around with Waylon but wasn't advertised."

"Not good. Is there a new Willie album?"

"Don't know that either. Willie's not on RCA anymore. They dropped him."

"Dropped him?"

"Doesn't fit in with the new stars like Dolly Parton and he never had any big Top 40 hits like Jim Reeves. Great songwriter. We just can't sell Willie's singing."

"Too bad. I like his nasal voice. Especially his phrasing."

Al sighed. "RCA dropped Pure Prairie League, too."

I frowned. "We must get a zillion requests for "Amie" off their *Bustin' Out.*"

"Great tune, but these days, accountants control RCA." He shook his head. "I *can* help you with Waylon Jennings, likely he'll be there. His new album ships in July, you can have my advance copy. Not yet for airplay, but I can get you copies for contests."

Al Mathias reached into his leather shoulder case and pulled out *Honky Tonk Heroes.*

2

About Willie

During the eighty-mile drive from San Antonio to Austin, I thought about Willie Nelson.

In early 1961 I had arrived in the Alamo City to do the all-night show on KTSA licensed to Gordon McLendon. I gave up my program director's job in Fort Lauderdale and moved to Texas—for less money—because I wanted to learn the nuances of McLendon's Top 40 format that had swept the nation. Top 40 consisted of personality deejays playing the biggest hits over and over again. It was a mix of rock 'n' roll, country, rhythm and blues, and pop ballads.

His stations featured happy and clever quipping local deejays, hourly five-minute newscasts, headlines on the half-hour, ever-changing contests, and jingles singing the station's call letters. Any station that was first to broadcast the format became its city's dominant number one... until another copied it and split their audience. That's how the ratings wars began. I found KTSA in a fierce ratings battle with KONO 860-AM for the top spot in town.

The late Pat Tallman was the station's program and music director, and into Willie Nelson. "Listen to this," he said one day.

I watched as he centered a 7-inch 45 rpm with a plastic

big-hole adapter onto his turntable's spindle. Tallman looked to be in ecstasy as he played a Liberty Records release of "Mr. Record Man." He closed his eyes to listen.

A few weeks earlier I had seen him do the same for blues master Jimmy Reed and "Bright Lights, Big City." Pat Tallman loved Texas country and Chicago blues and his tutoring greatly expanded this pop music fan's appreciation for both genres. My high school collection contained jazz, folk, classical, big band, easy listening, rockabilly, pop, doo-wop, R&B, but no country or blues. Okay, I had an Eddie Arnold and a Muddy Waters album, but that was it.

I later noticed Willie credited as the songwriter for the smash 1961 Nashville hit, "Hello Walls," by Faron Young. Also in 1961 his name was seen on one of my favorite songs, "Funny How Time Slips Away," by country singer Jimmy Elledge, and three years later it charted again, this time by R&B soul man Joe Hinton on Don Robey's Backbeat label out of Houston. Both versions were million sellers. Plus, in '61 I saw Willie credited for writing "Crazy," released by Patsy Cline. It was a huge year for the man.

Then in '63 it was "Night Life" by Ray Price. Four classics in three years!

In 1964 as program director for KONO, I played Willie Nelson's single, "I Never Cared for You," released by Monument Records. My hit-tuned ears heard a great melody with lyrics of poetic imagery, but surprisingly, it was the singer-songwriter's opening guitar artistry that held the hook.

Later I learned it wasn't Willie's guitar but a classical guitarist who provided those magic licks. It's still one of my top five Willie Nelson recordings. Most likely

Monument signed Willie because the company's big seasonal record was Nelson's "Pretty Paper," sung by another Texan, Roy Orbison.

That label challenged the established sound of Nashville's hit factories because its management had taken a different course than Grand Ole Opry and the major record companies. Its recordings were more like the Austin country-music-to-come and somewhat rockabilly oriented. Billy Grammer, Grandpa Jones, Boots Randolf, Leona Douglas, Tony Joe White, Dolly Parton, Larry Gatlin. They were the first to promote this new kind of country artist.

But to Nashville producers, Monument Records was an enigma.

Willie moved his music to RCA Records; however, in so doing, something negative happened to his recordings. Instead of treating his voice like a Hank Williams or George Jones, producer Chet Atkins—aka Mr. Guitar—with his Nashville studio orchestra, tried to sweeten bittersweet Willie. Thus many of those RCA sessions featured orchestral strings more suited for Sonny James or John D. Loudermilk.

Today, looking over the vast discography of Willie Nelson, it's clear those are his least important recordings. Atkins had managed to smother a great vocal style.

If you asked for my list of favorite Willie recordings, it would be his outstanding collection of duets that show off his cross-genre appeal. Those priceless collaborations started in 1962 with his first Billboard listed country hit, "Willingly." That duet was recorded with Shirley Collie and launched Willie into a lifetime of pairings with a stunning diversity of artists, such as Wynton Marsalis, Norah Jones, Leon Russell, Don Cherry, Juice Newton, Ray Charles, Timi Yuro, Bon Jovi, Julio Iglesias, and many others.

These duets have lasting value beyond record sales. They're worthy of the Smithsonian.

When I became KTSA's general manager in December 1967, my morning personality, Ron Houston, introduced me to a colorful wheeler-dealer aptly named Trader. Larry Trader. He sold used cars, did a little gambling, promoted country dances, and took Willie Nelson records around to radio stations to put the Nashville songwriter in front of San Antonio deejays.

You wouldn't hear Willie on KTSA because we played chart hits and he didn't have one. Still, Larry would invite me to see the singer and his band in action at the John T. Floore Country Store in Helotes. It is one of those celebrated dance halls that, after opening in 1942, hosted all the greats, including Bob Wills and Elvis Presley.

First time I went to see Willie, Texas had just adopted daylight savings time, so 9 p.m. that evening in 1968 still held some daylight. Yet when his first song began, folks packed the dance floor right away. Most aged in their forties and fifties.

One of the younger people in the place, I was also the only guy in the audience with long hair. Willie still had short hair and his clean-faced Nashville look and hadn't yet moved back to Texas. His relaxed stage presence and ability to charm was impressive. As Willie would catch people's gazes and smiles, most of the audience felt he was singing for them.

I got high and danced till closing.

After the show, Willie came out to sign autographs in the old tradition of country music. He signed for a half hour. This courtesy impressed me, very rare.

Garth Brooks set a world's record in 1996 by signing

fan autographs nonstop for 23 hours! Even Elvis, during the peak of his 1950s rocket ride, still took time out to sign. In the spring of 1956 after his show at the Sam Houston Coliseum, three hundred of us waited until the hall was empty and cleanup started. His sellout concert had a $5 ticket price. Elvis came out and sat in the bleachers near the stage, joked with us, and signed everyone's request.

Then, in 1965, after I attended The Beatles' press conference at the Sheridan-Lincoln Hotel in Houston, and met John Lennon, I saw the quartet play their 35-minute set in that same Coliseum, also sold out. Surprisingly, although it happened ten years later, the Beatles' tickets were priced at $5, same as Elvis.

Again, the screaming teen girls never let up and they even sounded more intense, or perhaps it just seemed that way because I was a decade older. Immediately after the band's mostly inaudible performance, the stage lights went dark, and the Fab Four were rushed, triage evacuation style, into a black stretch limo and whisked away. They were gone before the house lights came up!

Those mop-tops had set another trend. For years to come, rock stars, even if no one chased them, had to be rushed off in a limo. It became part of the act.

Willie, however, in 1968 still casually spoke with every fan after his show. Like Elvis, his parents had raised their small-town boy to be courteous in the Southern style.

Next morning, still hearing "The Party's Over" in my head, I phoned Larry Trader to thank him for inviting me to see Willie live. Larry drove right over to KTSA and handed me a worn RCA album titled *Country Music*

Concert: Live at Panther Hall.

"Listen to this," he said with a look of satisfaction.

I switched off my two radios that were simultaneously monitoring competing stations to hear the phonograph. Oh, yeah. This music was different from Willie's over-produced RCA studio albums. It sounded like the magic performance I'd experienced the previous night at Floore Country Store.

Larry looked at me knowingly. "You're hearing the real Willie."

"Powerful."

"Do you play golf?"

"No."

"Want to learn?"

Ron Houston later told me Larry was coaching Willie's game and they were playing with Ray Price. I never learned.

* * *

FOUR YEARS LATER, Willie left Nashville for Austin. Seeing the student popularity of the many progressive country musicians calling this hip college town "home," the forty-year-old singer decided he too would grow a beard and shoulder-length hair. Willie even punched a gold stud into an earlobe.

Yet while attracting this new audience of liberal urban hippies, he held on to his rural conservative redneck fans. Willie Nelson was the only country artist who could pull a crowd into both John T. Floore Country Store and the Armadillo World Headquarters. In those days the redheaded singer's drawing power was limited to packing Texas honky-tonks and small halls.

3

Leon Russell and the Bob Dylan Rumor

By the time I arrived at Tower Drive in the quiet Tarrytown neighborhood of Austin, several cars were parked on both sides of the street. I rang the front doorbell and Eddie Wilson's wife, Genie, opened it with a welcoming smile.

I walked into a living room where every chair was filled and several men were sitting on the floor. Eddie, who was standing, waved his arms, gave out a hearty greeting, and called out, "Everyone... this is Woody Roberts from San Antonio, and I've asked him to come up here and tell us what to do."

Willie Nelson rose from his chair and shook my hand. Glancing around, I recognized Hank Alrich from his bluegrass picking days in San Antonio. He now operated the recording studio inside the Armadillo and had financed the beer garden.

Beside him were the facility manager, Bob Hedderman, and the resident 'Dillo artist, Jim Franklin. CPA Randy McCall with his wife Diane sat on the couch. Legal counsel Mike Tolleson was there. And I recognized

Larry Trader and his running buddy from San Antonio, a fellow used car salesman, Billy Cooper.

A joint was passed my way.

"Anybody need a cold beer?" Genie said.

I listened to Eddie going over the plans. He called on 'Dillo department heads to give their overview: sound, fencing, porta-cans, lighting, the cost of a roof, security and finally... ticket sales. The room got quiet.

Larry said, "Well, it's still a little early, but we're not really selling any outside of Austin. And, ah..."

"How many in Austin?" Willie said.

"A few hundred."

"Dallas?"

"Less than a hundred."

"What about Houston and San Antonio?"

Larry had a slackened look. "I'm afraid they ain't sellin' yet, Will."

Eddie handed me the Jim Franklin poster. It was great: fireworks burst along the top of a banner-sized American flag stretched across a two-lane highway, and sneaking underneath was a lone armadillo nonchalantly carrying the Texas flag in its mouth. A perfect Fourth of July poster.

I looked at the performer list. Except for Doug Sahm, it had the same kind of lineup as the Dripping Springs Reunion the year before without its biggest stars. Another country music event.

I remembered Pat O'Day of Concerts West saying: "A show with many small acts doesn't add up to a big show. It's still just a show with many small acts."

I looked at Willie. "How was the Reunion's turnout?"

"A few thousand each day, didn't make expenses."

"Hmm."

Just last month, promoter Rod Kennedy had presented Willie Nelson, Michael Murphey, Jerry Jeff Walker—known for writing the Top 10 hit "Mr. Bojangles"—plus 18 other fine musicians, such as Peter Yarrow and Townes Van Zandt, in the Kerrville Auditorium. That concert's turnout was good enough, but its audience was not even close to festival size. And just like Willie's upcoming Fourth of July Picnic, that Kerrville show was on an extended holiday weekend. Memorial Day. Not a good sign.

"How are you guys promoting this event?"

Larry Trader spoke up. "Joe Jamail is doing Houston. Geno McCoslin has Dallas covered. Armadillo is doing Austin. We've been running commercials on every country station. Getting good extra promotion with ticket giveaways. I'm handling San Antonio tickets and working the album."

"What album?"

"Hold on, just released." Larry strode out to his car and returned with a copy of *Shotgun Willie*.

"Atlantic label," I said. "I know guys at Atlantic. Doug's latest is on Atlantic. Bob Dylan plays on it."

"Wexler's started a country division," Tolleson said.

I looked at the Picnic's lineup again. Nada. No big draw on this show. No one who could pack an arena. Still, a Fourth of July festival might...

"What do you think, Wood?" Eddie looked at me. He watched me staring deep in thought at the names on Franklin's poster. He said, "Not listed on the poster, but Willie added Leon Russell."

"Leon Russell!" My eyebrows shot up. "You've got Leon Russell?"

"We can't advertise him," Willie said in a firm tone.

"Leon's going to sing a song or two and help me emcee. He's trying to reach country music fans."

At this good news, I sucked in my breath. Leon Russell meant all the difference in the world! Now we had a show with a major draw.

Stardom comes fast in the hit music business. In the fall of 1971, the Allman Brothers and Leon Russell were not yet superstars and, with two other bands, had played an outdoor Austin concert at UT's baseball park, Clark Field. Now there wasn't a facility in town big enough for those acts.

There was no doubt in my mind that Leon would legitimize Willie Nelson's Picnic for the rock audience. Kris Kristofferson and Rita Coolidge were semi-known artists getting a tad of national FM airplay. But they weren't rock stars like Leon Russell. I could build a word-of-mouth promotion around that name.

"Well, guys, this is a fine music event. How many tickets do you need to sell?"

Randy spoke up first. "If we sold ten thousand, I think we'd pay our bills. Twenty's a home run."

"Problem is," I said, "counting today, it's only twelve days away. I'd say promote the rock festival aspect and go for walkup sales. You need a radio ad blast on Top 40 and rock FM."

"But those stations don't play Willie," Larry said.

"I can get rock stations to promote the Picnic," I said. "It's a festival. They'll come."

"There's not enough money for extra stations," Randy said.

I shook my head. "Hate to tell you guys, but this is not a major country music event. The hardcore country audience isn't about to drive from Dallas or Houston for this show."

People mumbled to each other. Willie had a slight frown. Eddie stood up, in his coveralls, looking somewhat like Jerry Garcia ready to play banjo with bluegrass group Old and In the Way. He waved a joint to quiet the meeting. "I recommend we turn this problem over to Woody Roberts."

Willie stared hard at me. "What do you say, Woody?"

"If I do it, I'm going to pull the ad money from Dallas and Houston and spend it in San Antonio and Austin."

Larry was concerned. "What about my Dallas and Houston radio stations?"

"Double their giveaway tickets. Promise VIP passes and interviews. But cut the ads."

He nodded.

"I'll need a temporary office and wall space to put up a promo timeline. Plus an assistant."

"There's a vacant room next to my office," Tolleson said.

Diane raised a hand. "I volunteer. Just tell me what to do."

With a cigarette smoldering between his fingers, Randy McCall chimed in. "Armadillo can't afford to lose on this. We need to make money."

When the meeting was over and folks headed into the night, everyone seemed enthusiastic. Larry Trader pulled me aside and spoke low. "I hope you won't pull the Waco ads."

"Waco?"

"Will's hometown is Abbott. He'd like the folks to hear about his Picnic. The station gets into Abbott."

"Done. And I'll run some ads in Hillsboro where he used to deejay. I think it was on KHBR 1560-AM. Is *Shotgun Willie* getting airplay?"

"Not much." Larry tugged his beard. "Some folks don't like the cover photo."

"They liked the short-haired Willie."

"Yup, they want the man they grew up listenin' to."

Billy Cooper called out, "Come on, Larry."

Willie was ready to leave. We shook hands again.

"Calling it a picnic is a great idea, Willie. The Fourth of July weekend is perfect."

"Thank you, Woody."

"Your poster should say: 'First annual.' "

Willie laughed. "I hope it is."

The man was worried, his big event was in the hands of a half-dozen latent hippies. His investment was on the line.

Back inside… a gift, two sparkling lines left on a mirror and two fat joints nearby. Genie said goodnight, leaving Eddie and me to talk into the wee hours. *Shotgun Willie* was on the turntable. It sounded great, his best studio capture since the Monument session.

Later Eddie turned on KOKE 95.5-FM so we could hear the world's only progressive country radio station. KOKE call letters had replaced KAZZ in 1967 when new owners upped the station's power to 3,000 watts. Now manager Ken Moyers and programmer Rusty Bell were using 95.5 to once again introduce a new format to listeners. The all-night deejay was sick and music director Joe Gracey was filling. His set was a mix of Dan Hicks and his Hot Licks, a Leo Kottke instrumental,

Lightning Hopkins, Maybelle Carter, Tom Waits, Steve Fromholz, and the Rolling Stones. Eddie lit an unfiltered Camel as we popped open the last two cans of Lone Star. "What are you thinking of doing with the Picnic ads?"

"We'll cut 'em crossover so they can play on three formats. I'm going to build the show around San Antonio and Austin rock FM and Top 40 listeners. For radio mentions, we'll give away a ton of Leon Russell albums, each with a pair of Picnic tickets. Deejays will be able to say Leon is flying in to be with Willie. Makes the rumor that Dylan might show up for Doug's set more believable."

"There's a Dylan rumor?"

"Why not? Could happen. He plays on Doug's new Atlantic album, same label as Willie. Gives our Picnic a rock star mystique for word-of-mouth, and gets some FM play for Doug. Folks are ready for Central Texas to have a rock festival. With Leon there, it won't matter if no other rock musicians show up. In fact, it won't even matter as to whose picnic it is, just where and when. It could be Jerry Jeff's Picnic, or Michael Murphey's."

Eddie laughed. "Actually, Jerry Jeff Walker outdraws Willie."

"Willie draws best in small Texas towns."

I took my time flipping through Eddie's collection of 12-inch albums. Tasty assortment. Heavy on folk. I noticed the lack of English rock bands, no Pink Floyd or Zeppelin. But here was Loudon Wainright, Jimmie Rodgers, Flatt and Scruggs, Mance Lipscomb, John Prine, Freddie King, Joan Baez, Delbert and Glen, Grateful Dead, Leon Redbone and...

"Wow, you have Willie's Panther Hall album."

Eddie nodded and turned off the radio. With slow and cautious hands, he removed the 12-inch platter from its paper sleeve, placed the hi-fi tone arm's needle in the opening groove, and reached for our last joint.

Today some consider Waylon Jennings' *Honky Tonk Heroes* to be the first "outlaw" album. Not so. A month earlier Atlantic had released *Shotgun Willie* recorded in NYC and Memphis and produced by Jerry Wexler, a man acclaimed for his R&B hits.

I'd say that was the beginning of the outlaw country albums.

* * *

EDDIE AND I WERE at the Armadillo World Headquarters office by 10 a.m. Diane McCall had beat us there and brought a box of croissants and a wide roll of butcher paper. Diane was a mix of voluptuous brunette and earth mother.

"Where do we start?" she said.

"Let's put up the wall planner and break it down into twelve days."

"Eleven days," Diane said.

The room was empty but for a rectangular wooden table and chair. A long window overlooked traffic on Barton Springs Road. I pulled in a second chair. We tacked up an eight-foot-long strip of butcher paper. Marked out eleven days.

"Okay, Diane, these are the elements. Quick as possible, we start commercials on every FM rock station in Austin and San Antonio. Five days out start the more expensive AM Top 40's. Larry's already bought the country stations. We need to mail press releases and special deliver Willie interview tapes all over Texas, from Port Arthur to El Paso. Need to secure live Willie phone interviews with big stations, especially all-night deejay Bill Mack at 50,000-watt WBAP 820-AM in Fort Worth. We'll set up contests using tickets and albums for prizes."

Diane took notes, then looked up. "What else?"

"I'll see to recording the ads and then set up Willie interviews. What you could do is get station ad rates, along with the program, music, and news directors' names. The names of national music magazine reviewers will be handy if you come across them. We'll need three dozen manila envelopes."

Diane took more notes. Very professional.

"I'm heading back to San Antonio this afternoon. I'll write the spots and set up production time at KEXL."

She looked up again. "Anything else?"

"No... oh yeah, first time we talk to someone at a radio station, let's say, to the best of our knowledge, there's no truth to the rumor Bob Dylan will be there. That he'll be hanging out with Doug Sahm."

"There's a Bob Dylan rumor?"

4

The Rock Festival Hook

Willie's Picnic had me excited. I had gotten hooked on festivals six years before when Jerry Wexler of Atlantic Records Group invited me to the Monterey International Pop Festival. His goal was to have me and other radio programmers see their new artists: Cream and Otis Redding. Turned out, Cream declined the festival appearance. Luckily, not long after, I got to see the short-lived power trio at the Psychedelic Supermarket in Boston.

Having this unique live music festival associated with Monterey's international reputation for hosting quality jazz performers meant these pop musicians had become legitimized as serious artists. Chet Helms introduced an unknown Janis Joplin, and the singer mesmerized the attentive crowd. Otis Redding and The Who scored rave reviews. Jimi Hendrix was described as rock music's Coltrane.

My musical paradigm shifted that weekend.

Flying home, my thoughts were about the music I heard and people I met. Everyone was friendly and peace-loving, with faces painted and flowers in their hair. This was the first event of its kind in the world, and it became the inspiration for a new kind of extravaganza: the pop music festival.

The year was 1967 and because of progressive rock's huge appeal, FM radio also would be forever changed. It was the beginning of the Summer of Love.

For outdoor concert fans, 1969 was more than just the year man first walked on the moon with a billion people watching. It became THE year in rock festival history! Five such events in six months. Three of them at auto racetracks and two at farms.

It all started August 1st with the Atlanta International Pop Festival. Two weeks later came the Woodstock Music and Art Fair, undoubtedly the peak event for the flower-power culture. The Isle of Wight Festival at Ford Farm in England followed in two more weeks, and then came the huge Texas International Pop Festival near Dallas.

That big event was the brainchild of Angus Wynne III. I recalled in 1965 seeing his name listed as co-producer for Bob Dylan's concert in Austin. I secured backstage passes for Texas Pop and with ragtop down sped my Triumph Spitfire north to pitch a tent and camp out on the land to set my soul free.

What a treat to see Janis, plus Led Zeppelin, B. B. King, Santana, Chicago, Freddie King, Herbie Mann, Canned Heat and more, even Shiva's Headband! Audio was superb with the sound system in control of Bill Hanley, who had also done Woodstock. In the blazing midday sun, I cooled down by skinny-dipping in Lake Lewisville where everyone claimed the naked man waterskiing with his penis erect was Wavy Gravy.

On the first weekend of December in that sensational year, this joyful series of rock festivals came to an abrupt end. During the superstar-studded Altamont Free Concert in San Francisco, Mick Jagger was prancing about on stage and singing "Under My Thumb" when a Hells Angel used a knife to kill a black man in the crowd who was brandishing a pistol. This violent act signaled the tragic finale for the Summer of Love and its flower-power culture's embrace of peace, love, dope.

Those five history-making outdoor events averaged over 200,000 music fans! Willie Nelson would be happy with a tenth of them.

5

A Deserted World's Fair

While at my desk jotting notes, I thought it over. Willie's team had missed the mark.

Most of the talent he booked for the Picnic was perfect for a fat-stock show and rodeo. But the country music audience, raised on Nashville hits and Grand Ole Opry, wasn't a festival-oriented crowd; they might like a county fair, but Woodstock wasn't their idea of fun.

The young album buyers, the maturing hippie types, would be the ones to bring this home. It was quite helpful that on July 28 a major rock music event called Summer Jam at Watkins Glen was scheduled and so outdoor festivals were again a hot topic.

Plus, in 1973 there was new liberty for boys to celebrate. The U.S. government, still at war in Vietnam, was forced by public blowback to end the military draft. Young men got their first taste of independence. No more their compulsory trips from high school to boot camp to battlefield and blood.

A mood of celebration was in the air.

But at this same time, a cloud of darkness formed over the U.S. Justice Department. On July 1 a brutal Drug Enforcement Agency would be established to escalate the newest government offensive, the war on recreational drug users.

I planned to use Leon Russell's superstardom for glitter while latching onto the country rock phenomenon for hipness. The "get back to your roots" thing was sweeping the nation. Perhaps it had started in 1965 with the Beatles and drummer Ringo singing "Act Naturally."

The mid-'60s also introduced the Lovin' Spoonful's "Nashville Cats" and the Rolling Stones with Brian Jones on slide guitar for "No Expectations" and their "Honky Tonk Women." The Byrds released *Sweetheart of the Rodeo* in 1968; the following year The Flying Burrito Brothers released *The Gilded Palace of Sin*, and Dylan used Bob Johnston to produce *Nashville Skyline*.

By 1970, album rock stations were playing Poco, Little Feat, Nitty Gritty Dirt Band, The Stone Poneys, J. D. Souther, Joy of Cooking, New Riders of the Purple Sage, the Eagles, and The Band. Even the psychedelic Grateful Dead acknowledged their workingman's roots, and by '73 Jerry Garcia sat down with a pedal steel for the New Riders of the Purple Sage and played a banjo with Old and In the Way. Gram Parsons and his "Fallen Angels" tour sold out the Armadillo and Liberty Hall in Houston.

My desk phone rang.

"Woody, it's Larry. I've got great news. Charlie Rich is going to be there."

Charlie Rich was fine. The man had the nation's #1 country song with "Behind Closed Doors" and he was getting Top 40 radio play. But I wished it was ZZ Top instead. Their manager Bill Ham had given KEXL a preview copy of *Tres Hombres* and the deejays were getting overwhelming requests for "La Grange."

* * *

NEXT MORNING, I set up a programming meeting at KEXL. Then stepped out of my cottage to stroll down the gravel driveway and walk a couple of blocks up Castano Avenue to a bus stop across from Alamo Heights High School. I caught the Broadway Avenue inbound. It wasn't rush hour so the bus was nearly empty.

As we passed the Pig Stand, four police cars sat in the parking lot; it was a counterculture joke that cops were always eating at the Pig Stand. When Royce Hailey opened his famous Pig Stand in Dallas 1921, it was the world's first drive-in restaurant.

I read the *San Antonio Light* newspaper until the bus let me off at HemisFair Plaza. The word "plaza" was my idea.

After the fair closed in 1968, most wanted to call it HemisFair Gardens or Park. But since there was only concrete, I advocated using plaza while the flowers and trees were planted. San Antonio could promote it as the largest plaza in the Americas. A good Texas brag. It would be decades later when those planted trees matured and the name was changed to HemisFair Park.

On the Plaza and heading to KEXL, I walked the elevated ramps alongside the unused monorail track. The system was decommissioned after the train fell off its track and killed one fairgoer and injured forty-eight others. Ahead of me was a majestic candlestick known as the Tower of the Americas. Noted psychic Jeane Dixon had predicted the 622-foot, poured concrete pillar would fall; instead it was the monorail. I had been among the dignitaries treated to the first dinner served in the Tower's revolving restaurant.

In 1973 this deserted 93-acre fairground was a site lifted from the surreal pages of J. G. Ballard. The view down from the ramp was of dry fountains and forgotten sculptures dotting the landscape. A sad comment about city planning. I could see empty buildings with rows of boarded windows. Today this kind of vacated area is hazardous. Back then, the Alamo City did not yet share our national shame of a large homeless population.

To my dreaming mind, the 1968 World's Fair was alive with its lines of excited visitors. I could see them wrapped around the Eastman Kodak building, with crowds waiting to view exhibits by Humble Oil, RCA, General Motors, and Southwestern Bell. Why, over there is the West Germany pavilion.

I've always sought out the unique and inspiring. Here it surrounded me. HemisFair Plaza was the ideal place to house San Antonio's most innovative radio station. Its transmitter was atop the Tower.

* * *

I STARTED THE MEETING. "Okay, gang, we need to score a few lids and fill our beer coolers. We're gonna have the biggest Fourth of July picnic in history."

They laughed.

I passed around Jim Franklin's poster and gave my report on the meeting with Willie Nelson. Now everyone was staring at me blank-faced.

Don White, late-night deejay and station engineer, said, "Woody, this is a country music show. We don't play these people, except sometimes Kristofferson."

Then I revealed Willie's co-host was Leon Russell.

Allen Grimm, the city's top rock deejay, wearing a

too-small cowboy hat atop his exploding brown hair, leapt to his feet. "Leon Russell? Help! Tow me away! Leon Russell? Whew." He shook his head as if trying to clear it.

"Just one hitch, Allen. Can't advertise him, but we can talk about him. No band. The Shelter People won't be there. Leon won't be in the ads. But he's co-host."

"That's heavy," said Ron Houston, now doing his morning show on KEXL.

"Whew." Allen sat down, straightened his cowboy hat, and grinned. "Do I get backstage?"

"One last thing. There's a rumor started that Dylan might show up to play with Doug... so far, just a *rumor*."

I had written the commercials to sound like a major festival blowout. Lots of fireworks, musical clips from artists, male and female voices calling out artists' names. Gordie Ham volunteered to produce the commercials in KEXL's studio. I asked Ron Houston and jazz singer/deejay Sunny Planto if they would be the Picnic voices. My planned campaign was backloaded from the afternoon of the show and these commercials would saturate radio just three days before the event. I aimed for a holiday walkup.

Only nine days until blastoff, tickets not yet selling.

6

Inside the Headquarters

The Armadillo World Headquarters was once a National Guard vehicle repair shop and storage facility. Its back office was at 521½ Barton Springs Road. This was a nondescript, two-story brick building with a few windows facing a traffic-laden intersection with 1st Street. On the roof was a giant painted billboard promoting the United Fund. Behind these offices sat the performance hall.

And sitting next to this former semi-armory was the Skating Palace, occupying a Quonset hut-style building with its rounded off roof like an armadillo's shell. Few knew it was a roller-skating rink, and first-time concert-goers figured they were looking at the 'Dillo's performance hall.

You passed alongside the Skating Palace when pulling into the Armadillo's dirt parking lot and it was easy to see why artist Micael Priest called it The Sea of Holes. Fortunately, for sold-out shows, people could also park free in the kitty-cornered Municipal Auditorium lot. Directly across the street from the Auditorium and displaying a big neon frozen custard cone was Sandy's Hamburgers. Some claim it's where Elvis Presley used to order double meat and cheese with fries and a large cone.

At age twenty, Elvis had sandy blond hair that he decided to dye black after seeing Tony Curtis in *City Across the River*. He was part of the *Louisiana Hayride*. When the *Hayride* with Elvis played in the Armadillo World Headquarters building, then called the Sportcenter, tickets cost 75 cents. Word has it, a riot broke out during his performance and ecstatic cowgirls ripped the clothes off the young singer's body. Our soon-to-be superstar quickly wrapped himself in the backdrop curtain to be ushered off stage.

This young singer from Tupelo had a history with Austin in the mid-1950s, having also performed at the nearby City Coliseum, on the outskirts of town for Dessau Hall, and in the redneck Skyline Club. In the late '50s, Elvis was drafted into the army and stationed in Texas at Fort Hood in Killeen, where he and his pals would grab a break from military life and drive the 70 miles south to Austin for some fun and milkshakes and girls. The superstar last returned in the spring of 1977 for his sellout show in the Municipal Auditorium. He was already familiar with the neighborhood... and Sandy's burgers.

Five months later, age forty-two, the King was dead.

Because I arrived early at the Headquarters, my entrance route to the hall was through the beer garden, the heart of all social life at the 'Dillo. It was the place to eat, relax, converse, smoke a cigarette, and sip a cold draft beer—$1.50 delivered a pitcher of Shiner to your table.

The crowd ranged from the media, politicians, blue-collar workers, and professors to artists of all types, students, and traveling hippies looking for a place to crash. No bigotry displayed, and cultural diversity greatly appreciated, but nonetheless, it was primarily liberal Euro-whites who frequented and maintained the Armadillo.

Every visit unveiled a new improvement for the facility; in all departments, the hippie-like crew sought excellence. The much-needed beer garden financed by Hank Alrich was still a work in progress. Hank was living in San Antonio when I met him. His bluegrass-themed band, Tiger Balm, often performed in that city's beautiful Sunken Garden Theater. In visits to Austin, Hank befriended Shiva's Headband and joined them for a while. Later, wanting to be near other talented musicians and artists, he signed on to do janitor's work at the Armadillo. For him, it was the righteous way to get access: earn it. He would one day own the beloved facility.

It didn't take long for 'Dillo management to figure out concert tickets alone would not meet all financial demands. The answer was to increase beer and food sales. When Hank heard about the essential, but unaffordable, idea of a beer garden, he stepped up to the plate with a $50,000 loan to build it. Many still frequented Scholz's Garten, founded in 1866, the oldest still operating in Texas; however, during the 1970s, the Armadillo Garden became the alternative respite from bustle and traffic. For lunch and dinner, the Armadillo Kitchen offered hungry music fans a healthy but tasty menu.

The beer garden was situated behind the hall, and from there I entered into the 'Dillo kitchen. As I walked past the large stove and ovens, the aroma of baking bread greeted me. Forty-odd years later, I still hunger for the homemade daily bread, the excellent green salads, delicious guacamole, thick soups, perfect brown rice, incredible shrimp enchiladas, giant nachos, and great big chocolate chip cookies.

That morning a smiling Jan Beeman was mixing a batch of brownies. We waved good morning and I stepped into the concert area. It was dim, and the air was still. High up, each of the side walls held a row of windows. The walls also housed a few large circular fans slowly turning heavy blades that flickered patches of sunlight across worn gray carpet remnants laid over the concrete floor. Two huge box fans rested on the floor and flanked the stage.

One of the mind-blowing factoids about the famous Armadillo is it had no air-conditioning, and people sat on the floor! To make the floor acceptable, we called it "festival seating."

Can you imagine such a concert hall being popular today?

Large metal double doors opened for the morning cleanup and to help air out the smell of cigarette smoke and stale beer. Bands used that doorway to load in their equipment and beer distributors used it for their keg deliveries. It was standing by these doors after helping roadies load out from the 1975 Pointer Sisters performance that artist Ken Featherston was murdered. He was one of the most promising young artists in Texas. A random bullet from the gun of a drive-by shooter hit Featherston. He died in the arms of his dear friend and fellow artist, Henry Gonzalez.

Perplexed homicide detectives had no clues. This

murder was so out of character for the 'Dillo that all of Austin felt a deep psychic-shock. Artist Jim Franklin took it upon himself to investigate the Ken Featherston murder case... and he found the killer! The creep was hiding in Waco.

More than anything else, Jim Franklin's art direction set the tone for the 'Dillo environment. First thing you'd see inside the cavernous hall of the Armadillo was mural art everywhere. Like the work of a madman. Who would put all this effort and talent into painting murals for concerts held in a darkened room?

Faint clouds and dozens of armadillo silhouettes floated on the walls. A large caricature of a frowning Guacamole Queen guarded the door to the women's restroom: "If I catch any of you guys in the girl's john... I'm gonna mash you up 'n SPREAD you on a Salad!" By the backstage entrance was a mural-sized fine arts painting of Freddie King in an intense guitar riff, with an armadillo bursting from his heart! The art was signed JFKLN.

I don't know who to compare with his style. Perhaps if Salvador Dali had grown up in Texas, moved to Austin, and chomped on peyote buttons, he might have created music posters. Jim Franklin painted surreal Texas landscapes with lots of bluebonnets and puffy cumulus clouds that are every bit as good as the work of Porfirio Salinas. Franklin also inked photo-real portraits and created elaborate murals in swimming pools and on appropriate walls.

It was Franklin who visually distinguished Austin's most famous venue from the Fillmore West in San

Francisco, Jam Factory in San Antonio, Liberty Hall in Houston, and a hundred other touring band concert halls across the U.S. His murals were so prominent and well executed that at the 'Dillo you had the distinct feeling of being inside a highly creative space. And you were.

By 1973, Armadillo World Headquarters was gaining statewide recognition from the musical, artistic, and intellectual counterculture to be a one-of-a-kind Texas venture. Here was an idealistic dream from the 1960s that most of us had given up on, yet somehow it remained alive in Austin. Moreover, that dream was manifested by a brave group of people who I believed deserved support and success.

In the back of the hall, cable-spool tables with brown metal folding chairs were placed on an elevated space called the Cabaret. I walked across the old carpeting remnants sewn together and tossed atop the hall's floor to help soften the cement and provide some acoustic balance. Eerily quiet at 10 a.m., like waiting for something to happen. The stage was dark and its only occupants were chrome mic stands and a grand piano. My route to the office took me past the main-floor bar and to stage right where the backstage entrance led to a narrow hallway with dressing rooms lining one side and the other a private hangout space for performers.

Here was where the Armadillo Kitchen got countless raves from touring musicians. Commander Cody, Van Morrison, and Frank Zappa requested Jan Beeman's shrimp enchiladas each time. And the musicians always received a bottomless urn of locally roasted black coffee served on a tray with a silver pitcher of cream, a bowl of honey, and white linen napkins. Tall and long-bearded, Bruce Willenzik had arrived fresh out of school with a business degree and started work as a line cook. He soon was managing the kitchen. Willenzik liked to say the Armadillo Philosophy was: "Do the impossible as best you can and have fun doing it."

During shows, the 'Dillo stage was swept with colorful Super Trouper spotlight beams, and guest-list folks wearing their silky access pass stuck on their pants and dresses packed the backstage. In the narrow hallway, you would detect the aromas of colognes, perfumes, and incense cut by smoke from tobacco and marijuana.

Behind the stage, a stairway led me up to the second floor. My footsteps echoed on the steel and cement steps. A thought went through my mind: "I'm living off the path of tradition, now. How fortunate I am with my hand-made cottage, KEXL on HemisFair Plaza, Armadillo World Headquarters... all visually exceptional."

Most of the second floor was an ample open space interrupted by metal support poles. The staff—and not just the security guys—used it for karate lessons. Emma Little used some of the space for her Armadillo nursery. I didn't know of any other business in Austin or San Antonio with a nursery for the workers.

To my far right was a door leading into a long room where Jim Franklin lived and created his extraordinary fine-art visions. Ahead of me lay the closed door to the offices. Light came from the crack underneath.

Diane was already at work. A young fellow in a beige suit was reading the latest *Crawdaddy*.

"This is Gary Holland, our sales rep at KNOW," she

said. "He's here for their commercials."

"Your schedule starts this afternoon," Gary said, anxiety in his tone.

"I know this is last-minute. Thanks for rushing us through."

I took the sturdy envelope and pulled out a small, square white box and opened it to make sure the plastic three-inch-diameter reel holding quarter-inch audiotape was inside. He took it and sped off for the station.

The door opened and in walked Mike Tolleson. Slightly receding hairline and boasting a full, neatly trimmed beard topped by a friendly smile. Tolleson carried the battered leather briefcase Beatle George Harrison had used in London for transporting the score of his *Wonderwall* soundtrack.

"You folks look busy."

We showed him our work and Diane walked him through the project's wall chart already displaying black strikeouts and red underlined notes.

"I hope it doesn't rain." He sighed. "I'm glad to see your end of the Picnic is more together than its contracts."

Opening the door of his office, Tolleson glanced back at me. "When you get free time, I have something that will interest you."

7

Armadillo TV

I've always felt Mike Tolleson had the best description of Armadillo World Headquarters. He called it a "cultural arts laboratory"—and it was. Ballet... comedy... healthy food... art shows... conferences... a recording studio... television and video... beer garden... political discussions... but mostly it was about music, about the national touring musicians with Austin talent opening the shows.

This completely meshed with my own vision of the 'Dillo's potential to become an Austin version of Grand Ole Opry by producing radio and TV shows and housing a record company's recording facility.

Tolleson said, "Have you met Bill Arhos?"

"Arhos?"

"He's the program director at KLRN in Austin."

When establishing publicly funded television for San Antonio and Austin, the founders thought channels 9 and 18 would be used for education, thus called them K-LeaRN. The transmitter for both stations was between cities in New Braunfels, and they broadcast NET—National Educational Television—programs. By 1973, education as a focus had been abandoned and PBS—Public Broadcasting System—was their new program source. Mainstays for both stations were NET holdovers *Sesame Street* and *Nova*, along with BBC reruns and WWII specials; not much local programming.

"Mike, I don't know the Austin staff, but I do know the KLRN management in San Antonio. Their studio is just a short walk from KEXL."

He leaned back in his executive level swivel chair. "We've been talking to Arhos about doing a TV show at the Armadillo. Willie said he'll do it after his Picnic is out of the way. Probably we can get Murphey or Jerry Jeff to be on it. Arhos thinks KLRN will go for it."

"Hey, I'd enjoy helping with that. Pretty sure I can get it shown in San Antonio, too. Let me give it some thought."

"We'll talk after the picnic."

"I heard a Houston group is filming on the fourth."

Tolleson shook his head in distress and leaned forward. "It's a mess. Willie hasn't any talent releases. Film investors are nervous. They had to deposit $15,000."

"What do the performance contracts say about the film?"

"Most of these musicians don't have written contracts with Willie, just a verbal agreement. Made on the phone."

"Eddie and I are going to visit him."

"Well, ask Willie about contracts. You'll get the idea."

Downstairs the Armadillo daytime staff was arriving for work. You could always tell by the yawns who had attended last night's concert, who had gone to the band's hotel room party, who got wasted at Soap Creek Saloon. Everyone was young, able to shake off the sluggishness, and ready to go for another day.

The morning scuttlebutt: Willie Nelson had shown up near midnight with Kris Kristofferson at Soap Creek Saloon, where they sang a couple of songs with Doug Sahm. That worried me. We had a 2 p.m. appointment at Willie's house. Would he be awake?

On my way down the stairs to meet Eddie in the beer garden, Randy McCall was coming up. "Hey, Woody, are we going to sell any tickets?" He had a prodding grin.

"Train has left the station, Randy. We'll know in five days. How's it lookin' to you?"

He twitched his cheek. "We're bleedin', man. Cost overruns." He lit a cigarette. "Money's going out the back door so fast my head spins. You think we'll sell ten thou by July third?"

"Presale? Don't count on it."

Randy shook his head and took a long drag. "Pray it doesn't rain."

8

Heading to Willie's House

Along one side, a sloping corrugated roof shaded the Armadillo Beer Garden. Eddie sat at a table with lawyer Dave Richards and his wife, Ann. She was called Ann but her first name was Dorothy, same as my mother. The beer garden was home for liberal-thinking politicos of that day. Texas Comptroller of Public Accounts Bob Bullock and friends, aka Bullock's Raiders, were frequent visitors.

A young and bearded Bill Clinton lived in the Timberlake Apartments just across the street on South First, from where he took advantage of the garden and Jerry Jeff concerts. His girlfriend, Hillary Rodham, had arrived in Austin the year before to work on George McGovern's presidential campaign against Richard Nixon.

Eddie had introduced me to the Richardses in 1971. A year when Janis Joplin had the nation's ear with "Me and Bobby McGee." And when the FCC banned cigarette ads from radio-TV and President Nixon froze wages as he decoupled our money from its gold backing and introduced the petrodollar. It was a year when LBJ's senseless war in Vietnam continued to wreck our society by sending thousands of eligible males off to kill people in a faraway jungle. These days, I can't find anyone who knows why the federal government insisted on this war that cost the lives of more than 58,000 Americans and 4,000,000 Vietnamese.

Eddie ordered a couple of cold draft Shiners for the drive to Willie's house. Among the Armadillo staff, Eddie, like Hank Alrich, was an exception, owning both house and car. Two cars. We climbed into his blue Dodge Charger, equipped with lap-crossing safety belts that we seldom used.

First stop was a fill-up at the Diamond Shamrock. The uniformed station attendant quickly came out to pump our gas, 39 cents a gallon, then he checked the oil, battery, radiator, tire pressures, and cleaned the windshield. Eddie paid $7.00 cash and off we went.

I lit a joint and relaxed. It was too early to smoke; the Armadillo's official hippie-happy-hour was five o'clock. Nevertheless, I passed the smoke to Eddie as we headed up Riverside Drive toward the expressway. "Tolleson says the guys doing the movie are on hold and waiting for talent releases."

"Don't think it'll happen, Wood."

"Hmm, so it could end up like the Dallas Pop Fest with a movie that can't be shown."

"My guess is this film won't even be shot."

He passed the joint back to me. It had gone out so I put the unsmoked half in the ashtray for later. Eddie wore blue jeans with western boots, and a T-shirt featuring a JFKLN armadillo busting out of the state of Texas. With his long dark hair and beard, the man looked the part of a music business hippie. Texas cartoonist Gilbert Shelton could have easily drawn him into his *Fabulous Furry Freak Brothers* comix.

Eddie was known for tossing out quotable one-liners

all day long. This man was a tireless worker and a self-promoter with excellent cultural taste, highly intelligent, literary, and a hell of a lot of fun to be around. His outgoing personality was larger than life and made him a dynamic team leader. We didn't know it then, but this was the start of a thirty-year collaboration between us.

"What kinda turnout do you see?" Eddie said.

"Well, there's nothing else like it happening in Central Texas, and it's a holiday. Rock festivals have appeal. Leon is huge." I stretched my arms to emphasize. "Charlie Rich is a major name, but his fans don't want to get drunk in a cow pasture."

"Did you say Charlie Rich? He's not on the show."

"I got a call from Larry Trader, said Charlie's coming."

Eddie frowned and popped his neck. "Woodman, this is out of control."

I crumpled my empty beer cup and stuffed it in the plastic trash bag hanging from a window roller. "Willie might even become a star."

He sighed. "One night I took Willie over to Mother Earth where Murphey was playing. He saw a packed house of mostly college kids getting off on a new style of country." Eddie smiled. "I think Willie had an epiphany that night."

"Heard he drew a big crowd at Armadillo... considering most kids never heard of him."

"Hippies and rednecks. Greezy Wheels was on that show."

"I didn't know that."

"Most of the audience, the hippies, came for Greezy. Pot smokin' dancers, lots of twirling, and hippie flail. Didn't take Willie more than a song to convert them. That night wouldn't have been notable if the 'Dillo had booked the Moods of Country Music or Dottsy instead of Greezy."

It put me to thinking. I knew Greezy Wheels—featuring Sweet Mary Egan on fiddle—had replaced Shiva's as Armadillo's unofficial house band. Their audience loved Willie. And Willie previously had played to hippies at the free and well-attended Last Bash on the Hill, featuring a reunion of the 13th Floor Elevators.

Now, Jerry Wexler had captured the singer and his band's unique Texas energy in the grooves of the *Shotgun Willie* 12-inch. "Maybe this is Willie's time."

I turned on the car's AM radio, hoping to catch a weather report, and heard: "Later on this hour K-N-O-W will give some lucky listener two tickets to Willie Nelson's dyn-o-mite Fourth of July picnic-plus… a copy of the three-disc *Leon Russell Live* album! Yeah, it's true. Leon *will be* in Dripping Springs. And you heard it first on K-N-O-W."

Then from the dashboard speaker came Leon's top hit: "I'm up on the tightrope…"

Eddie raised his eyebrows and nodded. He turned the car up Red Bud Trail. "I wonder if *Hank Wilson's Back* is selling at Inner Sanctum. It's a different kind of Leon than *Carney*. More like country."

"Leon trying for a country audience? Really? To me that sounds like the end of his string of hits."

A very pregnant Connie Nelson greeted Eddie with a hug and led us to a comfortable sunroom with large windows. The singer was recovering from his night with Kristofferson. I got out my cassette recorder and Willie, being a former deejay, easily handled my half-dozen questions.

He wasn't so pleased to hear I expected several live phone interviews. "I'm on the phone all day trying to coordinate musicians."

I explained how critical a media crescendo was for a walk-up. "We must have full access for all press. If this is going to be annual, we gotta have media excited before and great reviews after. During the event itself, I want to be sure all reporters, whether from *The RAG* or the *New York Times*, get their interviews."

Eddie spoke up. "Lone Star and Shiner will donate beer for a press party. Night of the third, we can pile up a mountain of barbecue and roll out the kegs."

Willie nodded.

* * *

WHILE RIDING BACK to town, I felt my tension mounting along with excitement. It was apparent Willie was feeling the pressure of financing the Picnic and juggling his talent lineup.

Eddie had left Willie a large box of Picnic T-shirts, white and blue trim with the JFKLN Fourth of July poster art on the front. The shirts lifted his spirit.

"Hey, Connie, look at this," he called to his wife, tossing an extra-large to her.

In the car I switched on KNOW 1490-AM, still hoping for the weather report. A McMorris Ford commercial was wrapping up; Dave Jarrott came on and told us it was 5:10 and 102 degrees on the concrete, no relief in sight. Then...

"Hi! I'm Willie Nelson."

The band strikes up, and Willie sings, "Stay all night, stay a little longer..."

The big voice of Ron Houston booms over the music: "Willie Nelson's Prospectin' Company invites you to a Fourth of July picnic at Dripping Springs, with a fireworks of country music stars…"

Crack! Bam! Boom!

Sunny Planto calls out over the music and exploding fireworks, "Waylon Jennings!"

Waylon sings, "Just forget I ever happened…"

Fireworks, then Sunny shouts, "Sammi Smith!"

"Take the ribbons from my hair…"

Boom! KaBoom!

"John Prine!"

"Your flag decal won't get you into heaven anymore…"

KaBoom!

"Doug Sahm!"

"Is anybody goin' to San Antone…"

And, finally, Willie comes back singing "Shotgun Willie's got all of his family there…"

And then Ron comes back, over fireworks. "Advance tickets only five-fifty. Kids under twelve's free. Dripping Springs is twenty miles west of Austin on Highway 290… See y'all on the Fourth…"

Fireworks explosion.

Gordie Ham's voice: "Get tickets at Armadillo Beer Garden, Inner Sanctum, Oat Willies, Broken Spoke, and Raymond's Drugs."

A cowbell rings and Kris Kristofferson says, "If it sounds country, man, that's what it is."

My jaw dropped.

Not a musician on that show who could draw 4,000 people. But Gordie's production and editing made it sound like the biggest thing since Woodstock was about to happen in Dripping Springs. Instead of Yasgur's farm, we had Hurlbut's ranch.

Eddie laughed. He reached down and took the half-joint from the ashtray, punched in the car's lighter, lit it, and passed it to me.

"Hippie happy hour," he said, with a wink.

9

How to Sell a Picnic

Now the die was cast. It became common to deny the Dylan rumor, and with each denial, more people came to think it might happen. Finally, we put the denial on our press fact sheet, along with confirmation of Leon as co-host.

We got lots of giveaway LPs from Atlantic. I knew Jerry Wexler and his label's president Jerry Greenberg. Inside word leaked that Atlantic had changed its mind about country music: One more Willie Nelson album, and then he'd be dropped.

Doug Sahm, due a second LP, was also dropped. Doug already had recorded for producer Wexler the best album of his career: *Doug Sahm and Band*. Cover artist Gilbert Shelton. It was a stellar return to his San Antonio roots. Dylan was on it, which made the rumor believable.

Sadly, Wexler's progressive country recordings by Freda and the Firedogs were not released; that was Marcia Ball's group in the day when she was Austin's only female bandleader. Six years later, Marcia did get her own national album, the country-flavored *Circuit Queen* for Capitol Records. This was a period when Capitol showed renewed interest in Austin by releasing the albums *Steven Fromholtz* and *Signs of Life* from the Lost Gonzo Band.

A couple of years later the Austin songstress changed her music's flavor from Texas barbeque to Louisiana gumbo, and over the next 30 years Marcia Ball recorded her albums for Rounder and Alligator. Few people today know the acclaimed swamp-boogie queen pianist was almost a country music star.

* * *

SHELTER RECORDS presented more of a problem. Since Leon Russell and Danny Cordell owned it, the label's staff knew Leon wasn't to be promoted at the Picnic. So why contribute?

Eventually they caved because they didn't want to piss off a bunch of FM deejays. After all, the label had other artists they needed to sell besides Leon. They had even released a Freddie King album with Jim Franklin cover art based on the mural above the 'Dillo's backstage entrance and featuring live tracks from his Headquarters concert.

Freddie, like Willie, had used the 'Dillo stage to cross over to the youth market. Enhancing his Shelter Records connection, Jim Franklin had traveled to Tulsa and painted murals on the walls of Leon's swimming pool.

Although radio played "Rollin' in My Sweet Baby's Arms," it only reached Billboard's chart at #78, and so boxes of *Hank Wilson's Back* were returned for a label buyback. We got a slew of those for giveaways.

Fortunately, we also scored dozens of *Leon Live*, his coveted three-record concert set. By the week leading into the Picnic, every rock station in Central Texas was giving away Leon, Willie, and Doug Sahm albums. Free tickets sprayed from radio speakers all over Texas and deejays always mentioned Leon would be there. And the

Picnic was often mentioned whenever a deejay played Dylan.

Two days out, Larry Trader called about San Antonio reporting the first good signs for success. Both of the Mr. Natural stores, two L&M Western Stores, and Green Earth were out of tickets.

The bad news was the stage roof had collapsed. It was now unusable. On a July afternoon in Texas, a roof is a must for shade as well as protection from unexpected rainfall. The moviemakers who decided not to film were supposed to pay for the stage roof. Now Eddie and crew grew frantic trying to solve the last-minute crisis.

* * *

WILLIE NELSON'S first Picnic was just twelve hours from liftoff. What could be more fun than driving out to Dripping Springs for the Fourth of July?

The name of the place made you feel better about having to drive forever down a narrow, dust-clouded dirt road so you could walk a mile to reach a parched empty pasture sizzled by Texas summer heat. The cattle knew better than music fans and would not be out in the hot sun unless fenced in.

Bordering the edges of this big pasture were sparse groves of Texas cedar with scattered elms and a few post oaks for shade. Most people coming to the concert didn't know there was a stream nearby, or that a short drive would take you to Hamilton Pool with its spring-fed waterfall, one of the best cliff-jump holes in Texas.

The first casualties of the event were the press. A few

arrived early that evening on the third. Felt like it was over 100 degrees. They had gotten lost and came in hungry and thirsty.

The remote Texas Hill Country site looked vast and empty. But it wasn't silent. The pounding of construction hammers and whining of drill bits on metal filled the parched air as the Armadillo guys built the stage and hoisted Eddie Wilson's emergency-made, urethane-over-chicken-wire roof, while the Showco team set up their sound and lights.

"Check, check, check... test, test, testicles..." said the giant speakers.

Showco was considered world-class and in demand by the likes of Led Zeppelin, Elvis, and Paul McCartney. Co-owner Jack Calmes also managed Freddie King. I first saw his name on a poster as the co-producer of Bob Dylan's 1965 tour stop in Austin. Showco was the perfect company to be in charge of lights and sound.

"Test, test, check... let's do the snare mic... "

Two big things went wrong at the press party.

First, that hoped-for heap o' brisket never arrived, but fortunately the Salt Lick was setting up their BBQ stand for the concert and had a supply of sausages. Kegs of Shiner were tapped, but no one had roped off space for the press inside a special tent. The work crews had been sweating since sunrise in the July heat, faces red from overexposure. They would have to work all night.

"Hey, look! Cold beer!" somebody hollered.

In less than one hour, the first keg was floating. Meanwhile, the press kept showing up only to discover nothing to munch on, and worse—plenty of beer, but no cups! Damn.

My second problem: the musicians were arriving

but heading directly for the two dozen air-conditioned Winnebagos. They weren't coming out until Willie got there. The small press corps was confused but understanding and hanging on with hope.

In the vast empty pasture, the solitary brightly lit stage looked like a shuttle launch. Later that night, the jet-black sky featured a crescent moon sailing in the awesome stream of our Milky Way.

At last the beer cups arrived. Musicians appeared. With the lack of city light pollution, stars shone like bright gemstones spilled from a black velvet purse and the ground below was scattered with flickering campfires.

Waylon, dressed in black, came out of his mobile home to sing a song or two. Kris and Rita joined in. Interviews began. Now and then, a circle of light revealed a TV crew filming (pre-video cameras); here and there flashbulbs lit a face.

By midnight, all had gone well enough, and everybody—the stars, press, promoters and work crew—was satisfied. By 1 a.m. magic was in the air and Hurlbut's parched land had cooled down. A few musicians chewed the fat with night owl fans and provided impromptu singing. People mellowed out.

Willie himself stayed up all night and stopped to talk with folks at the various campsites. Mostly out-of-towners who arrived unaware camping was not allowed. Ron Houston stayed most of the night and rushed off at 4 a.m. to do his morning show.

The final countdown was underway.

Just before sunrise, Willie Nelson took the stage. As the country singer waved good morning to his early picnickers, Willie, the event promoter, had to be wondering how this day would turn out. He plucked out the distinct opening notes to the "Star-Spangled Banner," picked as far as "the dawn's early light"... then, went into a duet with Leon Russell: "Amazing Grace, how sweet the sound..."

Leon then left the microphone to sit down at the drum kit and, signaling *more to come*, picked up the sticks. The all-day show was off to a perfect start.

Folks rubbed their eyes as they crawled out of sleeping bags to brew coffee over the remaining hot coals. Jackrabbits moved around now, startled to find strange two-legged critters in their field. White-wing doves cooed, a crow cawed, and a mockingbird called back. A big golden sun inched over the horizon.

Sunrise made Hurlbut's pasture look like a scene from *The Magnificent Seven*... or, like the opening to Kubrick's *2001: A Space Odyssey*.

We definitely had liftoff.

10

Independence Day: Hippies and Rednecks

In a few hours the Picnic got crazy. Ten thousand by noon—holy shit! The backstage was chaos because every musician had his own entourage. Maybe 20 bands and their spouses and road crew and friends had access to the small fenced area. Press invited their pals and designated them as helpers, which meant a backstage population explosion. Everyone brought drugs; some folks brought guns.

Bob Hedderman took on the hopeless challenge of stage manager. His stage crew worked nonstop to reset the mics and change amps for each artist. Workers had to fight their way through the backstage party to lug instruments up and down steep crowded stairs in roasting heat.

Coolest place around was under Eddie's urethane roof. Beer hospitality guys found themselves overwhelmed, out of cups again! By now a vast and constant flood of people carrying blankets, wearing backpacks, and lugging ice chests poured into the pasture. Traffic was jammed back up the dirt road for miles and snaking onto the highway. White dust clouds of *caliche* created a distant haze, like a fog on a cloudless day.

A happy Allen Grimm passed by me, tilted his too-small cowboy hat, and said, "Can you believe this, Woody? Whew!"

At four o'clock I knew we were in trouble. The crowd had doubled and the traffic jam stretched on forever. Eddie rushed by.

I called out, "I haven't seen Tolleson!"

"He's out on the road directing traffic." And Eddie was gone.

Crowd density made it impossible to find someone if he didn't hold a walkie-talkie. I couldn't believe it, people were still coming!

About an hour later, we received the first word that security was giving up. No way to tell who had tickets. Cars were hopelessly backed up and thousands of eager picnickers were trudging toward us.

Communications broke down due to a battery shortage for the walkie-talkies. Pre-cellphone days and with no telephone lines, real-time updates from outside were impossible.

In the Willie van, I heard news reports broadcast on KLBJ 590-AM and KTSA of a horrific mile-long traffic jam. By now backstage looked as crowded as the audience out front. Someone gave the order to clear everyone out of backstage—a desperate effort to regain control.

Wives, managers, press, everyone was ordered out. But now performers were blocked, and somewhere out there were reviewers Townsend Miller, Chet Flippo, and Jan Reid.

Hedderman rushed by, pointing at the security fence. "That woman over there, she's from *Time* magazine."

Billy Cooper tugged my arm, "Woody, there's a guy

from a magazine called *Crawdaddy*, says you told him to meet you backstage."

People outside the security perimeter got unruly. Deejays from KRMH 103.7-FM and KOKE demanded interviews. Dave Jarrott was looking for me. Ron Houston had changed into fresh clothes and returned. The Austin People's Clinic tent was maxed out handling cases of heat exhaustion; and since all cots were filled, their patients lay on the grass.

As the temperature hit 102, a KTSA newsman in a low-flying airplane recorded his bird's-eye view for playback: "Naked hippies and straight-laced country music fans are having the time of their life in Dripping Springs, Texas. DPS at 5 p.m. estimates 40,000 people at Willie Nelson's Fourth of July Picnic. And plenty more folks arriving... I can see a line of cars backed up to the Interstate... "

Many had been waiting for the heat of the day to end; they knew the night shows were the featured acts. Backstage kegs were floating. But the Lone Star beer team heroically rose to the occasion and lugged in extras—with more cups—while brewery executive Jerry Retzloff kept it flowing. Music was great.

It was a perfect Fourth of July mega-picnic.

At sunset, music was delayed briefly for a ceremony as Willie's black-cape-wearing drummer Paul English got married on stage! Waylon Jennings was best man.

What?

That wasn't on the schedule!

I guess about 10 p.m. is when it happened. Can't say for sure. I was pretty wrecked by that hour. Anyway, as the band started to play, a couple of Super Trouper spotlights lit up, and the electric power went down.

Ron Houston thinks he remembers Rita Coolidge was starting into a song. Then, total darkness with the Milky Way a glittering stream above the pasture. The only sound to be heard in that darkness was the rumble of the Winnebago generators from near the stage... and men frantically shouting instructions.

Car headlights were turned on and aimed at the stage. From a nearby radio, KRMH ballyhooed Willie's Picnic. The station seemed unaware of the current situation.

The power had blown somewhere. Rumors were flying. Had the power box had been shotgunned by an uptight rancher, like Hurlbut? Did someone hit a pole with their car?

At this late hour, the production crew was exhausted and stoned out of their minds, relying on instinct. Unplug this. Plug it back in. Try this. Try that.

Two guys raced off on foot with battery lanterns to trace the power line through the ranch. A harried county sheriff's deputy arrived to tell us the whole area was dark. He thought every transformer in Hays County had blown! No way to say when it would come back. Emergency crews were on the case.

Eddie rushed by with the look of a man trying to keep three balls in the air while riding his unicycle on Leon Russell's tightrope. He shook his head.

My immediate thought was of the press coverage. My second thought, the horrible possibility that one spooked rattlesnake could set off a stampede that would make worldwide news for days! I could see it: "Thirty people trampled to death at Willie Nelson's Picnic... five small children..."

I damn well knew more than one rattlesnake called this pasture home.

Bounding up the wooden stairs onto the stage, I stepped to the middle and leaned down to the people in front. I shined a flashlight on my face and shouted, "Power back in twenty minutes, pass it on."

The first row shouted the message to those behind them, "Power in twenty minutes, pass it on."

My hope was folks would stay put. I repeated, and then in ten minutes shouted, "Power on in fifteen minutes, pass it on."

I had to stall. We needed to make it seem like progress was being made, but actual reports were that we might be down permanently. An impossible situation.

Showco continued their efforts nonstop. Their latest strategy was to take the backstage Winnebago generators and hotwire them into the sound and lighting system. The guys had handled many emergencies. This was one for the books.

I shouted to the expectant faces looking up at me, "Power back in ten minutes, pass it on."

Again, the front row dutifully called the message back and you could hear it getting fainter and fainter as it went farther back into the darkness. Soon there arose a deep growl from the huge speakers like revving an outboard motor, and then I heard an engine starting.

I tapped a mic, tink tink. Thank god, the stage mics had power. Then lights. Dim, but lights they were.

A cheer went up! Showco had temporarily saved the Picnic from oblivion by connecting the motorhomes to their equipment. Sound volume was low but working. Rita stepped back up to the mic and restarted her song, as if nothing had happened.

One hour later the full power came back. Another big cheer! Some people had camped so far away they never knew the power had failed. To them, it was just a long set change.

But now, all these midnight picnickers were ready to party, and Willie didn't disappoint them. It was long after midnight before Willie began his traditional closing song, "Turn out the lights, the party's over; they say that all good things must end..."

Carrying a worn Martin guitar he named Trigger, and making his way down the overcrowded steps from the stage, Willie gave me a nod and then a happy one-armed hug.

I said, "Looks like an annual event, Willie. ABC-TV showed aerial film of the crowd."

He smiled. "Woody, I think we hit a home run."

A beaming Larry Trader came up to shake my hand, looked me in the eye, and said, "Willie will never forget you for this, Woody."

A frazzled Eddie Wilson sighed. "You did it, Woodman."

I felt great. The crowd was bigger than I'd ever hoped. Some media guessed, between the start and finish, up to 70,000 people might have come and gone. It was then I realized: not only did Bob Dylan not show up (wasn't expecting him, since he was only a rumor), but also Doug Sahm didn't show up. I shrugged my shoulders. Go figure.

* * *

FIVE A.M., back in the San Antonio neighborhood city of Alamo Heights. My ivy-covered home was a handmade cottage, German hatch style, cedar posts and stucco. The landlord was my good friend Pleas McNeel, who published the politico-arts tabloid *Eagle Bone Whistle*, a name suggested by Alan Ginsberg as he toured the city on a motorcycle with Pleas hanging on behind.

I lived there ten years. Never locked the door. Folks such as media visionaries Larry Yurdin and Lorenzo Milam would drop by to stay a few nights.

I pushed down the Dutch door latch and stepped inside. Fully wasted, I climbed the ladder into the loft and crashed on my king-sized mattress. I lay there dozing and thinking about the completion of my first project with the talented staff at Armadillo World Headquarters.

Wow.

The next day Connie Nelson gave birth to Amy Lee.

We definitely had liftoff.

11

Picnic Retrospect

Irecently saw a music reviewer claim the Dripping Springs Reunion was really Willie Nelson's first Picnic, or at least its prototype.

Not so.

It may have inspired Willie to do his own outdoor show, but these were two different kinds of events. The only connection was the venue and some of the musicians.

His Picnic was the start of an era, the Reunion was an ending.

Willie's name wasn't even on their playbill! It had been a decade since he charted a single in the country music Top 20. They didn't consider the singer a vital draw. On that Reunion bill were some of Nashville's greatest stars: Hank Snow, Roy Acuff, Loretta Lynn, Merle Haggard, Buck Owens, Bob Wills, Waylon Jennings, Roger Miller, and others. A Grand Ole Opry spectacular. Yet they couldn't turn out a crowd.

Until I stepped in, the Picnic was promoted as a country music event. Like the Reunion. My refocus using FM rock and AM Top 40 to promote Leon Russell (and the Bob Dylan possibility) repositioned the Picnic. It was transformed into a counterculture festival that coupled hardcore rednecks and back-to-the-country hippies with

Leon's rowdy rockers.

Mark it down: July 4, 1973. That's the date Armadillo Productions and Willie Nelson freed country music from the iron fist of Nashville's assembly-line producers.

It was truly an Independence Day.

12

Headband - Headquarters

Back in the summer of 1968, two long black beards walked past my KTSA office. Hmm, is *Fiddler on the Roof* in town?

It was Spencer Perskin and Shawn Siegel from Shiva's Headband. Turned out Spencer was indeed a fiddler. They handed us their first single, "Kaleidoscopic." We marked it for late night play.

A year later, they were back. The guys were promoting "Lose the Blues."

I liked it and, living up to its title, it wasn't blues. For example, Danny Galindo had recently brought me a Sonobeat Records demo called "She's a Country Gal" by New Atlantis, the Austin band he and his brother Bob played in with Donnie Erickson, Roky's brother. That was blues. It sounded a lot like Canned Heat in the style of "Going Up the Country." However, I must admit Spencer's psychedelic fiddle playing was in the country blues tradition of Gatemouth Brown and Austin hero Teodar Jackson.

Spencer and Shawn watched music director Johnny O'Neal flip the new Shiva's 45, "Let's hear this side." He put the needle down. It was "Take Me to the Mountains."

Johnny smiled. "Oh yeah, that's more like it."

The song was timely like "Kaleidoscopic" had been the year before. Across the nation, big city hippies adjusting to the fading idealism of their Summer of Love were now embracing rural lifestyles. Shiva's had a good tune.

But, strangely, what most captured my attention about this 1969 record was its label. Printed on it was a hand-drawn armadillo in front of a Victrola flower horn speaker. It was a visual pun on the original painting by Francis Barraud featuring a small black-and-white terrier mix that became the RCA Records logo.

Armadillo Records.

I laughed. Spencer proudly told me his new company was Armadillo Productions. And this was the first release by his new record company. Vulcan Gas Company poster artist Jim Franklin had drawn this weird critter for him. Spencer had seen Franklin drawing his contribution for *Dillo Toons Comix* with other Vulcan artists.

The drawings inspired him to ask if Franklin would create the critter for their record label. The armadillo instantly became the mascot for Shiva's, like the skeleton was for the Grateful Dead.

Today that 45 record is notable not as much for the songs as for its art: it represents the first use of the Armadillo logo. And the rare 1969 *Dillo Toons* comic book is sought after, not just because it holds some of Jim Franklin's earliest armadillo art, but also because it inspired Spencer to use the mysterious beast as a hip music icon.

Franklin was not the first.

Glen Whitehead had drawn cartoon armadillos in the *Texas Ranger* humor magazine and used them to promote student-related events for the UT cavers. Jim Franklin's animals were different. They were anatomically real armadillos placed in absurd and abstract situations.

The artist had introduced his version of the little critter in September 1968 for a concert in Wooldridge Park headlined by New Atlantis and Lavender Hill Express, featuring Rusty Weir on drums and Gary P. Nunn on keyboard. This first JFKLN armadillo of hundreds to come is smoking a joint! Hard to imagine now, but it was a radical drawing back then.

That year Franklin used the armadillo to promote a UT art exhibit, and Ramon, Ramon and the Four Daddyos. Soon his 'dillos were in *The Rag*.

I chronicle this small event because it demonstrates the power of an idea. The "smiley face" icon entered pop culture about that same time and has today has become a text emoji. Likewise, the armadillo has enlarged its territory, becoming *the* Texas music icon and Austin's official unofficial mascot.

After two months of KTSA's playing "Take Me to the Mountains" and my Gavin Report listings, I got a call from the Capitol Tower in LA. They were signing Shiva's! The guys came back at KTSA with their 1970 album, *Take Me to the Mountains*.

This was really a big deal. The 13th Floor Elevators and the Bubble Puppy had already gone national out of Austin, but their International Artists label was a Houston-based regional that farmed out distribution.

By now those bands were gone. The Bubble Puppy pioneered the use of dueling lead guitars in their album, *A Gathering of Promises*, and released the psychedelic "Hot Smoke and Sassafras" that rose to #14 on the charts. By including Sir Doug at #13, Roy Head #2, it meant Central Texas had placed three hits in the Top 15 in four years—San Antonio to Austin was a talent belt.

Soon the Puppy moved to LA, changed their name to Demian, released an album on ABC-Dunhill Records, and disbanded. The Elevators also broke up.

It should be noted the Bubble Puppy held the honor of the highest-ranked Austin rock single on *Billboard's* Top 100 until 1980. That's when Christopher Cross reached #2 with "Ride Like the Wind" and followed with nine more singles appearing in that coveted Top 100.

In 1962 The Bobby Doyle Three had been the first hometown musicians to sign with a major label, Columbia Records. They released *In A Most Unusual Way*. The following year that same label gave us *The Kooky World of the Geezinslaw Brothers*. Bobby Doyle later had a second album on Warner Bros in 1968; meanwhile Geezinslaws Sammy Allred and Son switched to Capitol Records where they created three additional '60s releases. Their 1967 album title was especially memorable: *My Dirty Lowdown Rotten Cotton-Pickin' Little Darlin'*.

However, Shiva's Headband was the first Austin rock group to be signed by a major label. The Beatles were part of Capitol. The Beach Boys. They had The Band and Steve Miller. Grand Funk Railroad sold millions. Their distinctive cylindrical office tower was a Hollywood landmark. Austin's new breed of long-haired pot-smoking musicians was excited. They too might score.

The year before, a long-haired Austinite named Steve Fromholz, wearing cowboy boots and white Stetson, driving a white double cab pickup, visited me. He and Dan McKinnen called themselves Frummox and had a new album called *Here to There*. It was on Phase, a sub-label that ABC Records launched to feature psychedelic music. It's a rare collector's album today.

This new release contained the now recognized masterpiece "Texas Trilogy." A song KTSA could not play because, for one thing, it was over ten minutes long. These guys were an acoustic duo, and unbeknownst to any of us at the moment, this beautiful recording became noted as the first album from the soon-to-explode Austin progressive country scene.

But Frummox was not a country band, and sounded much closer to Carolyn Hester or Willis Alan Ramsey than Michael Murphey or Jerry Jeff Walker. Proto-Americana. I walked Steve Fromholz out to the parking lot and his double cab pickup where the musician, looking at my hair tied into a ponytail, enlightened me. "Woody, let me clue you in: a man with long hair in South Texas better be driving a Cadillac or a new pickup truck."

I pointed to my 1969 T-Bird, he nodded and then drove off to visit KEXL.

In 2007, the Texas Legislature declared Steve Fromholz Poet Laureate for the State of Texas.

The cover art for the Shiva's Headband debut album, *Take Me to the Mountains*, was an outrageous armadillo painting by Jim Franklin. The surrealist artist depicted thousands of Armadillos stampeding like a herd of lemmings toward an earthquake's jagged open ravine. Any connection to the mountains was obtuse at best. Shiva's had recorded in the Grateful Dead's studio and used Santana engineer Fred Catero.

However, this band wasn't like the Dead. It turned

out keyboard artist Shawn Siegel was not even a partner, and over the years, Spencer changed sidemen like some folks change shirts. You could say it should have been called Spencer's Headband.

Their music was an original sound, even more distinctive than the Elevators. It impressed me that Shiva's sometimes performed without guitar—just drums, bass, keyboard and fiddle. Nevertheless, although their music was psychedelic in concert, Shiva's, like the Elevators, mostly played standard-length songs and not the long Grateful Dead jams I enjoyed.

This album was about to change Austin. The band had not only received studio cost, but they also got seed money to help Capitol Records find more Austin talent!

Spencer Perskin told me he was hiring a full-time manager for Shiva's. Next time I came to Austin, he'd introduce us. He was a neighbor and beer industry lobbyist named Eddie Wilson. This fellow had never been in the music business. Most bands would have ignored someone with such a lack of credentials, but Spencer believed Wilson's virginity was a plus. He also said the Vulcan Gas Company was closing and Shiva's was looking to lease a performance hall.

As Shiva's Headband manager, Eddie Wilson took up the assignment of finding his band a place to play. He spotted an empty structure that in the 1950s was the Austin Sportcenter where the *Louisiana Hayride* had performed, featuring its up-and-coming Elvis Presley. The deserted building was the perfect size for a hall, and the backstage area held air-conditioned space for offices.

To get it going, Shiva's Headband put up $3,000 seed money and Mad Dog Bud Shrake added $1,000. The group named their post-Vulcan concert facility

Armadillo World Headquarters. It was a perfect fit with the already established Armadillo Records and Armadillo Productions. From the music of the Headband came the music from the Headquarters.

Eddie told me one of the early considerations tossed around for naming Austin's newest music venue was Uncle Zeke's Emporium... finally they had settled on Armadillo National Headquarters. It was Bud Shrake of the Mad Dogs who recommended using "World" in place of "National." I remember hearing that Vulcan Gas Company was almost called the Electric Grandmother.

What's in a name?

Only a future legend.

13

Blown Away by Space City Video

Aterrible thing happened following the first Willie Nelson Picnic. I learned Armadillo and Willie had a falling out and would never work together again.

"What's the fight about?" I said to Mike Tolleson.

He leaned back in his chair. "Missing money and backstage guns."

"Guns? Not good. But it's an old story, Mike. The majority of Willie's gigs are rural dance halls. His night's cash earnings are carried across a dark parking lot after midnight. It's not uncommon for a promoter who lost money to stiff the man or pull a heist."

"I know. It's a culture clash. But you can't fault Bobby Hedderman for wanting the backstage safe from guns. He was threatened. Freddie King's guys don't carry guns."

"They used to."

Tolleson raised his eyebrows and nodded.

"What missing money?" I said.

"Randy thinks money is missing and Willie thinks money is missing. We're pointing fingers at each other."

Mike Tolleson sighed and leaned forward. "But I do

have some good news. Our television project is coming alive."

"Really?" I said.

"I've talked with KLRN program director Bill Arhos. He says they are going to bring a truck and cameras to record a two-part show."

"Great. Could be a pilot."

"Exactly. Willie committed to performing on this show before this money and guns problem. Eddie and Hedderman are working on booking some other musicians. Part one will be national talent and part two local. We're setting a date."

* * *

THE DRIVE BACK and forth to San Antonio was boring. The only notable stops of interest were the Aquarena Springs in San Marcos for Ralph the diving pig, or New Braunfels for the Snake Farm. So I usually boarded a nonstop Continental-Trailways bus to relax. The bus was always empty. I went for the back seats to muse over the Armadillo TV project and take a couple of tokes off a joint…

A few months earlier, Eddie and I sat in Tolleson's office watching black-and-white concert video of Freddie King at the 'Dillo. I was stunned, this recording was exciting! The cameras were handheld and provided intimate views of the musicians as if you were on the stage. Dark shadows from unaided lighting gave it a noir look. Here was a Burton Wilson photo come to life.

"Wow! Who made this?"

"Space City Video, they're out of Houston," Tolleson said.

Eddie laughed. "Used to be called Mother's Vidiots, worked with Mother's Family at FM-101, KLOL."

Why the name "Space City?"

Of course, it could mean spaced-out, which they were. But remember, back then the U.S.A. proudly rocketed men to and from the moon, and the hot phrase of the day was "A-OK." Via Mission Control in Houston, NASA monitored lunar space flights with their brave astronaut crews. During that period, the former Bayou City rebranded itself as Space City and became the home of Astros Baseball and the Astrodome.

The nucleus of Space City Video was five members, one of whom was Bill Narum. I recognized his name from his graphics credits on the early ZZ TOP albums. It was the age of the "big 12-inch" sold in shrink-wrapped covers with spectacular artwork. It was Narum in 1976 who had produced that magnificently eerie Texas landscape used by ZZ as their double-spread cover for *Tejas*. He told me it was a last-minute rush job done over a weekend and inspired by mescaline. It's my favorite Narum painting.

What the Space City team had done at the 'Dillo was carry Sony Portapaks and shoot video with available light. Portable video was a new technology and Sony had the only consumer-priced video camera recorders you could pick up and carry. Not many people had them; the units were heavy and picture quality was subpar for commercial use.

First released in 1967, Portapaks had become the tool of choice for the emerging guerrilla video movement and for media art collectives like the Raindance Foundation and the Global Village in Manhattan. Each cameraperson strapped on a 30-pound pack that contained rechargeable batteries and an open-reel half-inch tape deck. Its camera was cereal-box-size and connected by wire.

All this rigging gave the video team the look of combat commandos as they crept about on stage wearing backpacks and pointing their handheld cameras at the musicians and crowd. Poor video quality? Yes, but that Armadillo Freddie King tape was the best concert recording I had seen aside from the big-money documentaries, such as Michael Wadleigh's *Woodstock* or the Maysles brothers' classic, *Gimme Shelter*.

14

The Pilot for the Pilot of "Austin City Limits"

I was staring absentmindedly at my yellow Western Electric desk phone when Eddie Wilson called. "Woodman, I've got a name for the show: *Armadillo Country Music Review*. Along with Willie, I have OKs from Michael Murphey, Greezy Wheels, and Hank Alrich's band, Diamond Rio. We're still checking on Billy Jo Shaver and D. K. Little."

Eddie and Hedderman liked D.K. Little and his brand of country-style R&B, and it was D. K.'s beautiful wife, Emma Little, who managed the 'Dillo's nursery. The guys had booked a great mix of musicians with albums on major labels along with local unsigned artists.

Willie was the established war veteran, but it was young Michael Murphey who first broke into the national Top 40. He did it for A&M Records at #37 with the Bob Johnston-produced "Geronimo's Cadillac." And he was also getting progressive FM radio play with his album, *Cosmic Cowboy Souvenir*. *Rolling Stone* magazine was hot on him. His producer was the famous Bob Johnston, who had produced Dylan's *Nashville Skyline*: "Is it rolling, Bob?"

Johnston's initial country album for Murphey,

Geronimo's Cadillac, was groundbreaking with its use of progressive licks, sensitive lyrics, and a pinch of gospel flavor. This was in 1972, the same year Bobby Bridger, who then lived in Austin and published the Native American-inspired tabloid, *Hoka Hey*, released *Merging Of Our Minds* on RCA, and followed it the next year with *And I Wanted to Sing For the People*. It was also the year RCA released B. W. Stevenson's self-titled album, *Lead Free*.

The following year RCA delivered two more from Buckwheat, as his friends called him, including *My Maria* with its title song becoming a Top 10 pop hit. This big-voiced singer with a big bushy beard played a steel-string acoustic guitar and went on to round out the 1970s with three more singles in the Top 100, plus another RCA album, and two on Warner Bros. I often recall Buckwheat with a grin and saying, "You don't buy beer, you rent it."

Several years later Bob Johnston, under heavy duress from the IRS, moved to Austin, where he found Willie Nelson also hassled by the dreaded taxman. Both guys were going broke. Johnston took Willie into the studio and in 1992 produced *The IRS Tapes: Who'll Buy My Memories?* A beautiful album, most unique, two discs and twenty-four Willie songs performed solo with just an acoustic guitar.

* * *

KLRN CHANNEL 18 program director Bill Arhos in 1973 made a gutsy move. He dared to bring the very proper PBS viewers into a music hall run by hippies. The show's talent lineup was radical for the older public television audience who were accustomed to Nashville stars. Most people had never heard of progressive country. But the young 18- to 34-year-old Central Texas viewers had been exposed to the Picnic, and they would flip out seeing Austin's renegade country musicians on TV.

My interest in the show was immediate. "I think we can do this on TV in both cities. Have FM stereo simulcasts in both towns."

To dress up the stage, it was decided to hoist the backdrop used at both the Armadillo Confab in Victoria and Willie's Picnic. This elaborate mural was a collective masterwork painted by multiple Armadillo artists. The oversized canvas depicted cans of Lupita jalapeños framing the armored mascot while a singing cosmic cowboy sprang from a Texas-shaped belt buckle.

Looking closely, you could see this silver buckle was really a giant coke spoon complete with fresh snow flaking off the state's distinctive southern tip as if being scooped from a bag of blow. Fortunately, this excellent period piece was preserved for posterity by Leea Mechling. For decades the backdrop's spoon has been seen unrecognized by several hundred thousand shoppers at the city's famous Armadillo Christmas Bazaars.

Everything was set for a perfect event. The Austin branch of KLRN rented a video production truck from Trinity University in San Antonio. TV producer-director Charles Vaughn and his crew set up their equipment in a hot and jam-packed room. Soon the music started.

The station didn't yet own a handheld camera. Mounted on bulky pedestals, three heavy tube-based RCA color cameras required additional light. 'Dillo stage lighting was turned up full blast... and that made the unair-conditioned hall's temperature soar. The bar sold a lot of cold beer.

Then an unexpected thunderstorm rolled through, reducing the heat but also threatening the recording. Lightning knocked the power off and on during Greezy

Wheels' set. Thunder on the audio track!

A determined Charles Vaughn knew his low budget meant this show was a one shot. As the band played on, he kept recording and held the camera team steadfast throughout the storm. The man got his show.

Two weeks later Eddie Wilson and Mike Tolleson arrived on HemisFair Plaza to look at the edited program. We toured KLRN's studios in the Institute of Texan Cultures and I voiced the show's open and closing announcements. The next move was to contact Lee Gaddis, general manager at KRMH.

Television did not yet offer audio in stereo. Our goal was for both KEXL and KRMH to have stereo hi-fi simulcasts that were synced with the musicians playing on TV. No easy task back then.

Both radio stations would receive quarter-inch stereo audiotapes of the one-hour shows. KEXL's engineer, Don White, who later founded San Antonio's leading video postproduction house Match Frame, rented a specialized playback deck. It sported a heavy six-inch flywheel knob to imperceptibly speed up or slow down the tape.

That night, while standing in the KEXL master control, Don White monitored the show on a TV set. By hand, Don spun the giant knob back and forth to visually match the musicians' fingers and the singers' lips with the music.

For the younger public television and progressive FM audiences, this was a dream come true. Elated viewers lit up the KEXL and KRMH phones with compliments. Top-notch stereo complemented the high-quality images and bright stage colors. People were happy. Both shows were an enormous success for the broadcasters and a valuable learning experience for us.

Yet something was missing. With those giant studio cameras, Charles Vaughn couldn't have his people crawling around on stage for unique shots. Bill Arhos learned the best remote equipment couldn't capture the intimate live audience feeling. He needed to build a unique KLRN studio set featuring audience response as part of the performance.

Meanwhile, the Armadillo staff learned their future in music television had to be more like a Space City Video production. Otherwise, the magic vanished. It was like turning on the overhead lights at a high school prom. Still, everyone acknowledged the shows were a success and valuable data had been gathered.

KLRN's production of the *Armadillo Country Music Review* was historically significant. In addition to putting this new kind of country music on TV for the first time, that 1973 show was a pilot for the 1974 pilot of the *Austin City Limits* PBS series.

The show also turned out to be Willie's swan song for the Headquarters. He never again performed on the Armadillo stage, except for a duet with Tom T. Hall. Willie Nelson even bought a competing venue, the Austin Opera House, and hired Tim O'Connor, who had previously run the Bull Creek Saloon and managed Castle Creek.

Castle Creek was a small listening room that occupied the former Chequered Flag space and Tim strived to maintain its heritage of introducing singer-songwriters. Jimmy Buffet's signature hit, "Margaritaville," was a nod to his gigs at Castle Creek and *not* a club in Florida. It seems that one night in '73, he opened for Jerry Jeff Walker and was treated to his first margarita (of course, with Cuervo Gold) and the rest is boozer-music history.

15

Let's Go to Luckenbach, Texas

To cap off the successful Armadillo TV broadcasts, Eddie Wilson suggested a Hill Country getaway party in an unheard-of town called Luckenbach. This little bitty town's official slogan was coined by its squashed western hat wearing gray bearded mayor Hondo Crouch: "Everybody's somebody in Luckenbach."

Eddie's idea was to invite the staffs from KEXL, KRMH, KLRN, and Armadillo. The KOKE deejays, aka the Super-Ropers, were invited, too.

* * *

LUCKENBACH? I had been introduced to the itty bitty town in 1971 when psychedelic folk music pioneer Rex Foster and a band of San Antonio musicians pitched tepees and camped out for a few weeks. Most of the radio folks knew nothing of Luckenbach, though some had been there in August when Jerry Jeff Walker recorded *Viva Terlingua!*

But if Luckenbach was unknown, even fewer had heard of a guy named Kinky Friedman, who had recently signed with folk label Vanguard Records. Eddie had booked his band for the party. None of the deejays had any idea of what to expect from a singing cowboy with the name Kinky.

And the local beer drinking regulars in the Luckenbach General Store were uneasy about the name of his band. The Texas Jew Boys? When a mustached, cigar-smoking Kinky Friedman arrived wearing a black Stetson and dark sunglasses, folks took notice.

His drummer set up the drum kit. Soon there was a quick sound check and the band started tuning; and then, with an unusually brief Eddie Wilson introduction, the Kinkster and his Jew Boys played songs from their brand new album, *Sold American*: "We Reserve The Right to Refuse Service to You," "Ride 'em, Jewboy." "High on Jesus," etc.

Right away toes were tapping and soon people began to laugh. By the end of Kinky's first set, everyone had loosened up. Folks were in the mood to party.

As the late afternoon progressed into early evening, the Shiner beer kegs were put afloat as soon as they were replaced. At sundown, the party was still going strong. By the end of the day Hondo Crouch, budding actor Guich Koock, and Kinky Friedman were leading a rousing group sing-along:

> "Get your biscuits in the oven and your buns in
>   the bed,
> That's what I to my baby said,
> Women's liberation is a-going to your head..."

It may not surprise you to learn the National Organization of Women voted the Texas singer Male

Chauvinist of the Year. But the nonplussed Kinkster played on to become a cult star of notoriety, and over the next two years he released albums for ABC and Epic.

Late that night after the laughter had faded away, many a partied-out partier slept under the stars.

None of us at that magic event could have foreseen that in only five years these pioneering FM stations would disappear, talented staffs scattered to the winds... and Luckenbach's fun-loving mayor, Hondo Crouch, would be dead.

16

Austin-bred Armadillos

Got a phone call in the fall of '73.

"Woody, why don't you move to Austin and be part of the Armadillo? We want you up here with us."

That invitation from Eddie Wilson took me aback. What an honor! I didn't know how to answer him, and so mumbled something about needing to think about it.

Armadillo... I had no interest in being part of the concert or nightclub business. I let my imagination run wild. What I did like was the Armadillo venue had TV potential for live music. It could easily be the site for a radio concert hour, one more personal than FM's popular *King Biscuit Flour Hour*.

Armadillo Productions had inherited the groundwork for a record company from the Headband; thus it could become a major label with its own recording studio and publishing company. The mascot itself could be a syndicated comic strip in newspapers, like *Pogo* or *Peanuts*, and on Saturday mornings a TV cartoon show for kids.

It could be all that. The staff working at the Headquarters was a gifted lot and their weird little armadillo the perfect Texas icon.

But, what a long shot...

What most attracted me to Armadillo was the

professionalism Eddie Wilson drew to the project. Mike Tolleson was a copyright, trademark, publishing lawyer, Randy McCall was a CPA, and Fletcher Clark had been a Boston banker. I knew of Hank Alrich as a respected San Antonio musician, and Jim Franklin was obviously a most gifted artist. Bob Hedderman seemed rock steady as the 'Dillo's manager.

The icon?

As mentioned previously, its pre-Franklin origin traces back to UT's *Texas Ranger* parties and a few Glen Whitehead comic strips. That fixed the 'Dillo in humor from the start. Artists JAXON and Gilbert Shelton had been on that *Ranger* fun-loving staff. In fact, it was *Ranger* party revelers in Galveston who lured Jim Franklin to Austin.

This playful irreverence, along with protest, was at the heart of the Austin counterculture and could be seen throughout the Headquarters. It was evident on almost every 'Dillo concert poster. Many of the posters Micael Priest had drawn were outright cartoons, like the one for Willie Nelson's first concert that shows a big jukebox playing "Hello Walls" as a heartbroken cowboy sobs into his mug of beer. And Jim Franklin always got a laugh with his tee shirt displaying an armadillo humping the Texas State Capitol dome.

The phenomenal Armadillo World Headquarters was humbly born on Friday night of August 7 in 1970. At its beginning, AWHQ carried a strong presence of Vulcan Gas Company spirit. Spencer Perskin and Eddie Wilson were good friends of Vulcan co-owner Houston White. Jim Franklin and Bobby Hedderman came to the 'Dillo from the Vulcan.

And the needs of musicians ignited the initial sparks that led to the opening of both great venues. Conqueroo audio man and sometime 13th Floor Elevators manager Sandy Lockett helped Don Hyde start the Vulcan; and Shiva's Headband leader Spencer Perskin financed and inspired the Armadillo. Those guys were looking for halls where they and friends could perform.

Shiva's Headband had played the grand opening for the Vulcan Gas Company, and three years later they played the grand opening for the Armadillo World Headquarters. But as a sign of how quickly times were changing, the Vulcan's two most popular bands—Conqueroo and 13th Floor Elevators—would never perform in this newest Austin music hall. Nor would the Vulcan's premier artist Gilbert Shelton create any concert posters.

The founding Armadillo staff was a collective of like-minded people. Many believed that Eddie Wilson owned Armadillo World Headquarters, but it's not so. It was 2001 before he bought full rights to the name. But certainly the 'Dillo's collective attitude sprang from the philosophies of Armadillo Productions and partners Perskin and Wilson.

One writer said it best when he described Eddie Wilson as "the Armadillo's spiritual leader and trail boss."

Almost four years after its opening, Armadillo Productions finally registered as a corporation with eight equal shareholders.

Initially, like the Vulcan, the venue had no beer or liquor license. In those first days, staff worked for tickets and food, maybe a lid of pot and a hit of LSD. It was indeed a labor of love.

When money was made on a show, it went directly into bill paying and facility improvements. And those improvements were always focused on trying to provide a better event for the musicians and their audiences.

Eddie quickly became the glue holding everyone together. His mother and plumber-handyman dad helped a lot. His wife Genie did bookeeping. Entertainment lawyer Mike Tolleson arrived and opened an office to educate local musicians and artists on the rules of publishing and copyright.

No one else in Central Texas was doing this. Tolleson selflessly taught many penniless artists the basics of protecting their intellectual property.

So I sensed that with a dynamo like Eddie Wilson out front and the financial-legal flanks covered, plus the tremendous goodwill surrounding Armadillo, the management was in place to build a TV, radio, and record company that would rank among the nation's best. As usual, the missing element was money.

At that time, a handful of craft and art booths still operated inside the hall and, most notably, the excellent Daily Bread Bakery. Soon the hall's main stage was moved to its opposite wall and more floor space was needed. So the crafts booths departed for The Drag, where they established the Austin Renaissance Market.

It didn't take long for the staff to realize selling fruit juice and cookies wasn't the solution to cash flow problems. So they obtained a beer and wine license. Hank Alrich became interested in transforming the kitchen into a full-service healthy food operation. One day, out of the blue, he offered to lend the money desperately needed to construct the Armadillo Beer Garden.

This would be a revenue-generating addition. Beer and good food would change the 'Dillo's ambiance from a nighttime concert hall to a venue that enhanced and extended Austin's sense of community. It would be a friendly spot to hold a meeting or hang out with friends on a pretty day.

Hank then set about building an eight-track recording studio—Onion Audio—in two rooms behind the increasingly busy stage. Onion could record live concerts.

Draft beer quickly became the stabilizing revenue source for the 'Dillo. Income from tickets was used to pay musicians and production costs, while the beer sales paid staff and overhead.

The Armadillo World Headquarters became Lone Star Beer's biggest draft outlet after the Houston Astrodome! Lone Star's beer deliverymen rolled thousands of kegs through the 'Dillo.

"Come on up to Austin and let's have some fun."

I could hear Eddie's invitation in my mind. It would be a risky gamble for someone partially sustaining on savings while starting a new business. Eddie had surrounded himself with some of Austin's most creative professionals.

It was not just businessmen and lawyers who offered free advice but also volunteers, such as in-house physician Dr. John Luker. The man treated the staff and, because of their subsistence-level wages and zero health insurance, usually didn't charge them. Dr. Luker tells me he remembers the red-faced young man with his eyebrows and mustache singed off from a water-heater gas flare.

The good doctor later became a community leader in drug rehabilitation and a champion of elder care for poor folks. Meanwhile, Eddie's dad fixed the water heater.

How to earn my keep? There was nothing I could do to benefit the Headquarters. Everything was well taken care of.

Advertising and overseeing of posters were a combination of the 'Dillo's Ramsey Wiggins working directly with artists or with the Directions Company owned by visionary Michael Osborne, who later became known for his work with solar energy. Joe Gracey handled audio production for radio commercials and was the voice heard on 'Dillo commercials. Gracey was also music director of KOKE FM and would one day marry progressive country singer Kimmie Rhodes. He became a record producer, and in the late '90s, morphed into a food and travel writer of note.

The extraordinary Micael "Fast Draw" Priest oversaw the Directions' graphics department. Priest is the patriarch of Austin's cartoon poster artists, yet he never drew a comic book. His concert poster for the Grateful Dead at Manor Downs with skeleton jockey feeding a sugar cube to a racehorse is famous, but the Dead said it didn't fit their image. Thirty years later rare copies sold at $500 apiece.

At one time or another, Eddie Wilson and his wife, Genie, housed most of the 'Dillo founders in their backyard bungalow or two spare bedrooms. Eddie hospitably opened his home to traveling musicians, their managers, and record people.

Decades later, his talent as a host and his natural, open generosity would make him a famous Texas restaurateur. He even did some cooking for houseguests; everybody raved over Eddie's breakfast *migas* and his dinners with thick, well-seasoned pork chops.

Staying overnight a few days allowed me to meet the people at Armadillo. I could see the obvious differences compared to workers at traditional businesses. Folks were more relaxed and friendly. Employees were judged by actions and results, no matter their appearance. Bizarre creativity was appreciated.

What stood out the most was the respect people displayed for each other... the 'Dillo had one of every personality type on its staff, but without the backstabbing, or even loud arguments.

I liked it.

From a historical perspective, the Armadillo opened when the capital city's population was 283,000. It was a few days after category 3 hurricane Celia devastated Corpus Christi. The national champion Longhorn football team was set to begin its first integrated season. UT enrollment was $50 for *any* number of credit hours.

In Houston, listener-supported Pacifica station KPFT FM-90.1 signed on and was bombed off the air twice by a crazed Ku Klux Klaner. And in less than a year of the grand opening, Richard Nixon would introduce his awful phrase for that new kind of civil war, one he called the "War on Drugs."

17

Springsteen and the Fiddler

The first night of Springsteen's three Armadillo shows in March 1974 offered a $1.00 ticket. Didn't sell out. But you could tell by the number of music reviewers, deejays, and record company executives roaming backstage that headliner Bruce Springsteen was no ordinary guy. His band was not yet officially known as the E Street Band and the multitalented Little Steven Van Zandt had not yet joined him. I never figured out why Van Zandt was called 'Little' when he was about the same height as 'The Boss.'

Springsteen was tuning his guitar as the Central Texas hall filled with students and older Dylan followers. Bobby Hedderman worried they had blown a weekend of needed ticket sales by booking this unknown Yankee. Was the guy all hype?

The show's poster, drawn by Franklin, was confusing; the headbanger graphics could have been for John McLaughlin or Frank Zappa. Today his Springsteen poster is highly sought by art collectors, but I preferred the one drawn by Micael Priest and used later for the November show. It was based on a 'Greetings from ...' tourist postcard, as in Springsteen's *Greetings from Asbury Park, NJ* album. If you look closely, inside each letter Micael drew a scene from one of Springsteen's songs.

The opening act was the Austin-style country band Alvin Crow and the Pleasant Valley Boys. Springsteen's tour through New Orleans and his four shows in Houston had gone well enough, but here the Jersey boy was following a country act. He didn't know what to think about having that kind of band open his show, but he could tell the blond muscular guy with glasses, a pony-tail, wearing a tank top and carrying a fiddle, wasn't your everyday Grand Ole Opry musician.

'Dillo concerts always began at 9 p.m., with the first band playing up to an hour, depending on the encore. Audio from the stage performance leaked down the hall toward the band room. Everyone could tell Springsteen was getting anxious, pacing a bit. The fiddler had opened with "Dynamite Dina," went into "Faded Love," and onward to close his set with "Roly Poly." Backstage we could hear the audience cheering for more!

Now the band equipment was changed out, and it was show time. Bruce Springsteen carried his guitar through the narrow backstage hallway to the stage and scooted up its unpainted wooden steps. Micael Priest stood at the mic introducing the band while behind the curtain waited the rock musician in his black leather jacket, shifting his shoulders like a street fighter adjusting for a rumble. How would these Texas country fiddle lovers take to a Yankee boy?

Like he often did, he started out easy, as I recall, with "New York City Serenade." The unexpected slow and storytelling opener mesmerized the audience, and when he finished, the crowd stood frozen or sat quiet, staring… then burst into loud applause!

By the time he was into "Blinded by the Light," everyone was up, wildly dancing or cheering him on. All the musicians in his band were tight and first class. And that little Jersey dude was all over the stage, jumping and swaying in rhythmic motion, grinning, leaning back-on-back with sax-honking Clarence Clemons, aka the Big Man, blasting a jamming counterpoint to the Boss's hot guitar.

"Rosalita (Come Out Tonight)" put the Austin crowd forever in his pocket and well described the roots of this unknown rock poet. Not blues, not progressive rock, a live sound not unlike a Phil Spector production with Van Morrison sensibilities. I couldn't help but dance in place for the Rufus Thomas salute, "Walking the Dog." Finally I found myself lifted into rock 'n' roll paradise, hearing one of my favorite Fats Domino songs, "Let the Four Winds Blow."

With each song, the music reviewers and deejays grew more ecstatic. A couple of the bartenders climbed on top of the bar, dancing for "Twist and Shout!"

Springsteen's dynamic performance and the high quality of his band overwhelmed everyone in the hall that night. It was exciting, high-energy, exhilarating, top-notch rock.

Yet to me it wasn't quite real… wasn't genuinely raw and edgy. At the end of the night, I felt as if I had just seen a Las Vegas show band. Their performance almost looked choreographed. But it was obvious this dynamic singer-songwriter could become a pop superstar.

* * *

OVER THE NEXT two days, the Armadillo staff took a strong liking to Bruce Springsteen. He was easy to hang with, like the Marshall Tucker Band, Wet Willie, and Charlie Daniels. Of all the shows during the Armadillo's ten-year history, the Jersey rocker's legendary performances are the most talked about.

During his stay at the 'Dillo, as a bonus, our rising star found an early sweetheart in Karen Darvin, a beautiful, redheaded ballet dancer. She left Austin with Springsteen and they stayed together a couple of years. Rumor had it, he was attracted to redheads. In 1988 Springsteen helped confirm the speculation by marrying redheaded guitarist and E Street Band member Patti Scialfa.

The New Jersey band departed Austin feeling triumphant but quickly fell back to earth when they played to an empty theater in Dallas. Two months later, *Rolling Stone* writer and future manager Jon Landau would pen: "I saw rock 'n' roll's future and its name is Bruce Springsteen."

18

Lost Planet Airmen Set Beer Drinking Record

The front doors at 525½ Barton Springs Road opened at 10:00 each morning, though many workers showed up earlier. Departments included bookkeeping, talent booking, event publicity, beer ordering, and maintenance, along with cleanup and kitchen staff. The Armadillo payroll was huge for a music hall, though its communal roots were still evident in the egalitarian wages. Full-timers received $115 a week, management $125.

Bill Narum called it "The golden age of Armadillo."

By noon the former armory was abustle with visionaries and doers. Creative people came and went all day long: musicians, songwriters, artists, filmmakers, authors, dancers, politicians, chefs, thespians, and drug dealers. It was a never-ending parade of both rich and poor.

In early 1974 I didn't yet have an office, but a desk and a phone were always available for my use. The Skating Palace next door provided a surrealistic ambiance. The Palace would open for business, and by early afternoon, roller rink music could be heard in the downstairs offices. The skaters' favorite records were played over and over again: Percy Faith conducting "Theme from *A Summer Place*" and Billy Swan singing "I Can Help."

That one-eyed singer and hit songwriter had once played keyboard with Kinky and the Texas Jew Boys, Even today I can hear the muffled sound of those old hit tunes leaking through Eddie's office wall...

* * *

DURING A SOUND CHECK for Commander Cody and the Lost Planet Airmen, a Lone Star Beer representative named Jerry Retzloff introduced Eddie and me to the brewery's new marketing director, Barry Sullivan. The men had driven up from the brewery's offices in San Antonio. Retzloff had told Barry that Commander Cody sold more beer than any other act playing the 'Dillo.

It was easy to see different bands attracted crowds with quite specific recreational drug preferences. Freddie King and Roy Buchanan pulled in a lot of downer users; Legs Diamond drew methamphetamine freaks; Zappa's crowd used LSD; Willie Nelson drew pot smokers. Cody was cocaine.

But the common denominator for all was cold beer.

Barry said he wanted to find out who was buying all this Lone Star draft... and why? Retzloff was a specialist at promoting the brew in live music clubs and outdoor events throughout Central and South Texas. Their problem was sales were down for the regional breweries. The national brands—Schlitz, Budweiser and Miller—were outselling Lone Star and San Antonio's other brewery, Pearl. Latest beer scuttlebutt was Coors from Colorado would soon be sold in Texas. That made everyone nervous.

Next day, Barry Sullivan and Retzloff came by the Beer Garden for a cold Lone Star and lunch. Barry wanted to go somewhere where he and I could talk privately. I took him inside the empty and dimmed 'Dillo and we sat at a spool table near the closed bar.

The two Armadillo redheads—'Dillo partner and bar manager Michael Harr, and the most personable bartender in Austin, Dale Watkins—were setting out the beer pitchers for that night's concert. Dale pulled us each a cold draft of Lone Star.

Barry took a long sip and sighed. I liked him. He was a brewery marketing warhorse known for getting Hank Thompson to record the country classic "Rednecks, White Socks and Blue Ribbon Beer." No doubt, the man wanted to repeat that success.

"Woody, I want to hire you to direct our advertising."

Really? Lone Star Beer already had a Dallas-based ad agency.

"I know what you've achieved with ratings in San Antonio radio, and the huge turnout for Willie's Picnic. The ads were great. I saw the press coverage when 30,000 people showed up in Olmos Park for Save KEXL Radio Day. Woody, you understand the baby boomer market. The job pays $60,000 to start."

My brain was in high gear. Of course, I didn't want to be directly employed by anybody–been there, done that. But as his media consultant, this could be my way to earn an office at the 'Dillo. I'd be able to financially invest.

"Barry, my situation is I've already made a commitment to help the Armadillo brand go national. I can't work at the brewery. But if you pay Armadillo and let them pay me, I'll be available to you as a hands-on consultant."

"Let me think it over. I don't think the brewery can pay a venue because of alcohol licensing laws."

"Barry, one more thing. I don't want to handle the Lone Star brand itself. I want to work on a specific Lone Star product where my success will be easy to measure."

"Which product?"

"I like the Lone Star Handy Keg." It was a pull-top can designed like a silver keg and featured cold-filtered beer. To my taste, it was the best of canned beers.

"Hmm. That's Harry Jersig's favorite, too."

Jersig, a noted fly fisherman and collector of taxidermy trophies, was the flamboyant owner of the Lone Star Brewery.

I wanted to be sure the ad income was tied to the 'Dillo. My intent was to be fair to all who had worked so hard before my arrival. The Armadillo by itself could not afford to take on the financing of a national multimedia marketing effort. The hall was, as usual, behind on its cheap rent to generous landlord M. K. Hage.

Barry came back to report his attorneys said no way could the brewery legally pay the Armadillo, so I needed a separate corporation. Eddie suggested Mike Tolleson and Randy McCall as corporate partners in the venture. A perfect combination of talents: a former beer lobbyist, an entertainment lawyer, a licensed CPA, and me, the media guy.

We voted to make Eddie Wilson president of our new business, Randy would be treasurer, and Tolleson secretary. Eddie named our company Thought You'd Never Ask, The Austin Consultants, Incorporated. We pronounced initials TYNA TACI as "Tina Tacky."

The $60,000-a-year offer may not seem much today, but the online Inflation Calculator says it is the 2020 equivalent of $326,276.62. So with a $5,000 monthly retainer plus 17.65 percent of media production costs, our income would be about $7,000 and possibly more. I would take $125 a week. The rest would be for Armadillo. My company would rent office space and pay its own phone bills. And with a corporate board guided by Eddie and Mike and Randy, I felt the 'Dillo staff would know I was not carpetbagging.

Barry, Eddie, and I sat at a table in the Armadillo hall with a pitcher of Lone Star in front of us. Eddie had just shown Barry our state-approved corporate documents. Handed him a sheet of our TYNA TACI stationery using a letterhead design by Micael Priest. Plus, our first monthly invoice.

Sullivan grinned, nodded his large hockey player head. "I've decided on a product for you."

"Handy Keg?"

"Nope. The returnable bottle."

Eddie and I looked at each other.

"Huh, a returnable bottle?"

"They're in a 14-year decline. Nobody wants 'em. Returnable bottles take up too much space in convenience stores. Bars are afraid people will break them and start fights."

"I can relate to that," Eddie said, with a nod. Running the Armadillo and having worked in the beer industry, he could empathize with both clubs and brewery.

"Returnable bottles are good for the environment," said Sullivan.

What a dull-sounding product, I thought. There must be a hook. "Is there another name for this kind of bottle, or, is it just *returnable*? Maybe, recyclable bottle?"

"That could work. Our retailers, not the beer drinkers, call them returnable bottles. Old-time brewers sometimes referred to 'em as *long-necks* because of their shape."

Eddie looked over at my widened eyes. Right away, we had caught the phallic implications. I recalled the obscure Captain Beefheart track, "Long Neck Bottles," from his *Clear Spot* album. We could not have made up a better word.

"Longnecks?" I laughed aloud, "Oh, we'll have a lot of fun with longnecks."

And so it was to be, Thought You'd Never Ask, The Austin Consultants, Inc., would make that word "longneck" so popular it had to be added to *Webster's Dictionary*: "Beer served in a bottle that has a long neck."

19

Long Live Longnecks and Ramblin' Rose

To pre-test our commercials, I decided to enlist my friend, Dr. Thomas Turicchi, at the *Consumer Behavior Center* near Dallas. Part of his unique technique featured galvanic skin response coupled with the subject's conscious reactions. Dr. Turicchi's research was used by us radio programmers to spot hit records in advance of the Billboard Top 100 lists.

This was cutting-edge pre-testing in 1974, and I was the only one doing it for commercials. I tested several words, among them, longneck. When those tests came back, words like "recycled-bottle" and "enviro-bottle" had an acceptable response, but "longneck" blew off the chart! I also tested words to use in commercials: "high" and "fine" had great ratings.

Aside from radio, I needed Lone Star Beer posters and bumper stickers. My idea was to have each Armadillo artist do a poster. I could only imagine what Priest might draw, and Juke with his abstract side of art. Naturally we asked Jim Franklin to produce our first poster showcasing the bottle.

Franklin titled his striking art: *Long Live Long Necks.*

Brilliant.

Now we had a bumper sticker slogan, "Long Live Longnecks." I took Franklin's slogan to a San Antonio printer, asked him for a red-and-blue-on-white design to emulate the popular sticker of the day: "America Love It or Leave It." Said make the Lone Star logo tiny so a person will have to get down close to read it. With an initial press run of 50,000, those bumper stickers were soon visible on the expressways and in the supermarket, beer joint, and rock music club parking lots of Texas. We had a hit.

Franklin pitched us on doing an entire poster series by himself. Eddie thought it was a good idea, so I passed on the other artists and went for the series.

Those Lone Star posters made the eccentric Armadillo World Headquarters artist famous statewide. Gave him enough income to move from his digs at the 'Dillo and reopen the Ritz Theater where he would compete for live music shows.

Over the many years since, national collectors of art and brewery memorabilia have coveted our returnable bottle series by JFKLN. Jim Franklin often said he didn't want to be a commercial artist, yet in the end, he became noted for using his art to sell concert tickets and beer. Those posters are in high demand.

Eddie and I drove to Gary P. Nunn's home and met with him and Bob Livingston. They were the core of the Lost Gonzo Band that backed Jerry Jeff Walker, Ray Wylie Hubbard, and Michael Martin Murphey.

People really liked Gary P.'s song, "London Homesick Blues" with its great join-in round: "I wanna go *home* with the Armadillo..."

It would soon become the theme song for *Austin City*

Limits on PBS TV.

Jerry Jeff had first recorded the anthem in the Luckenbach General Store, using a stoned drunk sing-along audience for his chorus. This was a time when MCA Records was scouting Austin country talent. From 1972 through '79, they released six Jerry Jeff Walker albums.

When we met with Livingston and Nunn, I didn't ask for a 60-second commercial jingle. I wanted them to write a country hit tune and handed them a list of consumer-tested words to use with their lyrics.

The guys brought us a perfect Lone Star Beer flavored tune: "The Nights Never Get Lonely." TYNA TACI hired their Lost Gonzo Band to do a 16-track recording of the song, and we booked into the Odyssey Studio on 6th Street, a half-block from the Alamo Hotel.

Jerry Jeff often used Odyssey, soon to be renamed Pecan Street Studio, so the Gonzos felt comfortable in the room. Steve Shields and Jay Aaron Podolnick owned it, and Jay later became a producer for Bill Ham. In 1990, he had his own Warner Bros. album, *Inside Out*.

Mike Tolleson registered the new song with our Eddie-Wilson-named publishing company Rip-Snortin' Tunes.

* * *

LONE STAR BEER'S radio campaign needed first to establish the validity of Austin's live music scene. Hometown music journalist Chet Flippo would be the perfect spokesman. He was recognized as one of the best writing for *Rolling Stone*, *Creem*, and *Crawdaddy*. Flippo liked the idea.

Gordie Ham recorded Flippo in the KOKE FM studios and carried off the tapes to finish the commercials in his home studio. Electronic editing was not yet generally available, so Gordie had to take great care when rocking the audiotape back and forth across the playback head, and then use a grease pencil to mark the beginning and end of his splice. Then he laid the quarter-inch tape flat in a diagonally notched slot in an aluminum block and slid a razor blade through and cut at both ends of his marks, remove the unwanted piece of tape, and finally splice its two remaining ends together.

Tedious.

There might be thirty or more such edits in a single commercial. If done correctly, the listener can't detect that anything was cut out.

In one Lone Star commercial, Flippo announced the nation had a new kind of country music, and in the other, he promoted Austin as the home of that new sound. It was the place to be in Texas. Flippo's announcements were broadcast all over the state, plus Shreveport, New Orleans, and Nashville.

This was the first time Austin was commercially promoted in the media as a music town.

Soon after the ads ran, Chet Flippo announced a move to New York City for a job in the offices of *Rolling Stone* magazine.

"New York!"

To me it sounded crazy. Who would want to live in New York City?

"You're going to leave Austin for New York?"

"I just want the experience. We'll be back in a couple of years."

Flippo never returned and later moved on to reside

in Nashville, where he died.

Eddie and I contacted leading musicians to record their versions of "The Nights Never Get Lonely." Freddie King, The Pointer Sisters, Sunny and the Sunliners.

To get my nonjingle sound, I again decided to record complete songs and edit them down to 60 seconds. We commissioned WBAP deejay Bill Mack to do the voice tag. From this 50,000-watts station, Mack was the overnight voice for truckers in the continental U.S.A. He was also a songwriter whose tune "Drinking Champaign" was a hit for George Strait, while "Blue" earned a Best Female Country Vocal Performance Grammy for thirteen-year-old LeAnn Rimes.

Bill Mack is now known as the "Dean of Country Music Disc Jockeys."

Lone Star Beer wanted a campaign to reach young beer drinkers. I had once put together a popular series of KEXL Kid radio dramas with Ron Houston as the Kid. For years Gordie Ham had used an old-timer cowboy voice in San Antonio for ads promoting Harry's Western Wear.

My idea was to use these old-time sounding western characters in radio vignettes championing these old-time returnable bottles. Our pacing would be similar to the hilarious routines in *Statler Brothers Alive at Johnny Mack Brown High School*.

Gordie immediately liked the idea and booked studio time in New Braunfels with his friends at Prawn Productions. Ed Wood, Opie, Gary, and Dave were the

Prawn boys. They lived and ate together in Ed's parents' house while paying off a huge debt incurred in 1972 by producing their own failed version of the failed Dripping Springs Reunion.

Their event was called the Concert at Gattlin Creek. It had featured rocker acts like the Bob Seeger System, Bo Diddley, Captain Beefheart and His Magical Band, Freddie King, and Foghat. Super lineup. The Moody Blues had canceled on them at the last minute. The guys had borrowed heavily and lost a lot of money when it rained.

The young debtors assembled their Prawn recording studio in a wooden shed near the beautiful Comal River. It was isolated. Nevertheless, it was situated close to a great place for a refreshing break. San Antonio acquaintance Pat Molak was restoring Gruene Hall, built in 1878, reportedly the oldest dance hall in Texas. Perfect spot for a cold beer on a hot afternoon.

Gordie and I could have written longneck copy ourselves but outside inspiration would make it even better. I listened to the radio for interesting local commercials and one day heard a promo on KOKE FM that made me laugh.

This was about the time *Billboard* magazine proclaimed the station Trendsetter of the Year. I phoned and learned the writer was Carolyn Allen, aka Candy Kicker. I decided to use Carolyn to write our scripts and let our actors improvise from her scenarios.

I said we needed a character name like Ramblin' Jack, so Gordie called himself Ramblin' Rose. Carolyn made Ron Houston into Red Wade, which, if spoken by an old-time Texan, sounded like red weed. Ramblin' and Red interacted with a background gang that Gordie named the Sons of the Bunkhouse.

The job of these SOBs was to cheer and jeer throughout the skit leading to a Lone Star Beer punch line. They often shouted for more "LSB." Of course, each of our spontaneous-sounding commercials promoted the unpopular returnable glass bottle.

Our first two Ramblin' Rose productions from the Prawn studio blew the roof off Dr. Turicchi's emotive graph. The focus group loved Ramblin'.

Eddie Wilson flew to Los Angeles to record Freddie King's version of the "The Nights Never Get Lonely." Jack Calmes had arranged to have T Bone Burnett produce the session.

Eddie came back to Austin with a big winner. We tested the Freddie King recording and found it had Top 10 sales potential! Wow.

When our minute-long commercial first aired, Bill Young, the program director at KILT 610-AM in Houston, phoned and said, "Woody, playing this ad is like playing a hit record."

Eddie and I sat on a long red couch in the office for the marketing director of Lone Star Beer. From across his desk, Barry Sullivan wore a wide smile like a hockey player who had just scored a winning goal.

"I've been monitoring our longneck sales, and this is remarkable." He pointed to a wall chart, "Woody, do you realize you've reversed *a 14-year decline* in returnable bottles?"

20

A Hill Country Hooraw

Mike Tolleson leaned back and said, "Do you remember Bill Arhos?"

"KLRN," I said.

"Exactly. Well, he just called and is thinking of producing an Austin Music special for PBS. He asked if we would handle the talent."

"Interesting. I think you should tell him that we'll act as consultants to program development."

"They want B. W. Stevenson for their first show."

"That's awful."

He was an excellent country singer with a big tenor voice but had no stage pizazz. Fortunately, the Arhos crew messed up the audio and their already recorded pilot would have to be scrapped. They needed another local musician.

Tolleson leaned forward. "They also like Willie Nelson."

"Willie is great. Do they have a producer?"

"Paul Bosner. He's from Dallas."

They didn't yet have a name for the TV show. One idea was *Hill Country Hooraw*. Because KLRN was in both Austin and San Antonio I was lobbying for an inclusive name, but not *Hooraw*.

One afternoon, Paul Bosner was driving in from Dallas when before his weary eyes appeared a sign: Austin City Limits. *Aha!* he thought.

Of course, I was disappointed the Alamo City was excluded by the show's name. But *Austin City Limits* was perfect. It promoted the exploding Austin music scene.

KLRN asked for a list of potential shows and I wrote it out longhand. Tolleson made a copy and sent it over. I suggested a variety of talent mirroring the Armadillo concerts.

Arhos, the programmer behind *ACL*, said it was too soon for an eclectic mix of styles. He pointed out the only country music show on PBS had recently been canceled, so country was the niche to fill. And PBS was a four-year-old public television program distributor hungry for new content to offer local affiliates. PBS stations had to buy their programs. So those earliest ACL seasons focused on progressive country with some folk rock and little else.

Remember, producing those *Armadillo Country Music Review* shows in 1973 taught Bill Arhos that a studio-housed set would have to be used for this pilot. The goal would be to recreate the Armadillo experience for television.

Bosner, wearing a silk ascot, came to the 'Dillo and we walked the inside hall.

"To get the Austin live music feel," I said, "the audience reaction needs to be seen along with the musicians."

He nodded. Bosner dramatically swept his hand past a group of cable-spool tables. "This area looks good. Tables are important."

My turn to nod. "What do you think of these bleacher risers?"

"I like them a lot."

Later we walked the space KLRN had allocated to shoot the pilot. A Spanish-language children's show, *Carrascolendas*, had just wrapped up its season.

I pointed. "Look... bleachers."

The estimated budget for the pilot was $14,000. If he could use these bleachers for his set, money would be saved. Bosner crafted a theater-in-the-round by placing the bleachers behind his stage while out front were tables with chairs as in a large music club. Meanwhile, a talent search for a director was underway. Finally, Bosner and Arhos decided to bring in Bill Scafe from Southern Illinois University where he had been directing a music series.

An underwriter would help with any unexpected cost overruns and distribution.

TYNA TACI pitched the show to Barry Sullivan in his Lone Star office. He agreed to sponsor it, plus, if PBS liked *Austin City Limits*, the brewery would underwrite the entire first season. Lone Star Beer could ride the wave as the Austin music scene went national.

Barry was out to win, and the man was a visionary. A 'whatever it takes' kind of guy.

There was a rule of no alcohol drinking on TV. We negotiated the placement of Lone Star longnecks on the tables but no drinking on camera.

When the show's theme music was chosen, it was Gary P. Nunn's great chorus from his song, "London Homesick Blues."

"I wanna go home to the Armadillo..."

This made a perfect fit for Sullivan because Gary P. was already part of his new Lone Star image as theme song writer and singer-musician with the Lost Gonzo

Band we used in the radio commercials.

Tolleson contacted Willie Nelson. My feeling was this show would better represent the local scene if there were two featured artists. Then we could recreate the jams that even today play a significant part in the Austin live music experience.

Still wanting a San Antonio tie-in, I suggested Doug Sahm. A duet by Willie and Doug—Wow!

Their careers had intertwined when Jerry Wexler flew into Austin to sign Doug for Atlantic Records and discovered a bearded Willie Nelson. He signed them both.

I drove out to Doug's home to talk, but we ended up next door at Soap Creek Saloon where he was meeting his running buddy, Speedy Sparks.

"That sounds like a hoot," Doug said. "What kind of show is it?"

Next day, Tolleson broke the bad news. "Willie's people said they don't want Doug Sahm on the show."

21

Austin City Limits

Jim Franklin had leased the dilapidated Ritz Theater on 6th Street for a concert hall. To redo the shabby décor, Franklin partnered financially with his dear friend and silkscreen perfectionist, Bill Livinggood, who owned Slo Printing.

When I first entered the Austin scene, my mind would confuse Bill Livinggood with Ben Livingston, the city's internationally recognized neon-light sculptor and inventor of the infinite phosphorescent color palette... and Bob Livingston, the Lost Gonzo's bass player. Franklin preferred Slo Printing for his T-shirt art, and today many consider Livinggood's early '70s shirts among the finest relics in the huge JFLKN catalog.

After Jim Franklin vacated the 'Dillo, artist Henry Gonzalez moved into his second-floor studio. Most people immediately identify Franklin and Micael Priest with Armadillo, but Henry lived there longer than Jim Franklin. He used the studio for public exhibitions of photographs and art, portending that 40 years later he would help start and become the curator for the Austin Museum of Popular Culture, while his wife, Leea Mechling, served as its executive director. His forte was large murals and designing stage props.

In the years between AWHQ and AusPop, Henry worked at the Austin Opera House and for Stevie Ray Vaughan. I asked him to describe the difference between the Armadillo and the Opry House. "Tim O'Connor was a good employer and fun to be around, I enjoyed it, but he made all the decisions for the Opry House. He was the boss. Working at the 'Dillo was like being part of a family. Everyone made decisions."

Later, Stevie Ray Vaughan would trust Henry to handle the guitars and Double Trouble's band equipment. The night of that fatal Alpine Valley helicopter crash in Wisconsin, Henry was driving the band's gear back to Texas when the news first blared from the radio. Stevie was dead!

Unbelievable. But everyone was reporting it! His friend was gone.

With tears streaming down his cheeks, he continued towing the acclaimed guitar hero's equipment southbound through the Midwest night. Henry Gonzalez told me he would never forget hearing local station after station playing nonstop Stevie Ray Vaughan.

* * *

I LEARNED WILLIE NELSON would be featured during Jim Franklin's grand opening week of The Ritz. His grand opening show had been Doug Sahm with Paul Ray and the Cobras.

Gordie Ham and I set out to ask the singer why he didn't want Doug to play on the pilot.

When the historic theater was constructed in 1929, it was the first local movie house built to show talkies. For his reopening event, Franklin rented a huge brilliant searchlight to beacon across the Austin sky. The poster-artist-turned-promoter had transformed the dingy movie theater into an elegant concert hall. Franklin outdid himself by painting giant highly realistic Ritz crackers on the lobby walls and ceiling. Somewhat like a Warhol but more three-dimensional. Of course, Andy would have replicated the Ritz box, not its contents.

Inside the theater, Uranium Savages co-founder Rick Turner airbrushed sky blue walls with fluffy clouds. Turner, the year before with Tom Bowman and Karry Awn, painted a landmark wall mural for the People's Renaissance Market on The Drag. Over several decades that work of art has been preserved so to be viewed anew by the latest crop of UT students. The old Ritz that night looked sparkling and stunning.

In front of the Ritz milled a turnout of Austin's counterculture who's who dressed in costume ball extremes. Big Rikke aka the Guacamole Queen—the gal who inspired Frank Zappa to dedicate "Inca Roads" to her—took my hand and led us backstage to Jim Franklin.

I explained that Gordie and I wanted to see Willie Nelson and find out why he didn't want Doug Sahm on the PBS show. It was approaching 10 p.m.

Franklin said we could likely find Willie in his motorhome out back in the alley. We made our way through the packed backstage crowd of celebrants and into the narrow alleyway. Willie stood outside smoking a joint and passed it to me. I took a hit; the bud's taste was excellent.

"Willie, we got word that you don't want Doug Sahm on the *Austin City Limits* pilot."

"Huh, I never heard about Doug being on the show. I didn't say no."

I looked at Gordie and then back to Willie. "Will you agree to have Doug open and then maybe do a song together?"

"Woody, I better find out who said what on my side and get with 'em. I can't commit to anything without talking to Neil Reshen."

That ended that. He referred me to his manager. Obviously, Willie could have made that decision. Going further would be pointless.

* * *

IT CAME TO PASS that in 1974 Austin introduced a music phenomenon to the U.S.A. Willie Nelson's performance on the pilot *ACL* show is renowned. The audio isn't the best. I had brought recording engineer Chet Himes to help KLRN but they wouldn't let him in the control room.

Here was an old-time country singer with a new interpretation of how to play country music. PBS viewers had *never* seen anyone like this bearded, long-haired bandleader and his devilishly goateed drummer wearing a black cape with a red lining.

"Whiskey river don't run dry..."

A few PBS stations broadcast the program in their fundraiser periods and record pledge calls lit up their phones. Word of the strong response spread to other pledge drives and soon the idea of a live music series from Austin appealed to PBS.

None of us back then understood Willie's true greatness: that over the decades he would, by instinct or intent, transform himself into an international folk hero. And not one of us imagined that *Austin City Limits* would become the longest-running music show on television, and *Time* magazine would name it one of the ten most influential music programs of all time, or that *ACL* would become the first TV show to receive a National Medal of Arts award.

22

Red Headed Stranger Goes Platinum

Karry Awn's cartoon album cover for Doug Sahm's *Groover's Paradise* put out by Warner Bros. Records is the perfect symbolic map of Austin's 1974 live music club scene. There's Soap Creek, armadillos, the state capitol with Oat Willie atop, and a silver coke spoon. A collector's prize. Should be framed and hung at city hall to remind incoming councils from whence their valuable live music reputation came.

That nightclub art seen on a nationally distributed record was a sign to all that Austin was a happening place, and for the music industry, there was money to be made. Other albums featuring the city's talent soon followed.

Homegrown progressive country singer Rusty Weir recorded three national albums: *Stoned, Slow, Rugged* for ABC Records in '74, *Rusty Wier* on 20th Century Records '75 and in the following year *Black Hat Saloon* for Columbia.

Then London Records arrived to sign Greezy Wheels and, in the tradition of Shiva's Headband, the group used a local artist for their album, Micael Priest. In 1975 they released *Juz Loves Dem Ol' Greezy Wheels* with Priest's armadillo chomping up a car tire on its cover; next London shipped *Radio Radials* to the nation's record stores. By the closing of Armadillo, Greezy had set the record for most performances, 123 times, and Priest a record for over 100 posters.

And in '75, Toy Caldwell of the Marshall Tucker Band commissioned Ken Featherston to create the album cover to *Searchin' for a Rainbow*. Toy liked the bucking horse cowboy that Ken had used for their Armadillo poster. Also in '75, MCA signed and released *The Lost Gonzo Band*. Those were the days when Austin's great music writer, John T. Davis, was on their road crew. A year later, the label released its second Gonzos album, *Thrills*, and that same year WB introduced *Ray Wylie Hubbard and the Cowboy Twinkies*.

MCA then dropped the Gonzos. Capitol Records picked them up to bring out *Signs of Life* in 1977 while MCA released the self-titled *Joe Ely*. Its song, "All My Love," got onto the Top 100 country list. Starting the following year, after Ely met the Clash in London and then hooked up with them at the Armadillo, his next five MCA albums would be considered more rock than country. The year 1977 is when Polydor Records gave us *High Ridin'* by Alvin Crow and the Pleasant Valley Boys. His album held the South Austin tribute song, "Broken Spoke Waltz."

During the 1970s, records like these and dozens of touring musicians created an international awareness of a music town unlike any other. None of those albums sold very well, but each is a genuine progressive country classic.

* * *

IT WAS THE DAY of the 'Dillo... but also it was the time of the preacher. So it was that in early February of 1975, Willie Nelson, excited about scoring a Columbia Records contract, drove north to Autumn Sound studio in Garland, Texas. The studio was but one month old and housed the first 24-track recorder in Texas.

The singer recorded four platinum albums there. His first session, costing only $4,000, produced the groundbreaking country music concept album *Red Headed Stranger*.

This wasn't his first concept album. Two years before, Jerry Wexler had produced (in Muscle Shoals) *Phases and Stages*, telling the poignant story of a divorce, and in '71 RCA had released *Yesterday's Wine*, and way back in 1968 Chet Atkins produced (in Nashville) *Texas in My Soul*. Its concept was a Willie Nelson tribute to the Lone Star State with cover art featuring San Antonio, that year celebrating its 250th birthday.

Along with depicting the obligatory Alamo, the art showed the HemisFair Arena, the notorious Monorail, and the Tower of the Americas. From *Texas in My Soul* came the single "San Antonio," written by Alamo City steel guitarist Jerry Blanton, then playing with George Chambers and The Country Gentlemen. Unfortunately that album was terribly overproduced and, in spite of its title, completely soulless.

Willie wrote some of the tunes for *Red Headed Stranger* in Austin and, except for drummer Paul English, his band lived in Central Texas. Two local artists designed the LP with its cover portrait and story-telling graphics on the back; one of those designers was

Lynn Capri, Eddie Wilson's secretary at Armadillo. Austin's music community rightly claimed the *Red Headed Stranger* as its own.

The release of this underproduced LP sent a music shockwave through Nashville. A renegade Texas outlaw, using acoustic instruments in an "unknown" studio, had picked up a Grammy for Best Country Vocal Male Performance and crossed over into the pop charts with "Blue Eyes Crying in the Rain."

But it almost wasn't to be.

My friend, record promoter Joe Mansfield from San Antonio, had moved to NYC to go upward in the ranks of the marketing department for Columbia Records. He was one of the guys who had to fight A&R department executives for the album's release. The pros considered the record a demo. They expected a full-sounding band and not an unplugged solo artist; they wanted a more Nashville-like production.

Mansfield and the marketing guys won out and released *Red Headed Stranger*. The LP went gold to become a hit on the country charts! A decade later, the redhead turned double-platinum for Columbia. But meantime, RCA Records had scored the honor of having the first million-selling country album.

RCA got into the game with *Wanted: The Outlaws*. Its cover featured wanted-poster photos of Willie, Waylon, Jessi Colter (married to Waylon), and Tompall Glaser, and on the back cover were liner notes by Chet Flippo. A fix-up album pieced together from older recordings, it quickly scored country music's first Platinum Award.

In the spring of 1977, RCA released "Luckenbach, Texas (Back to the Basics of Love)" by Waylon Jennings, with Willie joining in and Jerry Jeff saluted in the lyrics.

It won a Grammy for Best Country Vocal Duo or Group Performance.

Sadly, Hondo Crouch wasn't around to enjoy his little town's newfound national fame. The colorful and beloved mayor of Luckenbach had died the previous year.

* * *

COUNTRY MUSIC TRIVIA: It was most appropriate that Texas musicians broke the million-seller barrier for country albums, because in 1924 Texan Vernon Dalhart had the first country single to do a million with his double-sided smash, "The Wreck of the Old 97," backed with "The Prisoner's Song." And, like *The Outlaws* album, his record was from RCA.

The 1970s decade was but a moment in time, yet its creative people inspired the course of Austin culture well into the 21st century. At the close of this formative decade, however, only two music icons dramatically stand out: Armadillo World Headquarters and Willie Nelson.

23

Lure of the Big Apple

Things were going well for the Armadillo, concerts were drawing sellout crowds, and the beer garden filled with people for lunch and happy hour. Now, with TYNA TACI's cash flow assured, we could set plans for marketing Armadillo Records and syndicating Armadillo programs for radio and TV.

Grand Ole Opry had announced it was moving from its original home in the historic Ryman Theater Auditorium. They were readying a brand new 4,400-seat theater custom-built for TV productions.

We could do that in Austin! Except our TV shows would be Austin eclectic and not Nashville-style country. Ditto our radio shows.

Eddie had Priest draw a map of the Armadillo Headquarters that depicted our new production facilities on an undeveloped corner lot directly across First Street. Today occupied by a Whataburger. He dubbed this combined real estate the Prime Eight Acres. Might cost a million to build.

Let's go for it.

* * *

BE IT RECORDS or TV, we knew our production money had to come from New York or Los Angeles. We chose the Big Apple. To find those deep-pocket investors, TYNA TACI planned to launch a full assault on unsuspecting Manhattanites. Ours would be the first orchestrated push to promote Austin as a music capital and source of talent on par with cities already recognized for music. New Orleans, Nashville, Memphis, Detroit.

Before starting the assault, we needed a media-press kit. I wrote a script and with Gordie Ham went into the Onion Audio studio to simulate a demo of *Armadillo Radio Headquarters.*

Micael Priest, working aside Mike Osborne at the Directions Company, produced our handouts and designed the printed materials to fit into a 7-inch reel box for audio tape. Bill Narum and the Space City Video gang had begun operating the city of Taylor's cable channel... from their living room! They changed their name to TaylorVision.

We hired the collective to do our videocassette presentation and I did the voiceover. Very high-tech for that moment. Phillips had released the first affordable Videocassette Recorder in 1970 and by 1974 your local department store was selling video recorders. Their primary use was to record a program from a TV set.

The popular VHS format used for movie rentals from places like Blockbusters didn't come on the scene until 1977, the same year the Apple II and Commodore PET (personal electronic transactor) computers were introduced.

For weeks our adrenaline-pumping team rushed around the 'Dillo getting everything in place for the upcoming Big Apple sales trip. In the meantime we set about mailing our media kits to major electronics firms, airlines, breweries, automakers, and record companies.

My friend Bill Bland had left his deejay post at WPOP to become sales manager for a nationally syndicated radio promotion called Bridal Fair. This highly successful event built around weddings was held annually in the nation's top markets. TYNA TACI flew Bland in to advise us on how to sell 'Dillo syndication to advertisers.

Former RCA promotion chief Augie Blume became our consultant to secure an Armadillo record contract. RCA assigned Blume in 1971 to launch Grunt Records, their sublabel for the Jefferson Airplane and its spin-off band, Hot Tuna.

Jorma Kaukonen, cue stick in hand, alongside the pool table in the Airplane's black-and-gold Victorian mansion, told me RCA wouldn't let the guys call their new band Hot Shit, so they called themselves Hot Tuna. Because of the smell. I don't think he was joking.

TYNA TACI commissioned Bill Narum to bring his Portapak video recorder to NYC and document our historic trip. Eddie and I rolled up enough high-grade marijuana joints to fill a Marlboro cigarette carton. Party favors. For this ambitious excursion, Lone Star Beer contributed 50 cases of longnecks and 100 JKFLN posters to hand out in our hospitality suite.

* * *

BEFORE HEADING NORTH, we needed a half-dozen songs by Uncle Walt's Band to play for Mary Martin, the east coast A&R head of Warner Bros. Records. This lovely woman carried heavy credentials, having put Bob Dylan together with the Band, as well as orchestrating the launch of Canadian Leonard Cohen's career in the U.S.A. She once managed Van Morrison and her latest find was an unknown singer named Emmylou Harris.

We hoped an Uncle Walt's album would be released on a WB sublabel called Armadillo Records. She liked the boys' music and provided demo money for TYNA TACI to record the trio.

Mike Tolleson first introduced Eddie and me to Uncle Walt's Band at Castle Creek. The trio had formed in Spartanburg and moved to Nashville, then to Austin.

Walter Hyatt, David Ball, and Champ Hood were inseparable in those days. Each musician contributed equally to the clean sound of acoustic instruments with young male voices singing from their melodic songbook of original tunes.

Thing is, this was not folk music, not country or rock. Champ on guitar and mandolin wove perfectly in and out of Walter's understated lead guitar. David plucking his upright acoustic bass gave depth to their mountain-air sound.

Eddie right away liked their lyrically crafted songs and healthy-looking faces. My ears heard the trio's melodies and superior harmonies. David's high tenor voice was stunning. Willis Alan Ramsey was in the club that night and praised their music. The audience wanted encores.

We decided to represent the band to record companies. A year later, it became my good fortune to produce Uncle Walt's Band. Their music was pure Americana. A genre not yet labeled.

The boys chose Arthur Smith Studios. This was the Charlotte, North Carolina, studio of the renowned Arthur "Guitar Boogie" Smith. It was the first commercial recording studio in the Southeast. His song, "Tale of the Red Headed Stranger" had inspired Willie Nelson. In addition to Smith's three-million-selling hit "Guitar Boogie"—the first instrumental to make it on the country record charts—he garnered even greater fame with his tune "Dueling Banjoes." It was featured in the 1972 movie *Deliverance*. He was the first country musician to have a national television show.

For the Warner Bros. demo, I intended to record seven Uncle Walt's Band songs. But the guys had been apart for a few months and thus had fresh ears and were sounding better than ever. No way could I possibly stop their musical reunion. Arthur Smith himself stepped into the control room to listen.

We kept the eight-track Ampex rolling and recorded twenty songs! Picked out seven for the demo.

24

Armadillos in Manhattan

Our door at the TYNA TACI suite at the Warwick Hotel in New York City stayed open 24 hours. Word spread quickly among the promotion-jaded New York cosmopolitans that we Texans were a rare event. Poets and musicians, record industry people, ad agency buyers came parading through.

Here was a weird traveling party the likes of which the Big Apple hadn't seen since the days of the Merry Pranksters! Elizabeth Ashley, starring in *Cat On A Hot Tin Roof*, had befriended Eddie and came by after her performance. Loudon Wainright III dropped in and borrowed Gordie's old gut string Framus to play a few songs. Freddie King stopped by. So did Bill Oakes, president of RSO Records, and Jerry Greenberg, president of Atlantic. Mary Martin was there each day, and Texas expat Chet Flippo of *Rolling Stone* arrived to greet and party. Two attractive women arrived to supply an infinite rail of cocaine for those so inclined.

The room filled with a perfect mix of management and talent, and Eddie Wilson, the ideal host, greeted each of them. Meanwhile Bill Narum videotaped this Austin-style moveable feast.

During office hours, we pitched more decision-makers

in five days than many ad agencies do in a month. I was shocked to learn our video presentation was ahead of its time and corporate offices in this worldly metropolis did not yet have playback decks.

On the third day, we grabbed a cab to the Bottom Line for a performance by Freddie King. The new club was one of three distinct NYC showcase venues for the record industry. One club demonstrated the power of our Austin music scene by calling itself the Lone Star Café. They regularly booked Austin artists such as Ray Wylie Hubbard, Doug Sahm, and Rusty Weir. Another was CBGB, which featured alt-rock proto-punk, Patti Smith Group, Television, Ramones.

Jack Calmes had built a youth audience for Freddie King. It sprang from the national reviews of his shows at the 'Dillo. Most people identify Armadillo World Headquarters as THE progressive country hall. But in the early struggling days, Freddie King was one of the few acts that could be depended on to make money. Armadillo was referred to as "The House That Freddie Built."

Spencer Perskin sees it differently: "Freddie helped the 'Dillo, but Armadillo helped Freddie get bookings aside from his usual blues gigs."

Good point.

Jack Calmes had the vision. He used the Armadillo press clippings and his industry connections to get Freddie King on Leon Russell's own Shelter Records, and FM rock radio play followed. After three albums, he moved Freddie onto Robert Stigwood's new RSO Records out of London. Stigwood built his reputation by launching Cream and the Bee Gees. Eric Clapton was his client.

The Bottom Line was a perfect listening club. That night, its 400-capacity main room was "standing room only." For a while, I hung out in the cramped backstage where Freddie and some band members were taking the edge off the special evening by playing a few rounds of poker. The Bottom Line that night saw an unending string of well-wishers—executives, music press, fellow musicians—and Calmes greeted them all.

Freddie King's brand new album, *Larger Than Life*, had one entire side recorded live at the Armadillo. Everyone thought that was too cool for school.

My old friend, Jerry Wexler, invited me to sit at his table. He told me he liked Freddie's recording of "Nights Never Get Lonely." Wexler also told me he thought the Spanish language version of the song by Sunny and the Sunliners was a Tejano hit.

The moment Freddie King took the stage with his crackling guitar, the music-savvy audience instantly melted. It was Texas blues-rock. It was ZZ Top or Johnny Winter, but more black and more blues.

Songs such as "Big Legged Woman" were getting FM exposure and getting requests from young Hendrix, Page, and Townshend addicts. The Texas Cannonball was the only black blues player getting such exposure—more than B. B. King—although BB's version of "The Thrill Is Gone" had been a Top 20 hit.

Freddie received standing ovations that night and great reviews the next day. The musician was elated and his showbiz future looked bright.

We checked out of the Warwick Hotel with a feeling of mission accomplished. On the flight back to Austin, we stayed high and considered our trip a big success.

* * *

ANOTHER IMPORTANT EVENT occurred in 1974. The Heidelberg Press in Austin published *The Improbable Rise of Redneck Rock,* by Jan Reid. Even today I still believe this edition is the perfect accounting of the optimistic spirit and naiveté of that exuberant moment in Austin's music history. His book was one of the fundamental elements birthing the roaring era of "redneck rock," "cross-country," "progressive country," "cosmic cowboy," and "outlaw country." In those days I'd often go to a meeting with a music executive and see Jan Reid's book on their desk.

KLRN director Charles Vaughn told me: "I was sitting in Bill Arhos's office when Paul Bosner, a visiting professor from Dallas, stormed in and slapped a copy of Jan's book on Arhos's desk and declared that Bill should read this and if he didn't start a music series based on this opportunity, he would. Arhos read the book and took the first steps in creating *Austin City Limits.*"

25

Disco Arrives ...
'Dillo Goes Bankrupt

In 1976 TYNA TACI and Armadillo World Headquarters ran out of money at the same time. RSO had passed on our research-tested hit by Freddie King to cash in on the disco craze and released "Boogie Bump."

I can't imagine a worse tune for the guitar master. Best suited for Chubby Checker.

It was the start of the end. Our problems mounted and we next lost the Uncle Walt's Band album deal with Warner Bros., then we lost the *Austin City Limits* series... and finally, we lost the Lone Star Beer account.

That disaster hit when the Glen Agency from Dallas convinced the brewery they were the proper ones to direct Lone Star's advertising, not those hippies from Austin.

I learned the inside skinny afterward. Harry Jersig was negotiating the sale of his brewery and felt he needed a more "professional" looking agency to present to the buyer. Our returnable bottle success had made national beer industry news and taken the value of his Lone Star brand's stock up in the eyes of brewery investors, but TYNA TACI was too far out to suit their taste.

I had inadvertently contributed to our decline by

producing a controversial television commercial. The disco and anti-hippie lifestyle trend was emerging. With it came the fern bars, gourmet burgers, fried mushrooms, and dress codes.

I wanted to position Lone Star Beer to be accepted in these new venues filled with dancers instead of listeners. But we didn't want to alienate the brand's redneck and hippie customers. I was making this image adjustment a couple years before *Saturday Night Fever* took the nation by storm.

Believability called for a handheld documentary appearance, so I asked Ken Harrison from Dallas to produce. Noted for 16mm work, he had just finished editing his now famous Texas vérité documentary, *Jackelope*, shot in Central Texas. It focused on three artists, one of whom is venerable Austin sculptor Bob "Daddy-O" Wade.

Harrison filmed our commercial in 16mm at Jim Hasslocher's soon-to-open million-dollar Austin restaurant-disco called the Magic Time Machine. Colorful, its wait staff wore outlandish costumes. The salad bar was a shiny red 1952 MG.

I asked This fashionable lifestyle with its social upscaling affected live music's preferred environment. Willie Nelson at the Austin Opry House had inherited motel carpeting along with air conditioning and he could sell mixed drinks. More upscale.

Many young gals wore cocktail dresses and high heels at concerts, while their guys kept dressy shirts loose-buttoned to show off a gold neck chain dangling a small gold coke spoon. For those particular music lovers, watching a band while sitting on the floor with a pitcher of beer was not an option. Not even if you pretended it was hip by calling it festival-style seating. our Austin co-producer, Sheri Nelson, to give the dining beer drinkers and dancers a costume-party look. We had afternoon tryouts on the 'Dillo stage. The disco music I used was our English version of "Nights Never Get Lonely" by Sunny and the Sunliners. All of us agreed the finished commercial looked great and the well-dressed young dancers were exciting.

Barry Sullivan exploded. "Woody! What the hell are you trying to do?"

"What?"

"Our distributors went ballistic after seeing that black boy and white girl dancing together..."

"Huh?"

We reviewed the ad. For the briefest part of a moment, the commercial flashed what Lone Star interpreted as an interracial couple dancing. It had zipped right past Harrison and me during editing. It was just a 2D optical illusion; they weren't dancing with each other.

No one else had noticed it. Nevertheless, Lone Star killed the commercial.

Then came a split over live armadillo races. They were a common redneck event in Texas, but we at the 'Dillo had realized how inhumane it was to capture them and make them race. Some people even painted on their armor. Very harmful, like painting on a turtle's shell.

Barry and Jerry Retzzlof insisted on sponsoring the races. Then after TYNA TACI had laid out the plans for a weekly barter TV Austin music series, Barry took our idea to Leon Russell's ShelterVision. They would film the progressive country scene in the city's nightclubs. The Armadillo staff said, "Not in here, not as long as you sponsor those dastardly races."

So the brewery went on without the participation of the most famous music hall in Texas. It was a typical Willie outlaw kind of series and was highlighted when Tim O'Conner pulled his pistol and shot at something in front of the Alliance Wagon Yard. His bullet hit the Columbia Records executive visiting the set. Barry had a lot of explaining to do and O'Conner left town for a few years.

* * *

OUR TYNA TACI disasters happened between January and June of 1976. We went down as fast as we'd gone up.

And on top of everything else, attendance numbers at the Armadillo World Headquarters dwindled. Artists such as Commander Cody were given a guaranteed minimum, based on previous shows.

Now the musicians were attracting fewer people and income projections were not met. The Headquarters was coming up short. Financial numbers dropped further into the red.

Still, the venue maintained its huge payroll, believing business would improve. My first alert that further adverse changes were in store came from the *Austin American-Statesman*.

"Eddie, look at this. UT sorority and fraternity pledging is up 300 percent!"

Frats and sororities—the Greeks—had been in decline for years. They were thought to be obsessed with social-class and emblematic of the American establishment that hippies and outlaw country cultures rejected. However, this newest generation of college students was starting to dress in high fashion. They wanted air conditioning, mixed drinks, and comfort when attending concerts.

I had anticipated the implosion of the civil rights movement when the military draft ended. Young men were free at last to build their social lives and not die in a swamp. It was time to celebrate, not protest march.

As a programmer, I understood pop music changed generationally from emphasizing melody to emphasizing rhythm. I expected the sound of lead instruments to change with the times. And the lyrics.

But the speed of this shift in the mid-seventies was startling. Many hit records featured synthesizers. Yuppies were taking control.

The Me generation had arrived.

This fashionable lifestyle with its social upscaling affected live music's preferred environment. Willie Nelson at the Austin Opry House had inherited motel carpeting along with air conditioning and he could sell mixed drinks. More upscale.

Many young gals wore cocktail dresses and high heels at concerts, while their guys kept dressy shirts loose-buttoned to show off a gold neck chain dangling a small gold coke spoon. For those particular music lovers, watching a band while sitting on the floor with a pitcher of beer was not an option. Not even if you pretended it was hip by calling it festival-style seating.

In fall of '76 when UT students returned, a Memphis deejay named Rick Dees had claimed the nation's #1 hit by selling six million copies of... "Disco Duck."

Give me a break!

To climax that year of darkness, Freddie King at age 42 suffered a heart attack and died. It seemed a strange coincidence that only a few days later, Armadillo World Headquarters—"the house that Freddie built"—applied for Chapter 11 bankruptcy.

26

It's a Wrap

Among the most vivid memories of my Armadillo years are times I sat across from Eddie Wilson at his dining room table. In front of him would be a yellow legal pad scribbled with lists and lists of lists. Drawings and proposals scattered about. There might be a plastic baggie of pot, an Alamo Sweet cigar box for rolling joints, a couple of beers or cups of coffee, and a pack of Camels. Our ashtray was a brass cast armadillo.

At this mahogany table, many dreams were born and decisions made.

I was honored the day Eddie looked across the table and said, "Woody, we have to incorporate the Armadillo. There are eight of us, we talked it over, and we'd like you to be one of us. We're only an eight-banded Armadillo, but the real animal has nine bands."

I wanted to join them, but I couldn't. There were others who for low pay had already put a few years of their lives into the Headquarters. It wouldn't be right for me to barge in ahead of them. My decision that night embodied the latent hippie ethics of the moment. They never offered that ninth position to anyone else.

My saddest Armadillo memory comes from that same table. It was a day in the fall of 1976. Money was gone.

TYNA TACI had no clients. Armadillo was bankrupt.

Eddie said, "Wood, I don't know what else I can do except hand the Armadillo over to Hank, if he'll take it."

Bill Narum's "golden age" was ending.

Hank accepted.

Of the eight partners, seven received one percent of the stock and Hank Alrich got the rest. In effect, 'Dillo ownership and guidance had gone from a loose collective to a partnership, to a corporate board of directors, and now a proprietorship.

Randy McCall helped Hank file the bankruptcy forms. Eddie, Genie, Tolleson, Bobby Hedderman, and I left the 'Dillo. Hank and a small team of minimum-wage, part-time employees plus a larger number of volunteers pushed on, worked hard, and made sacrifices, all the while adding to the hall's musical heritage. And then Phoenix-like, they raised Armadillo from its insurmountable debt. It could actually make a profit.

Then one fatal day in early 1980, the landlord told Hank Alrich he was going to sell the property so it could become an office building. He could stay till the end of the year.

27

Remember the Armadillo

By the 21st century, our grandiose Armadillo World Headquarters plans had fully transitioned into folklore and legend. Examining the immense archive of the Armadillo's posters, photographs, videos, audio recordings, and press clippings creates an impressionistic vision of a ragged band of dreamers parading through the 1970s. When it closed the doors forever, Eddie Wilson, like me and a thousand others, sensed the nag of something missing. The feeling of something left unfinished.

I have to agree with Governor Ann Richards, who said, "I saw a little of everything at Armadillo. And it was truly one of the great experiences of my life."

Ramsey Wiggins described us best in words he wrote for our TYNA TACI marketing kit. He intended the piece to be an introduction to the Armadillo World Headquarters. It now serves as the eulogy:

Armadillo World Headquarters is a concert hall, restaurant, and beer garden. On occasion it is also a ballet theatre, art gallery, and center for the performing arts.

It is also a musician's referral service, a music publishing company, a recording studio, and a media consulting firm, about which "We thought you'd never ask."

It is also a business, complete with executives, accountants, bookkeepers, secretaries, and at least one documented case of ulcers earned as part of the over a million dollar gross recorded in 1975.

We are also over a hundred barkeepers, security men, waitresses, maintenance people, audio engineers, lighting specialists, cooks, food handlers, electricians, carpenters, plumbers, musicians, actors, artists, and stage crew, as well as several people whose function has never actually been determined, but who are nevertheless considered indispensable to the operation of the world's largest full-service honky-tonk.

Finally, we are a community within ourselves. We care for each other and love each other. We firmly believe that any hurt to any of us diminishes us all, and that all of us together can do anything that needs doing. We're something that has never happened before. We are the Armadillo.

SNAPSHOTS OF A MUSIC CAPITAL

The only truth is music.

Jack Kerouac

1

Post-Midnight Encounter

I left my Fort Lauderdale radio program director's job and moved to San Antonio. I wanted to work for Gordon McLendon and learn his Top 40 format that had swept the nation. KTSA's studio, offices, and transmitter were on the edge of the city's suburbs in a big pasture. Most of Eisenhower Road leading to the studio was unlit, unpaved dirt.

I was alone in the station and it was the first week of my overnight show. At 3 a.m. someone tapped on the window glass. Cautiously, I crossed the room and peeked around the closed drapes and into the darkness to see a skinny guy, about my age, in a cowboy hat.

He shouted, "I've got a new 45!"

Oh?

"Hey, it's me. Doug Sahm."

Doug who?

He waved a cherry red vinyl record. I left country music crossover smash, *El Paso*, by Marty Robbins spinning on the turntable. It would give me about five minutes to meet this guy. After I unlocked the steel backdoor, there stood Doug with his friend, Rocky Morales.

"Hey, man, we brought you my new single." Doug was chewing gum real fast. "Wait till you hear these horns."

I took the record. Noted it was a hometown label, Renner Records.

"You gotta come see my band, this weekend." He took out a pencil and scribbled an address on back of a Handy Andy Supermarket receipt. "Your name's at the door. No cover."

His single was "Crazy Crazy Feeling."

Doug Sahm's scribbled instructions led me downtown to a cellar club called the Purple Onion—likely named after the famous beatnik cellar at North Beach in San Francisco. Cellar clubs were hip, their underground setting recalled Prohibition-era speakeasies.

San Antonio's popular club, the Tiffany Lounge, was considered a step up, with its ornate décor that encouraged a fashionably dressed crowd. Sunny and the Sunglows played there, so did the Royal Jesters.

But while the Tiffany was elegant, the Purple Onion was a true dive.

I inched down the steep, purple-lit stairway to a closed door. Pulling it open, I saw a hazy red-lit room full of blue cigarette smoke. A hot guitar solo with three horns wailing twelve-bar blues pierced the haze. On stage Doug leaned forward and moaned into the mic: "The eagle flies on Friday…"

That night Doug Sahm did right by upbeat classics "Stagger Lee" and the "T-Bone Shuffle," but he excelled on ballads such as "Wasted Days and Wasted Nights." When the band slid into a hot version of "C. C. Rider," the gals pulled guys from tables to the dance floor. Texas Push-style swing, also called the whip, involved a lot more spins for the ladies.

Watching Doug in action, I remember thinking, how can that guy sing and chew gum at the same time? Then he stunned me with the Johnny Ace classic, "Pledging My Love," followed with a Sahm original, "Two Hearts in Love."

Slow dancer shadows in the red haze bodies snuggled close.

2

A Night on the Town

Doug took me around San Antonio to meet other musicians and "interesting" people. He drove east to introduce Johnny Phillips, owner of the Eastwood Country Club. This was the home of famed stripper Miss Wiggles and the destination for touring R&B bands. Like the Victory Grill in Austin it, too, was on the Chitlin' Circuit.

At Eastwood we saw local blues star Big Bertha, and I met local music hero Spot Barnett, a saxophone king. Spot, who in the '60s would become the bandleader for Ike and Tina Turner, is today known as the Father of San Antonio Blues.

Next evening, Doug took me to Latino radio station KCOR 1350-AM, where I shook hands with R&B deejay Scratch Phillips. Scratch was a black deejay at a Mexican-American station. Thanks to Sunny Ozuna, Freddy Fender, and others, there was a love for R&B and blues-flavored music among Mexican-Americans, especially because of the horns.

So KCOR hired Scratch Phillips and a new Spanish-language TV station, KWEX 41, hired Scratch to do a Monday night show. As it turned out, that little TV station was a seed that grew into the Univision Network.

We visited trashed-out station KMAC 630-AM, owned by Howard "Stinky" Davis. Doug wanted me to meet deejay Joe Anthony.

Here was a man who got to play his personal favorites, who one day would be the first deejay in the USA to feature only heavy metal bands, and who would become known as "The Godfather of Rock Radio." But in his early days, Anthony favored obscure blues records and called his program *Harlem Hit Parade*. His late-night theme song was the instrumental classic "Harlem Nocturne" by sax virtuoso King Curtis.

He especially liked that I was using saxophonist Jimmy Forrest's version of "Night Train" as my overnight bumper music. Anthony was also part owner of Harlem Records, and Doug's "Why, Why, Why" was a local hit for the label.

Later that night Doug took me to the Big House, where upstairs smoke-filled poker games were running hot and heavy as soulful blues horns blared up through a worn oak floor. Being the new kid on the block, I appreciated Doug Sahm taking me around town.

All the while, he raved about Freddy Fender and Sunny Ozuna being his favorite singers. Sunny, with his national hits later, would become of major importance to all local blues musicians as well as Mexican-American bands. To understand his influence on Doug Sahm, you have to hear an early track like "Ooh-Poo-Pah-Doo," recorded during Sunny Ozuna's high school years, and compare it to Jessie Hill's hit.

For my ears, his soul singing was equal to the blues masters. His recording of "Talk to Me" is superior to the Little Willie John original. Both singers' vocals are great, but the Sunglow's band arrangement is superior.

I first heard the hit played from a master tape at Texas Sound studio as Jeff Smith used his acetate lathe to cut an early dub. This version of the R&B standard opened with sweeping violins! The idea of using violins came from Sunglows' bandleader, drummer/producer, Manny Guerra. By using strings, he created a mood that set the listener up to hear Sunny pleading: "Talk to me, talk to me..."

It gave me goose bumps.

One night I picked up Doug in my white 1959 Plymouth Fury, anodized gold side trim with large tailfins, four headlamps, push-button transmission. Doug pointed the way to the Farmer's Daughter dance hall.

At the door they told the cover charge guy I'm with KTSA and he let me walk. Everyone was dressed western. The floor was filled with line dancers—this is when no one outside the Southwest had heard of line dancing— and the band was playing the "Cotton-Eyed Joe," which many Texans consider their national anthem.

After that rousing instrumental, the star of the night, Charlie Walker, stepped forward to sing his country hit, "Pick Me Up On Your Way Down."

I learned the noted singer had a day job as a country music deejay on KMAC. Twenty years later, Charlie Walker was inducted into the Country Music Radio DJ Hall of Fame.

Leaving the Farmer's Daughter and driving to downtown, we as usual talked about Texas music scenes in Houston, Corpus Christi, Lubbock, and Dallas.

The city never mentioned was Austin.

3

Yesterday

Today Austin is called the "Live Music Capital of the World," but until the mid-1960s, San Antonio's music scene was far ahead. Some claim Austin's live music scene first happened in the 1850s and sprang from the German bier gartens, of which only Scholz's remains as a place where singing groups drink and make merry.

I'll trace San Antonio's live music heritage back to the Alamo in 1836, where Santa Anna arrived with a full military band of drummers and horn players to announce his presence. Inside the old mission, a musical duo—fiddler Davy Crockett and John McGregor on bagpipes—played spontaneous jams and buckdances for their doomed compadres. Davy Crockett was a popular fiddle player in Tennessee and known for his original reels. One still played today goes under the names "The Route" or "Jenny on the Railroad."

In the early 1960s, country-western artists Charlie Walker and George Chambers, with his band The Country Gentlemen, were the biggest draws in Central Texas. San Antonio's only chart-topping star of the 1950s was million-selling deejay singer Charlie Walker with his #2 country hit, "Pick Me Up On Your Way Down." The singer continued selling records into the 1960s with

Top 10 country hits: "Who Will Buy the Wine," "Wild as a Wildcat," and the novelty "Don't Squeeze My Sharmon."

George Chambers was known for mentoring musicians such as Grammy winner Bobby Flores, songwriter Jim Chestnut, and prodigy Steve Earle. Willie Nelson got both of his bass players from the Country Gentlemen: Bee Spears, whom the military drafted in '68, and his replacement, David Zettner, who stayed with Willie 40 years before passing on to his new gig in the sky.

In those days, the Alamo City was home to the celebrated Leon Payne, aka the "Blind Balladeer." Henry Lebermann had tutored the lad at the Austin School for the Blind, and Payne later became one of the Playboys with Bob Wills.

In 1948 Payne was living in Houston when Hank Williams had a hit with his song, "Lost Highway." Williams soon adopted it as his signature tune. The following year Payne wrote a second classic and this time sang the hit record himself, "I Love You Because." In 1954 Elvis Presley recorded the song for Sun Records.

In 1969 Leon died at home in the Alamo City. Then a decade later Elvis Costello recorded Payne's song, "Psycho."

Leon Payne holds the honor of being the only composer to have two different songs recorded by *two* different Elvises!

The Alamo City once had active hometown record companies and a busy pressing plant where the vinyl "biscuits" were squashed into 7-inch, big-hole 45s to be pasted with colorful labels. Those mid-1950s years were a transition period, as some consumers still bought 10-inch, 78 rpm shellac discs.

Columbia had introduced the microgroove vinyl

12-inch LP in 1948, and stereo was on the horizon. Hi-fi audiophiles bought recorded music on 7-inch reels of quarter-inch tape that played back at 7½ inches per second. Their brand of choice for an in-home reel-to-reel deck was Viking.

But predominant in this era of black-and-white TV and AM radio was RCA's 45 rpm, a two-sided single that was first sold in 1949. It took a few years for the 45 and LP formats to dominate. The source of all this recorded music emanated from professional studios using Ampex monaural tape decks with 10-inch open reels running at 15 inches per second.

These decks were initially made for singer Bing Crosby so the superstar could prerecord his radio shows on the new ABC network. Bing played an out-front role in this new medium by promoting the use of magnetic audiotape and heavily investing in the tiny company named Ampex. Then he became a leading player in the development of videotape.

Der Bingle was more than the most popular singer in America and a top recording artist of the last century, having sold over one billion records. His "White Christmas" is the *best-selling* single of all time! The man was also a visionary.

Bing Crosby gets credit for saving the record industry. In 1934 he endorsed the radical idea of lowering the price of his Decca singles from a dollar to 35 cents and taking a royalty based on records sold, rather than a flat fee.

San Antonio used to be the home of TNT Records, featuring regional artists such as the rockabilly kings Johnny Olenn and the Jokers with their ballad "Candy

Kisses." It sold 35,000, and that was a lot in 1955, the year pocket transistor radios came on the scene.

That label as well had Ray Campi from Austin doing an upbeat Elvis-like number, "Play it Cool," and the Traits from San Marcos doing "Live It Up." Bill Anderson, an unknown singer from out of state, recorded his new tune, "City Lights," for TNT.

A singing deejay named Willie Nelson also cut a demo, but they passed on him.

People in the local music business were excited when Ray Peterson of "Tell Laura I Love Her" fame moved from his home in Denton, Texas, to San Antonio. I suspect these days he would have moved to Austin.

Noted for his four-and-a-half-octave voice, Peterson had left RCA and started his own record label, Dunes. He was a man ahead of his time. In 1960 I especially liked his Top 10 version of "Corrine, Corrina," produced by genius Phil Spector.

It was released after Spector's time with the Teddy Bears ("I Love How You Love Me") and before he became famous with his "wall of sound" recording technique used for a host of million sellers by artists such as his wife Ronnie's group the Ronettes, the Righteous Brothers, George Harrison, and John Lennon.

San Antonio musicians used to survive on gigs at the five military bases and a handful of nightclubs, plus Central and South Texas dance halls. But the city's earliest Latino bands made good money by playing the annual pickers' circuit for income—and we're not talking about guitar pickers.

During harvest season, these professional folkloric

bands, which also added pop hits to their repertoire, followed migrant farmworkers from Mexico as they harvested crops throughout the Midwest and up and down the West Coast. Live music dances for migrant laborers provided an important break in otherwise strenuous work.

At these dances, families held reunions and often wedding engagements were announced. Some bands contained a dozen musicians. Their sound wasn't yet called *Tejano*, but they played traditional Mexican music mixed with U.S. big band standards and occasional R&B. The forms evolved into new chart arrangements, always requiring the horns out front to punctuate the lead singer. Many of those vocalists wished they could reach higher octaves like Ray Peterson.

* * *

AUSTIN HAD A different dynamic than SA. In the 1950s, music people in Austin were excited when "You Cheated, You Lied" by McCallum High School students, the Slades, hit the charts for Domino Records, a homegrown company.

Of course this wasn't Austin's first label. For example, in the late 1940s, Lasso Records issued Dolores and the Bluebonnet Boys playing her "Austin Waltz." Dolores Fariss has the honor of being Austin's first female bandleader. She didn't sing but, like those swing era leaders of big bands, played an instrument: piano.

In 1958, Domino Records staked its claim as the city's only label to have a national hit. Fifty years later their claim still held.

Eleven people who met attending a YWCA song

marketing class started the little record company. Eleven partners? Sounds crazy, like it could never work.

Yet here were the Slades, heard on Top 40 radio stations from Boston to LA. Domino again grabbed national ears by releasing "No Way Out" by Joyce Harris and the Daylighters. It was a soulful record, with a black R&B band from East Austin backing Harris, a white girl who sang like a merging of Etta James with Brenda Lee.

Truly, I would say it was this single and her recordings of "Got My Mojo Working" and, as Sinner Strong, "Don't Knock It" that first pointed the way toward the Austin blues vocal styling of Roky Erickson and Janis Joplin. Joyce also recorded a couple of ballads with the Slades. Music chronicler Dave Marsh listed "No Way Out" by Joyce Harris among his music industry's Top 1,000 singles.

Domino Records only made it three years. But its two most successful recordings seeded a local crosstown blues-rock appreciation scene that would influence many Austin musicians to come.

That small town indie label from Texas had produced a pair of 45s internationally sought by today's collectors.

I've watched dozens of Austin labels bud, flower, and wilt. A total collection of their recordings would present a side of the city no other media can duplicate.

To understand a musician, you can't just look at a photo or read a description of their music. You gotta hear it! Such a catalog would be a hometown version of *Smithsonian Folkways*.

Most impressive to me of Austin's record companies were Sonobeat, Fable, and Antone's. They not only had exceptional catalogs, they were also formative in creating a scene. Already I feel guilty about not mentioning great local companies such as Amazing ("If It's A Hit, It's Amazing"), Rabid Cat, Loudhouse, and Watermelon. There were so many.

And not enough can be said about the culture-building role of Bill Josey and Bill, Jr. Like the John and Alan Lomax team, the Joseys went into the field to record on site. But this father-and-son team also broadcast the live music direct from places like the New Orleans Old World Night Club on Red River Street. Broadcasters refer to such a remote as a NEMO: Not Emanating Main Office.

From 1967 to 1976, their Sonobeat Records output was 24 singles and two albums, and all were in-club recordings. The Joseys produced *The Progressive Blues Experiment* by the Johnny Winter Trio.

Recorded during the daytime in an empty Vulcan Gas Company, the album was Winter's first, with Tommy Shannon as his bass player. That 1967 master tape eventually sold to Imperial Records and their 12-inch release featured photographer Burton Wilson's first album cover photo.

Burton is considered the dean of Austin's live music photographers. He shot with available light in black and white and his style had been greatly influenced by his teacher/mentor, the acclaimed Russell Lee, who in 1965 became the first professor of photography at UT. Interesting that Russell's dad was named Burton.

This period was also when noted Armadillo artist Jim Franklin produced his first album cover art. It was for Sonobeat and the record was *Jazz to the Third Power*. No, it didn't feature armadillos.

4

Austin's First Hitmakers

The Texas Capital was definitely a university town in 1961. Culturally its main claim to national fame was Billy Lee Brammer's novel, *The Gay Place*.

"Gay" did not yet have a homosexual meaning. Brammer referred to its original use for merry, lively, given to social pleasures. Here was a highly acclaimed work of literature written by a hometown author. Texas history through allegory. Much of it takes place in the Scholz Garten, then a political insiders' hangout, and today the oldest continuing business in Texas. The book is the definitive novel on the political beginnings of Lyndon B. Johnson.

The Gay Place signaled the beginning of the "New Texas" literary movement and portended the blossoming of the creative arts as a primary driving force in the Capital City of Texas.

Ten years before Brammer wrote his game-changing book, an Austin gospel group, The Bells of Joy, recorded their historic 1951 crossover hit, gospel to R&B (then called race pop), "Let's Talk About Jesus." Austin musicians scored this chart-topping hit, and the city's jive-talking, R&B radio deejay and pianist, Lavada

Durst, aka Doctor Hepcat, wrote it.

The man is often credited as the first black deejay in Texas for his 1948 radio show on KVET 1300-AM, the *Rosewood Ramble*. Part owner of that station was future Texas governor and secretary of the U.S. treasury John Connally.

Meanwhile, two hundred miles east of Austin in the Bayou City lived Don Robey. He owned the Bronze Peacock Nightclub. He also owned the successful gospel and blues label, Peacock Records. Robey had produced the original "Hound Dog" by Big Mama Thornton that Elvis later took to #1 on the *Cashbox* charts. It surprises most folks to learn the writers of this famous down-home blues classic were two Jewish fellows in LA named Leiber and Stoller.

Robey discovered his fascination with the yet-unnamed genre of rhythm and blues played in his nightclub. He decided to purchase a Memphis label called Duke that would bring him new talents such as Johnny Ace and Bobby Bland.

However, success came to Robey from another town and genre, Austin and gospel music. The Starlight Singers had changed their name to The Bells of Joy and their sound broke new ground for Robey. They were an *a capella* quintet singing gospel music that decided to use guitars along with a drum set.

Most importantly, The Bells introduced what came to be the dominant R&B vocal style of call-and-response singing. In 1951 A. J. Littlefield was lead singer for The Bells of Joy when they recorded "Let's Talk About Jesus." To everyone's surprise, it became a million seller!

And it was this gospel classic by The Bells that changed the vocal styles of newly emerging performers such as Ray Charles and Aretha Franklin. Here was a sound turning the recording business on its ear.

In hindsight Jerry Wexler, the acclaimed producer who coined "rhythm and blues," said he should have called it "rhythm and gospel."

The Bells of Joy avoided temptation and stayed true to gospel music, although many producers wanted them to record a secular R&B record.

But this was not Austin's first charting record. That honor goes to Cactus Pryor and the Pricklypears. In 1950 on 4 Star Records they released a parody of Frankie Lane's big smash "Cry of the Wild Goose" and called it "Cry of a Dying Duck in a Thunder-Storm." It went all the way to #7 on the Billboard country chart.

The local humorist was named after the Cactus Theater on Congress Avenue run by his dad, and he was front man for the First Family of Austin's professional announcers: his brother Wally Pryor was the city's foremost sportscaster, and his sons Paul and Don became political talk show hosts.

In 1958 when the Slades had their national pop hit with "You Cheated, You Lied," Austin's population was fewer than 150,000. These young hit makers were white boys and originally called their group the Spades but were "convinced" by the record company to change their name.

Seems deejays were reluctant to say their name because some used it to describe Negroes, as in the phrase, "He was blacker than the ace of spades."

The boys were ultimately a doo-wop group. "You Cheated" was pure, street corner doo-wop and perfect for slow dancing. Teens could get close with her head on his shoulder, his hand on her ass.

The Slades' accompaniment was bass and rhythm

guitar, no drums. They were more traditional than The Bells had been.

Meanwhile, in Los Angeles, an opportunist record producer quickly assembled a black group to cover the Slades. He called them the Shields.

They released their own recording of "You Cheated" just as the Slades' tune was starting up the charts and, by using a better distributor, had the bigger hit and broke into the Top 20. The L.A. version was slicker than the Austin boys', yet, except for a soulful falsetto wailing in the background, it was identical.

This is a rare instance of a black group covering a white group's hit. When the Shangri-Las, a white girl group that gained international fame for their '60s novelty, "Leader of the Pack," recorded "You Cheated," they added drums and piano.

McCallum High-schooler Don Burch had penned a doo-wop classic.

Tommy Kasper had written the Slades' first release, "You Mean Everything to Me." It didn't sell. But two years later the Fleetwoods out of Seattle recorded his song for the flip side of their million-seller, "Mr. Blue."

So the Slades officially were Austin's first pop chart musicians and pop hit songwriters.

The Slades also were Austin's first band to appear on national television when the guys made their debut on *American Bandstand.* It would be 1961 before Arthur Godfrey booked mandolin-playing humorist Sammy Allred and guitar picker Dewane "Sonny" Smith—known as the Geezinslaw Brothers—for his famous CBS TV show.

Until the Slades did their *Bandstand* lip-sync, the only Texas rock group seen on national TV had been the Crickets.

* * *

USING A STANDUP BASS, blind child prodigy Bobby Doyle played with the Slades on their big hit and he matured to become a musician's musician. Doyle developed into a jazz-oriented piano player who could sing with the best. He formed a trio, which included University of Texas student and music superstar-in-the-making Kenny Rogers on bass.

Kenny Rogers' story, of course, is huge, the man growing from those early Austin jazz trio days to Las Vegas headliner and resort owner. I had the pleasure of seeing the Bobby Doyle Trio at the Tidelands in Houston and Kenny Rogers' vocals were then in the style of Frank Sinatra.

Bobby Doyle was the first blind student to graduate from McCallum High. He had moved from Houston at age seven to attend the Austin School for the Blind and be tutored by Henry Lebermann. This music teacher himself was a blind pianist and orchestra leader, who had already nurtured other great blind musicians, such as Whistling Fred Lowery.

* * *

LEBERMANN HAD STARTED young Fred Lowery with birdcalls and encouraged the boy to develop his whistling talent as a way of making a living in a sighted world. Lowery left Austin and soon joined the bands of Vincent Lopez and Horace Heidt.

By the time his life was over in 1984, Fred Lowery had performed with stars such as Bing Crosby, Stan Kenton, Jackie Gleason, and Mary Pickford. He was known as the

"King of Whistlers." Many consider his album, *Walking Along Kicking the Leaves*, for Decca Records a tour de force and the best whistling record ever made.

Years later, in 1954, the movie theme song, "The High and the Mighty," moved into the coveted Billboard Top 10 with **three different** singles all by large orchestras. The one that hit #9 on that chart was an instrumental version by the LeRoy Holmes orchestra featuring Whistling Fred.

But ultimately Fred Lowery's most famous recording was his 1939 version of "Indian Love Call" that sold two million 78 rpm 10-inch shellacs. Incredible for its time, and that old recording today continues to sell as a ringtone.

5

Janis Meets Mr. Threadgill

At the dawn of the '60s, the only thing musical I knew about Austin was folk singer Carolyn Hester and her husband, Richard Farina, hung out there. She lived in New York City. It was the period in the East Village when Phil Ochs, who also lived a few years in Austin and San Antonio, was a major part of the scene, as were Peter, Paul, and Mary.

This community was the East Coast's ground zero for an emerging folk music happening that had been reignited from the olden days of the Weavers by the multi-million-dollar sales of albums by the Kingston Trio. Carolyn Hester, known as the Texas Songbird, was recording a self-titled LP for Columbia when she introduced already famous producer John Hammond to her unknown harmonica player Bob Dylan. Hester was a notable artist in the flourishing coffeehouse circuit and had there met Dylan.

At that same time, Rod Kennedy championed folk musicians and was living in Austin. While a student at UT, Rod had been a driving force in establishing the first public radio station in Central Texas, KUT 90.5-FM.

In 1957, Rod bought KHFI 98.3-FM and focused on classical music but also programmed a few hours of jazz and folk. It was a standard format when newly emerging FM radio used the marketing slogan, "FM Means Fine Music."

No doubt in the early 1960s, an inherent weirdness sprouted in our Texas capital. It was most obvious in 1963 when another long-lasting tradition started: a free, costumed event in Pease Park called Eeyore's Birthday Party. It was a celebration for kids of all ages and it packed the park full of Winnie the Pooh lovers and local crazies. Today crowds of people still dress up to attend.

In those days, no one realized the future importance of a renegade group of UT folk musicians heading to a hillbilly music beer joint and Gulf service station on the outskirts of Austin. They and other artists lived communally in run-down apartments and a dilapidated converted army barracks they dubbed The Ghetto. These residents—musicians Powell St. John, Tary Owens, John Clay, artist Jack Jackson, photographer Stephanie Chernikowski, and others—were the "who's who" of Austin's eccentric new creatives.

Kenneth Threadgill owned the service station and sometime music club. Wednesday nights were for hootenannies, a predecessor to the open mic pass-the hat-format. Threadgill would pass around his upside down tambourine so listeners could donate coins.

The friendly proprietor was known for stepping out from behind the bar to yodel a few tunes, Jimmie Rodgers-style.

In the early 1930s, Rodgers owned a two-story hilltop home in Kerrville and did weekly radio shows out of San Antonio on KMAC. He died from TB in 1933.

That same year, Willie Nelson was born and our twenty-four-year-old Austin entrepreneur bought a Gulf service station on North Lamar Boulevard and sold bootleg liquor from its back lot. Never raided. By the end of 1933, the young proprietor had snagged the first beer license for Travis County. What a lot of people don't know is this singing bartender graduated as an honor roll student from Austin High School.

Rodgers had been proclaimed the Father of Country Music, yet the Blue Yodeler never recorded in Nashville. Aside from NYC, L.A., Camden, and Louisville, the yodeler frequented studios in Dallas and did three sessions in San Antonio. One of his songs that Kenneth Threadgill especially liked to sing, "Jimmie the Kid," had been recorded in the Alamo City. It's fitting; Threadgill would be proclaimed "The Father of Austin Country Music."

In time, local musicians arrived at the old service station to sit around tables, sip beer, and trade guitars, while passing a microphone to sing for one another. Some, such as Bill Malone and Stan Alexander, were graduate students.

The "audience" might include music promoter Rod Kennedy and psychedelic visionary Chet Helms. Eventually, along with a procession of UT folkies, came Janis Joplin.

Janis played a seminal role in launching Austin as a music center. Her burst of superstardom lit a bright ray of hope for aspiring local musicians.

The story goes that one day musician Julie Joyce picked up a hitchhiking Janis and took her to meet a silver-haired Mr. Threadgill. Julie played bass regularly in the singer's 1960s band, the Hootenanny Hoots, and she often was his drummer. A female drummer in a band was a novelty then.

Kenneth Threadgill, who sported a beer belly and wore a white bib apron while tending bar, was a musical trailblazer. His bands leaned toward progressive instrumentation by mixing jazzy Texas swing with traditional country songs. Good hillbilly music often had him out on the floor dancing solo.

Kenneth loved all kinds of music. In time he became a second father to Janis.

His friend Moon Mullican from Beaumont was a piano-playing singer pre-Jerry Lee Lewis and is one of the founders of country oriented blues-rock. Another friend was fiddler Cotton Collins from Waco who had written the Central Texas standard, "Westphalia Waltz."

Tarry Owens brought visiting blues master Mance Lipscomb from Navasota to meet the bartending yodeler. Kenneth's sidekick and running buddy, Bill Neely, is considered Austin's first singer-songwriter. His western folk music grew from the same rural country blues tradition as had Mance. They were friends and Mance Lipscomb often stayed at Neely's home when visiting Austin.

The welcoming atmosphere at Threadgill's was informal enough that musicians were comfortable trying out new songs and jamming. Janis sang and played her autoharp in a trio called the Waller Creek Boys.

During those Austin years, Janis Joplin dressed frumpy with unkempt hair and no makeup, and she was a victim of a cruel UT hoax that voted her Ugliest Man on Campus. The Waller Creek Boys especially liked to play songs with blues roots like "St. James Infirmary," "Trouble in Mind," and "San Francisco Bay Blues."

And Janis loved to sing them!

Kenneth Threadgill really liked the young woman's loud voice. He mentored her to not hold back on emotion. Her weekly appearances soon became a cause for many to drive out from the city to the edge of town.

When you hear her recordings made at Threadgill's, they demonstrate Janis took Mr. Threadgill's advice to heart. The singer belts out folk tunes such as "Walk Right In" and "Silver Threads and Golden Needles."

For reference, I've heard another Janis recording that was made by photographer Burton Wilson's son, Minor Wilson, in his San Francisco apartment. This is a solo recording accompanied by her autoharp, and Janis sounds vocally close to Joan Baez.

Many female singers doing Janis songs miss the fact her range had a rare and distinct high end to complement her bottomed-out, guttural, whiskey blues sound. Janis truly had a lovely voice.

Along with Janis, the rest of the Boys were Lanny Wiggins on guitar and Powell St. John on harmonica. St. John would later form the band Conqueroo and write songs for the 13th Floor Elevators.

Powell and another of the Threadgill's regulars, Chet Helms, decided to move to San Francisco where a hip music scene was blossoming. St. John became a founder of the band Mother Earth, fronted by blues singer Tracy Nelson. Helms took up with The Family Dog production collective that eventually lured Austin comic book artist Jack Jackson to California.

Helms became involved with band management as well and produced shows for that acclaimed center of '60s psychedelic music, the Avalon Ballroom. He managed a band called Big Brother and the Holding Company and they needed a singer.

St. John reminded Helms that Janis Joplin sounded real good singing at Kenneth Threadgill's place. They phoned Austin for Janis and myth has it she hitchhiked to San Francisco.

This new San Francisco quintet hit #1 on the album charts with their 1968 psychedelic blues-rock album *Cheap Thrills* sporting its famous R. Crumb cover.

Then Janis permanently engraved her place in pop culture history. She left Big Brother, taking lead guitarist Sam Andrew with her to form the Kozmic Blues Band. Janis added Memphis-style horns to accent her soulful vocals, and in 1969 became rock's first female bandleader.

Janis Joplin is godmother to Austin's famous lineage of blues-rockers.

6

A Crazy Cajun Invents Sir Douglas

It was the peak of the Dave Clark Five's hit-making era and they sold out their initial San Antonio concert. But the British mod rockers didn't want to go on stage. The quintet's unique sound—"Bits and Pieces" and "Glad All Over"—was built around drummer Clark's prominent 4/4 beats, Danny Payton's gritty saxophone, and singer Mike Smith playing a transistorized Vox Continental organ. It was broken and that model Vox wasn't sold in the United States. Smith refused to play a Hammond B3 with its fatter sound.

Local keyboardist Augie Meyers stepped forward and offered his new organ.

"No, thank you."

"But it's a Vox."

Augie, who played in the Goldens, backing Elvis-style rockabilly singer Denny Ezba, had seen an early photo of the Beatles using a Vox Continental. He immediately knew this small portable organ had to be in his future. Augie put down three hundred dollars and had one shipped from England to the Alamo City.

That fateful night, the Dave Clark Five played to a

cheering Municipal Auditorium, with Mike Smith using the only "wheedling" tone Vox in Texas.

Record producer Huey Meaux—aka The Crazy Cajun— was backstage at that event. He wanted to study the British hit makers' act.

After the show, in a backstage dressing room, Huey saw Doug Sahm and Augie Meyers, whose separate bands had opened the show. He said, "You guys already have kind of long hair. Why don't you grow it out longer, put a band together, and I'll produce the British sound with you."

The two guys looked at each other, eyebrows raised… why not?

Months later Doug dropped by the KONO studios and in his raspy whisper told me I had to come see his new band. Augie Meyers was no longer with Denny Ezba and the Goldens. He and Augie were groovin' together.

"Listen to this." He held out a 45 test acetate. On the label someone had scribbled "Blue Norther" and the name Sir Douglas Quintet. The band's sound was inter- esting, but was it commercial?

Then I heard "She's About a Mover."

* * *

ON A FRIDAY NIGHT in January of 1965, I drove to the Blue Note Cocktail Lounge on Blanco Road to see this new band. It was an intimate room with small round tables centered with blue globes holding flickering candles. There was a small eight-couple dance floor with a slight rise for the nicely lit stage.

It was not yet legal to sell mixed drinks in Texas so the Blue Note served beer and wine and setups of soft drinks and juices for the BYOB brown baggers. I carried a silver pocket flask of rum to mix with a glass of Coca-Cola. The club was packed. Right away you knew something exciting was happening.

Light applause and scattered whistles greeted Doug and the band as they came on stage. Wow. The guys were dressed Carnaby Street-mod with Beatle boots and long hair! Even drummer Johnny Perez looked as if he had just stepped off the plane from Liverpool.

Doug was chewing gum. He raised his arm and the room went quiet. His electric guitar leads into the bass and drums and the 12-bar rhythm grabs everyone's attention, then Augie's Vox punches in, as Doug leans toward the mic and, "She was walkin' down the street, lookin' fine as she could be…"

The little dance floor was instantly jammed with undulating bodies. This band had a different sound from any other in town. The feel of this new music came from Doug's years of playing Westside soul and Augie's years of rockabilly keyboard. The guys had family roots that encouraged a love of rural polkas, both German and Mexican. I was more than impressed.

Doug and Huey, in effect, had copied the Dave Clark Five, called initially the Dave Clark Quintet—it was the identical configuration with Augie on the Vox and Frank Morin on sax.

But the music Doug's quintet played was Alamo City flavored; it was polka-influenced Texas country blues. Augie's style of blending in Tex-Mex riffs with his Vox gave the Quintet a commercial hook. Manfred Mann also had organ and sax but was more jazz oriented. Eric Burdon's Animals featured a lead blues Vox for "House of the Rising Sun." But no one had experienced anything quite like this San Antonio homegrown musical blend. Sir Douglas kept the jam-packed Blue Note Lounge cheering and dancing past midnight's last call. I ordered a paper setup cup of Coke to go, while on the stage five guys wrapped up the night with an extended reprise of "She's About a Mover."

* * *

I WAS CALLED in December of 1965 to host a Sunday afternoon Teen Canteen dance in the Wonderland Shopping City mall. This gig would be the antithesis of my weekend dances at Lake McQueeney.

Sam Kinsey owned the alcohol-free, young people's live music club, and if I'd agree to MC and promote his event on my KONO show, he could book the Quintet.

I said okay. Doug said okay, but he planned to leave early for a press interview scheduled in Corpus Christi.

On the day of the gig, Augie wore his best mod clothes: thick-roped corduroy bell-bottoms, wide belt, overlarge buckle, and a wild paisley shirt. We had a sold-out crowd made of early teens and a few well developed twelve-year-olds who had sneaked past Kinsey's watchful eyes.

The site was a big white room in the basement of Wonderland Mall, so it was boomy. I opened the door to an echo of excited chatter. Fortunately, Kinsey had cut the fluorescent lights for the SDQ performance. As the band walked to the stage, cheers and squeals greeted them.

Doug opened the set with "Sugar Bee" and the kids instantly packed the dance floor to do the push. In a way, this wasn't much different from the first time I saw him five years before at the Purple Onion. Except these dancers were all teenyboppers.

The five guys played a quick set. Their encore was a Tex-Mex arrangement of Gary "U.S." Bonds' million-selling hit, "Quarter to Three," showcasing tenor saxman Frank Morin, who blew the house down. Everyone was happy. The band waved *adios* and drove off as Doug headed south to his press interview.

Next morning's front page of the *San Antonio Light*: Doug Sahm Arrested, Possession of Marijuana at Airport. They had busted him and Frank Morin and Austin guitarist Charlie Prichard in Corpus Christi. Augie told me Doug had the weed stashed in a Prince Albert tobacco can.

I couldn't help but think of the irony that Doug Sahm had been nabbed for pot just like his hero, Freddy Fender. Doug later told me he was moving to San Francisco and *never* coming back to Texas.

* * *

IT'S NOTABLE THAT in 1965, Huey Meaux produced Top 40 hits for both Doug Sahm on Tribe Records and Roy Head on Back Beat Records. Huey recorded both artists at Gold Star Studio in Houston. It was the Sir Douglas Quintet in the spring, with Roy Head and the Traits in the fall. Two different sounds using blues as their rhythmic touchstone. Roy Head hit #2 on the *Billboard* chart and outsold Sir Doug, who made it to #13.

But over the years, it was the Quintet, with its bright tones from Augie's out-front Vox, that forever meshed the genres of Tex-Mex and Cajun blues into a new sound. A year later, two other bands were duplicating Augie's distinctive riffs.

Sam the Sham came out of Dallas and played a Farfisa for his band, the Pharaohs. The five guys unleashed their "Wooly Bully" and had the first American record to sell over a million copies during the British Invasion. In actual fact, it sold three million and became *Billboard's* Number One Record of 1965.

A year later the Vox of Frank Rodriguez was driving ? and the Mysterians to count "96 Tears" and sell three million copies. A Michigan-based quintet, children of migrant farm workers, but ? and others were born in Texas. It was San Antonio bandleader Rudy Tee Gonzalez who produced this monster hit for San Antonio label Pa-Go-Go Records.

So within a year, like out of nowhere, we had three hit records by American quintets that featuring a Texas singer and a Vox organ. These bands excelled at playing the kind of 12-bar blues that made you get up and dance or at least dance in your seat. But among their lead singers, only Sir Doug continued evolving to leave a lifetime of original songs in an unparalleled diversity of genres, styles, and arrangements.

Doug Sahm is a bona fide Texas music genius.

Along with Sir Doug's hit, San Antonio that year had another important hit single in the Top 100: "Peanuts (La Cacahuata)." And it let everyone hear the Mex in Tex-Mex.

From the studio of Abe Epstein came this recording by the Sunglows, who had split from Sunny Ozuna. Once again Manny Guerra had produced a national hit for the Sunglows band on the orange-and-white Sunglows Records label. Reached #64 on the chart and that's unheard of for an instrumental polka. It was a game changer. Music historians claim the record launched Tejano music!

In the previous year, Epstein had scored by getting Rene y Rene into the *Billboard* Top 50 with their bilingual recording of "Angelito." San Antonio was vying with Dallas as the focal point for the Texas music industry.

In those days at KONO, we often had phone calls and visits from Huey Meaux. He first scored for the Alamo City by taking Sunny and the Sunglows to #11 with "Talk to Me" on Tear Drop Records out of Conroe, Texas.

Without a doubt, the generous hospitality Huey Meaux extended to dozens of us deejays in Texas and Louisiana helped get his critically needed radio play. I recall our shucking oysters and dining on T-bone steaks at Big John Hamilton's restaurant on the Austin Highway. It's where Huey told me having back-to-back hits by two unknown Central Texas bands was "jus' pure ol' Cajun luck."

7

The Silver Fox

In 1966 Lee Baby Simms and I were by far the top-rated deejays in San Antonio. As the KONO program director, I wasn't happy when station ownership messed with my version of Top 40. I decided to jump ship and go to competitor KTSA. Lee Baby wanted to come with me.

KONO immediately filed a breach-of-contract restraining order and our four-month-long court battle ensued. It was a South Texas media event with continuing newspaper and TV updates on the trial. It ended when the jury found us innocent but the judge, friend of the KONO owner, overruled and said "guilty."

We couldn't work in San Antonio radio for the next eighteen months. Thus we became exiles in Connecticut and lived as expats in Hartford. I was program director at WPOP 1410-AM and did the morning show, while Lee Baby took care of the nights. Much fun and good money.

One day I got a phone call from an International Artists record promo man in Houston known as The Silver Fox. The Fox was Lelan Rogers, prematurely white-haired brother of Kenny Rogers, then lead singer for the First Edition. Lelan told me the 13th Floor Elevators had a new album.

It is interesting *The Psychedelic Sounds of the 13th*

Floor Elevators on IA charted for Lelan, and his brother Kenny's first hit was a psychedelic version of Mickey Newberry's country tune, "Just Dropped In (To See What Condition My Condition Was In)."

Newberry, also from Houston, is often tagged as the first of many Nashville country musicians to go Outlaw. Later, Newberry extended the reach for the Austin brand of country music by helping Guy Clark and Townes Van Zandt connect with Nashville publishers.

Before the Internet era of indie music, songwriters trying to make a living desperately needed someone in New York City, L.A., or Nashville. The idea was to find a person who could hook them up with a recording artist looking for new songs or wanting to *hire* someone to write their songs. Few nonmusicians understand the importance of this relationship with music publishers, record producers, and top-selling artists.

Lelan Rogers was aware our hip music director, Bob Paiva, had listed the first Elevators' single, "You're Gonna Miss Me," for nighttime air play and Lee Baby Simms had played the song. It was the second time around for Lee, however, because in 1966 we had played and charted the song top ten at KONO in San Antonio.

But most importantly, my friend Bill Gavin had listed "You're Gonna Miss Me" in his top hits report used by the nation's most important programmers. Being in his tip sheet could make or break a hit. And I was one of his exclusive reporters.

Lelan Rogers was hoping for another influential review and offered to fly me—and other Bill Gavin program directors—to the band's record release party in Houston at Love Street Light Circus & Feelgood Machine.

The album was *Easter Everywhere*. Walt Andrus, an engineering genius with whom I had worked at KILE in Galveston, recorded the band in his Houston studio. Unfortunately, I couldn't make the Light Circus date.

Lelan then suggested seeing the group in a new hall opening for Halloween weekend in Austin, the Vulcan Gas Company. Show was early November, a few days before the presidential election.

"Austin?"

"Sure. I'll set it up, come on."

8

My 13th Floor Elevators Trip

Upon arriving in the capital of Texas, I took a white Austin Cab to my reserved room at the brand new Holiday Inn on Town Lake. It was still being completed. My top-floor room in this unique round building overlooked the Lower Colorado River. A beautiful view.

Unfortunately the flight leg from Dallas had been delayed and I missed the opening bands. At the time it didn't matter because I'd never heard of Conqueroo or Shiva's Headband. Later I realized that night's Vulcan Gas Company show had featured the city's three most popular bands, each distinct from the other. It was the apex of Austin rock band music events for the 1960s.

Adding to it was the show's poster, created by underground comix pioneer and progenitor of Austin's music poster artists, Gilbert Shelton. It's theme was Winnie-the-Pooh, lots of silly annimals having fun. On one side a pig stood on its head, on the other was a dancing Pooh Bear, while in between a cartoon armadillo was on hind legs and jumping. The first use of the armored critter for a music event.

These early Vulcan posters were colorful with a

much larger format than Armadillo's posters and, due to a limited run of only 100, are prized by art collectors.

My cab took me through the deserted nighttime streets to an intersection where the only non-decrepit building was the Greyhound Bus Station. Kitty-corner from it, a large group of people filled the sidewalk in front of the Vulcan Gas Company and spilled onto Congress Avenue.

Congress Avenue was then known as the widest street in the U.S.A. Unfortunately, 20 years in the future Mayor Lee Cooke would narrow Congress Avenue for head-in parking and end that brag. But the broad avenue still leads directly to our nation's tallest capitol, with its Goddess of Liberty standing atop a dome that rises fifteen feet higher than the U.S. Capitol in Washington, D.C.

Vulcan Gas Company was a hippie version of a rural country dance hall, or perhaps a psychedelic version of a grownup's Teen Canteen. No alcohol sold, so all ages were there. Big shows were packed with stoned college students and high school kids. Because of the hall's no-smoking rule, a lot of lit cigarettes appeared among the outside band break crowd on the sidewalk.

A guy with a cloth shoulder bag, along with his girl-friend, clad in a long tie-dyed gown, nonchalantly sold mushrooms. I wondered if they had peyote buttons. Both of these entheogens grew wild just a short drive from Austin. The cactus buttons had been deemed an illegal substance two years before, but LSD and the mushrooms were not yet federally illegal.

The Vulcan had quickly gained statewide notoriety for its stunning psychedelic light shows covering entire walls. The light show was promoted along with the music. They installed a platform holding the projectors, with the stage wall and a side wall painted white for screens.

These multimedia pioneers used a combination of slide and movie projectors with overhead projectors to display pulsating gels of amebic oils with eclectic still images, film clips, and loud music. Billy Lee Brammer's daughters, calling themselves the Light Show Debutants, LSD for short, were crowd favorites among the Vulcan's luminal artists.

Lelan Rogers waved to me and led me backstage. A joint was passed, but the band was on edge waiting for their equipment change and setup.

Roky didn't remember me from KONO and didn't know WPOP had played "You're Gonna Miss Me." He seemed embarrassed by it and called me Mr. Roberts. I found him naturally friendly.

Danny Galindo from San Antonio had joined their band on bass. We recalled going to a fun party after he played my Woody Dance at Lake McQueeney. Tommy Hall and Clementine were gracious and polite.

Tommy was the soul of the 13th Floor Elevators, Roky was the star.

Dark room, dim lights. No smoking, yet pot aromas subtly fused with sandalwood incense. Moving about, I sensed flowery whiffs of patchouli. Seating benches were available but folks were already standing. The Austin crowd was high and ready to rock. I wasn't sure how the band would sound live. They walked onto the stage and plugged in.

No disappointment. Great music!

Psychedelic, but driving: more like a later era's garage punk than a San Francisco approach to the LSD-inspired genre. I had never heard anything like it in the northeast. My surprise was how good-looking Roky Erickson was; like a teen idol, the appeal of a Jim Morrison.

The intense singing of this young talent was raw edged and he excited the crowd. Roky's screaming vocals and Tommy Hall's rhythmic electric jug gave this high-energy band a sound like no other before or since. The Fugs and Jim Queskin's band featured jugs, but they sounded like jugs. And unlike them, Tommy didn't blow across his jug, he vocalized into it.

Easter Everywhere was a concept album. Musically the recording was a groundbreaking work like *Sgt. Pepper*, but it represented the other extreme in studio production. George Martin had used a 4-track deck at Abbey Road to record elaborate *Pepper* orchestrations and electronic effects, while in Houston engineer Walt Andrus switched on his 8-track machine to record the completely unadorned Elevators.

Of course, these boys weren't the Beatles. There was no way I could play anything from *Easter Everywhere* on a Top 40 radio station. I had tested "It's All Over, Baby Blue" and results were negative. But after seeing the group live, I had no hesitation in believing this was a major band.

Their next album could very well hold that important hit song to push them over the top and onto the lucrative touring circuit. Hearing the guys play a greatly extended bridge for "Slip Inside This House"—with Hall's jug hooting in and out of Stacy Sutherland's brilliant guitar licks and Roky frantically strumming rhythm while belting out the lyrics with his lips practically touching mic—made my night. I noted both guys played Gibsons. It was powerful. Lelan Rogers had something here.

The group's driving out-front rhythms and searing lead guitar would adapt perfectly to large arenas. And though it hadn't yet been proven, I sensed Roky Erickson might be more than a rock star. He might become a music legend.

Little did I know Roky would crash and burn. He became a legend for his tragedy as much as his talent. And the band fell apart before they could record that hit album.

After cheering encores, people headed into the night. Lelan said the Chequered Flag had an after-hours show. Along with San Antonio deejay Joe Anthony, we rushed to grab a sandwich and a cup of coffee, too late for a "last call" beer. Anthony told us he was playing *Easter Everywhere* on AM station KMAC.

The Flag was the new club in town and used an auto racing décor for its theme. The room was packed. We met proprietor Rod Kennedy, who by then was the premier Austin promoter of folk arts concerts and music festivals. He was now well known as a music champion. Kennedy introduced us to his talented club manager, folk singer Allen Damron.

Over the following years, Rod treated Damron as his protégé while they worked side by side through dozens of music events, most notably every one of the promoter's famous Kerrville Folk Festivals. By the late '80s, Kerrville supplanted Newport as the U.S.A.'s premier folk music event.

That night, Damron took his guitar to the stage

and, under its black-and-white-checked canopy, sang a couple of songs before calling up singer Carolyn Hester. In a while, Stacy Sutherland quietly joined our table and whispered, "Had to hear this lady, great songwriter."

Late next afternoon I went out of my way to order a Top Chop't at Harry Akin's Night Hawk Restaurant. His now defunct steakhouses were once prominent dining stops for movers and shakers in Austin and San Antonio. And in addition to serving Black Angus steaks, Harry Akin served as the city's mayor.

Finished with dinner, I set off for Robert Mueller Municipal Airport to board a Trans-Texas Airlines shuttle into Dallas Love Field. There I would catch a lavender Braniff 727 and head east.

9

UT Meets ZZ

Bill Ham had negotiated with the University of Texas to host ZZ Top's First Annual Rompin' Stompin' Barndance and Bar B.Q. in Memorial Stadium on Labor Day 1974. Their event's name was an obvious parody of Willie Nelson's well-known Picnic and this humongous Bar B.Q. would take place in Willie's hometown.

It was the first major rock concert to promote ZZ Top as the headliner. And it was the first time the UT regents let a concert promoter use their hallowed football field. A sellout was expected for the biggest concert ever in Austin. It would attract a larger crowd than a Longhorns football game because spectators could also sit on the field. Eighty thousand people!

Santana, Joe Cocker, and a new band called Bad Company were on the show. Bad Company had played in Austin the night before and thrilled a crowded Armadillo. Not kids, these pro musicians had been signed by Led Zeppelin's new record label and Jimmy Page was traveling with them. I expected a jam tomorrow. Their first album for Swan Song Records, *Bad Company*, ended up multiplatinum, selling five million copies.

After the Bad Company gig at the 'Dillo, I stayed up way too late with the boys and did a little too much cocaine. Next afternoon my head was buzzing as I zombie-walked through 100 degrees of bright sunlight toward the looming venue that in 1996 would be renamed the Darrell K. Royal-Texas Memorial Stadium.

By the time Coach Royal retired, his UT football teams had scored a record three national championships and 11 conference titles. The man was a local hero and civic leader.

In the early September heat, three long and winding queues shuffled past ticket takers. I headed for the security entrance with my backstage pass to look for someone I knew.

10

Crowd Roasts, Ham Sizzles

On that fateful Labor Day, the giant UT stadium was fully packed with reddened sun-blazed faces. The ZZ Top Rompin' Stompin' Barndance and Bar B.Q. was underway. People were crowded in blistering heat on a tarp-covered football field where all day long the Fahrenheit registered over 100 degrees.

Backstage was a happy gang of friends and reporters. Each band had its entourage. A shaded VIP area offered cold beer and a TV showing the newly sworn-in President Ford praising U.S. factory productivity at a United Auto Workers' picnic.

I drank a cold Lone Star with a smiling Bill Narum, who had created the Barndance poster. Narum, with his artistic eye, noted the exceptional number of good-looking girls backstage.

Bill Ham was upbeat and excited. "Woody, good news, ZZ Top just sold out UT Stadium. This is rock *history*." He paced off toward the stage to hug impressario and rock concert promoter Bill Graham.

Just three hours later rock history took an unexpected turn. Concessionaires were running out of food and drink and shutting down their stands. No more barbecue.

They had stocked food like it was a football game and hadn't taken into account the concert's extended length of time and thousands of extra people sitting on the playing field. Now the heat of the day was peaking and only those sitting in the grandstands facing east escaped a blinding sun.

Doug Sahm whispered, "I hear the crowd is getting crazy."

Understatement. The thirsty and irate audience was baking. They could not even get ice. One by one, the concession stands had to close their windows. Soon the only spots to drink were public water fountains located in the hallways of each level between the ramp entrances. Long lines. Some were trying to fill water bottles, which slowed it all down.

Then came the catastrophe.

One fountain quit squirting water so it was pulled out of the wall to get at the pipes. Next level up was another fountain hanging loose and running water. To solve this problem, the University of Texas staff decided to shut off the water to all stadium drinking fountains.

When Bill Ham frantically strode my way, his smile was gone. "They've ruined my concert! Ruined it."

He squinted as I pointed to a top row. "Darrell Royal is in that box. He has influence."

"Let's talk to him."

We jogged up the stadium ramps past milling crowds of unhappy thirsty people. No one had been allowed to carry beverages or ice into the stadium. The afternoon heat was now oppressive and, with the fountains off, bathrooms had developed lines of thirsty folks hoping to get water from sinks and others with pained expressions needing the toilets. Exiting glaze-eyed patrons reported toilet conditions inside those bathrooms worse than a horror movie.

At last, we reached the top floor and I saw the familiar pressroom with its perfect view of the field below. A disheveled Joe Cocker had just finished his encore. The door was closed but unlocked. I opened it to find a group of seated onlookers, including Darrell Royal and Willie Nelson.

The singer looked toward us. "Hi, Woody."

I used Willie's acknowledgment as the chance to attract Royal. "Hi, this is Bill Ham. Came to see The Coach. This is Bill's event and he really needs help."

Bill Ham and Darrell Royal talked. Darrell was distressed but said there was nothing he could do. I said goodbye to Willie and followed Bill Ham out the door.

In the hall, he said, "I'm going to sue their ass. They've ruined my concert. I'll sue their ass."

Bad turn... yes; however, it was still rock history. For posterity, Ham put a crowd photo from that infamous barnburner on the record sleeve of *Fandango*.

11

Home of the Blues

In 1975, a twenty-five-year-old Clifford Antone brazenly started a live blues club directly across from the landmark Driskill Hotel on East 6th Street. Then at the edge of a run-down area. There were no other live music nightclubs on 6th, as the 11th Door had closed years before.

Even the clubs on Red River had gone dark but for the One Knite, "The Dive Too Tough To Die." The joint with a coffin door and after-hours hot knife parties: two machete blades heated red hot, buds of marijuana lined up on one and then pressed with the other, filling the room with smoke. Around town, T-shirts with crossed blades proclaimed "Hot Knives Forever." The One Knite is where you'd find Austin's blues-rockers.

Sure. There were a couple of beer bars where a hat would be passed and you might hear an accordion player or conjunto trio. However, the big draws on 6th Street were the Pecan Street Café and Gordo's Pool Hall. That's it. The area was in keeping with the blues.

I decided to check out this unopened club. Next to it, the OK Record Store sold blues 78s and 45s to collectors. Had to stop and browse, met the owner Steve Dean. Likely his OK Record Store influenced Clifford a decade later when he opened Antone's Record Shop with a similar inventory.

Ahead of me, on the corner of 6th and Brazos, a bunch of guys stood around smoking cigarettes and talking. Two glass front doors for the new club were propped open and workers carried in stacks of long wooden planks. I looked inside. The place had once been a furniture store and had zero aesthetics.

One of the guys standing on the corner wasn't in blue jeans. He was overweight, plump but firm, hands stuffed in trouser pockets, the tail of his white dress shirt hung untucked. It was Clifford Antone. He was smiling. I introduced myself and shook hands.

"You're only going to book the blues?"

"These are old artists, Woody. Some over 70, like Pinetop Perkins. My job is to bring them, to bring *all* the greats to Austin for a new audience. Albert Collins, Barbara Lynn."

Clifford was a missionary, and his passion was the blues. "Led Zeppelin, Grateful Dead, Cream, Pink Floyd... Elvis: They all owe their success to these blues musicians. These rock 'n' roll bands stole their licks."

"Sure, blues is their rhythmic backbone. But Appalachian music played a major role," I said. "Remember that first Sun Record for Elvis had an Arthur Crudup 12 bar song on one side and a Bill Monroe song in 4/4 time on the other. A lot of rock licks are hillbilly influenced. Chuck Berry's first hit was rockabilly."

Clifford wasn't fazed. "The first rock and roll was 'Good Rockin' Tonight' by Roy Brown. 1947. 'Rocket "88," Jackie Brenston with Ike Turner's band, 1951."

The man knew his music.

"Nah, I'd call them jump and roll. Rock needs a lead guitar with the drums and bass line: "Crazy Man, Crazy," Bill Haley, 1953. Had the first album, *Rock with*

Bill Haley and the Comets. He even had a steel player."

Clifford thought about that. "Little Richard and Fats Domino didn't have guitars."

"Yeah, but they were transitional, like Jerry Lee Lewis. The modern rock era started with the Beatles in '63, "Please Please Me." Brits using electronics pioneered by Les Paul, Link Wray, Duane Eddy. Since then, most have that lead guitar. Grateful Dead, Cream, new bands such as Rush."

Clifford lowered his head and shook it. "Bo Diddly's been ripped off so many times. John Lee Hooker. Johnny Otis... the list goes on and on."

Two men inched past us carrying a long wide flat board, I guessed for the stage.

"Doubtful you can support a club this big without rock or country bands."

"I'm going to try. I'm honored to do this for these great musicians. It's humbling."

In the mid-1970s, a handful of Austin blues musicians maintained a loyal following; they played with Paul Ray and The Cobras or Jimmie Vaughan and the Fabulous Thunderbirds. Clifford needed touring bands to pack the house. Blues talent draws, such as Paul Ray, Lewis Cowdrey, Lou Ann Barton, Jimmie and Stevie Vaughan, appeared regularly at Soap Creek Saloon, a roadhouse, or the One Knite, a dive.

Antone's would be different, a nightclub. Larger capacity. But still...

* * *

IN THE MIDDLE of July 1975, I went to the new club's grand opening and became Antone's link to the Armadillo. His other link was talented artist Danny Garrett, who designed the club's Little Walter logo and through to Clifford's death in 2006 produced many of his posters. For music poster collectors, Garrett art is for Antone's what Franklin is for Armadillo and Karry Awn for Soap Creek.

Opening night featured Clifton Chenier and his zydeco squeezebox. I thought, very appropriate for his first booking: Clifford presented Clifton. A line of people snaked out the front door onto the sidewalk and around the corner. The young entrepreneur was off to a great start. Sixth Street never rocked like that before... ecstatic midnight sidewalk dancers making the best of a sold-out club.

Clifford had snatched Chenier away from Soap Creek Saloon where his Red Hot Louisiana Band regularly packed the place. Not a bad reflection on Soap Creek hospitality.

In the music business, like any business, there are personal relationships, and there are business relationships. No matter how befriending a promoter or venue operator is to the artist, if someone else offers more money, that artist has to go with the money.

Many musicians loved the special attention, friendly people, and backstage food at the 'Dillo, but they would switch to the Austin Opera House if the guarantee were larger. Like a sports star, the musician has a limited number of years in the big bucks spotlight.

With fondness I recall those magical Antone's years on 6th Street. The club was serving up po' boys and the blues. Clifford was often standing on the sidewalk, his dress shirttail out, looking up and down the empty street. If not, you'd find him inside by the door or see him chatting with the featured artist.

The club had a long bar and a great bartender named Roy. Patrons found a seat at polished dark tables with padded chairs, plus a nice dance floor with a foot-high stage. If the band were the Cobras or the Fabulous Thunderbirds, then likely there was a good turnout.

For big shows with touring performers, such as Jimmy Reed or Bobby Blue Bland on stage, Clifford's sister, Susan, photographed the event. Many a night I ordered Cuba Libres from Roy and turned to see the club's manager and blues singer, Angela Strehli, with a home model Teac tape deck recording the performance.

It became common to see her standing at the Teac and it helped me realize the potential for a syndicated radio show. FM rock stations required drawing power and it would be easy to get younger rock stars to interact with these aging blues greats. Jimmy Page, Billy Gibbons, Eric Clapton. We could produce a blues-focused show right after the launch of the *Armadillo Radio Headquarters*.

Yes, I was a dreamer.

Clifford Antone loved Angela Strehli and respected her singing. He told me her voice was "a whole lot better than Linda Ronstadt's." It was true.

Clifford told me he started his record company for her. Many a night found Angela on stage performing with the band. And many of those nights the club was practically empty. Hookers would come in from the street to smoke a cigarette and watch from the back tables while friends of the musicians sat near the front and danced. Maybe a half-dozen of us would be at the bar listening to great music played by unknown Austin blues wizards.

Since Austin's Home of the Blues on 6th Street sat directly across from the Driskill Hotel, touring musicians of all genres often dropped in. One night it was Elvis Costello, and a few weeks later, Joni Mitchell.

Boz Scaggs got decked trying to force his way backstage. "Don't you know who I am?"

"Nope."

"Let me by!"

Bam! And he was down for the count.

I was there when Bob Dylan came in about midnight. Word of his presence spread like wildfire among the forty people in the room. He sat by himself at one of the back tables listening to Antone's house band.

What impressed me that night was nobody bothered Dylan. They let him enjoy the music. He left by himself and walked back across the street to the hotel.

Clifford, as usual, stood by the door, eyes closed, groovin' to the late night jam.

12

Pistol-Whipped at Randy's Rodeo

January of 1978 a magnitude 10 culture quake occurred in San Antonio that most people never heard about. Jack Orbin was the head honcho of Stone City Attractions and he booked the Sex Pistols into Randy's Rodeo. There were only five concerts scheduled on their U.S.A. tour and Orbin had bought one.

Four years prior, Jack Orbin, one of the great Texas rock concert promoters, had volunteered his company to help Friends of KEXL produce their free "Save KEXL Radio" concert in Olmos Park with Shawn Phillips, John Nitzinger, Rex Foster, and Augie Meyers. And it worked.

Thanks to a turnout of 30,000 fans, the station's progressive rock format was not killed off by its ownership and lived to play another four years. I'm sure Jack Orbin didn't realize his bringing the Sex Pistols to San Antonio would catalyze a hierarchical shift in the creative leadership of *Austin*. A changing of the guard as punks replaced the hippies.

Here was new raw energy music. Punk rock. Now sold

at Inner Sanctum, but only heard on Austin radio when deejay Rev. Neil X spun his personal records late night at KUT FM. Students went out of their way to tune in and hold listening parties.

This latest form of rock 'n' roll was no secret but it was considered too crude and unmelodic for radio play. And its lyrics were scary. None of the San Antonio stations would touch punk rock. For most ears, it sounded too much like kids thrashing a tune in a garage. Which, in many cases, it was.

Remember, these were the years of stadium rock and big hair, the years of Aerosmith, Kansas, Boston, and Journey. Bands traveled with a caravan of 18-wheelers filled with equipment and stage props. Yet everyone working in the pop music business had been exposed to Sex Pistols hype and most of us had listened to "God Save the Queen."

The quartet from London was one step beyond the already-considered-hip Ramones, who had blown away the 'Dillo crowd in the summer of '77. That loud quartet hailed from NYC and was Austin's first introduction to garage band punk.

The mainstream slant for these new baddest-of-the-bad-boys claimed the Sex Pistols were a pop-art statement out of control. Their manager, Malcolm McLaren, assembled this edgy young group of musicians. It could be said the band had roots in the Monkees, also assembled for commercial purposes.

Stylistically the Pistols shot out a raw sound like an unrehearsed New York Dolls with the stage mannerisms of Iggy Pop. All necessary ingredients for stardom were there—young and good-looking guys with a new type of hairstyle playing a new type of rock—and McLaren had done a brilliant job of marketing them to university students.

But the boys weren't selling many records or drawing big crowds to match their super hype. This tour was carefully placed into locations where tickets would be sure to sell out. Randy's Rodeo could hold a couple thousand. They should have been performing in Austin for UT students, but a suitable venue wasn't available.

So, instead of performing, the band spent a day hanging out in Austin. No matter, the Sex Pistols could have played in Poteet and drawn over a thousand rockers. Word was out. This was a rare opportunity to see these megastars. Some music biz people believed the Pistols were a pop music breakthrough.

I asked Jack Orbin for a backstage pass.

* * *

RANDY'S RODEO, like Panther Hall, was a bowling alley converted for country music dancing. It was a place you might hear George Jones or do a two-step with the Moods of Country Music. On Sunday, January 8th, its gravel parking lot was filled, so I pulled into a vacant field.

Joe Pugliese worked with Orbin and was in charge of the show. He told me people had come all the way from Austin. He and his younger brother Frank were part of the Vamps who played that night in front of local metal heavies Ultra. From Kathy Gibbs with Stone City, I learned they had sold out with 2,200 tickets. Security was tight and the headliners were already backstage.

Johnny Rotten wore a garish wide-plaid suit and T-shirt and loose necktie. He was appropriately dressed to be either a rock 'n' roll singer or a rodeo clown. But he sure wasn't Steven Tyler.

The guys had all spiked their hair, just less than shag length and unkempt, it looked like they had cut it themselves... with no mirror. This was all a new look back then. It signaled the end of the big-hair bands.

Drugs? I didn't see any cocaine. A fifth of whiskey was passed around in a stream of Lone Star beer. I smelled a trace of weed, but nothing like backstage Austin.

I looked around the packed hall while Ultra cranked it out on stage. Crowd was mostly under age twenty-five. The people in the audience from San Antonio included several musicians. Young rocker Hector Saldaña and folkie Steve Earle were there. I even saw a few of the older guys, including rockabilly singer Denny Ezba.

I spotted two music reviewers from Austin, my friend Margaret Moser and Jeff Whittington. I wondered if Moser was on assignment for *The Austin Sun*, didn't see her backstage. Whittington penned for the UT *Daily Texan*.

Nearby was bassist Jesse Sublett, had he cut his hair? Rumor had it Sublett was putting together an all-girl band.

Someone told me nineteen-year-old Kathy Valentine was there but I didn't see her. Carla Olson showed up. Olson would soon join with Valentine and Sublett to form seminal Austin punk band the Violators, after which the girls headed off to L.A. land to start the Textones. Then Valentine left for the Go-Go's and Olson moved on to collaborate with guitarist Mick Taylor. Both inspired feminist-punk cult followings.

Many years later, I learned culture makers Nick Barbaro, Louis Black, Lois Richwine, Nick West, Debra

X-it, Rick Turner, Bill Bentley, Ken Hoag, and Artly Snuff were all part of that loose and distinguished caravan motoring south on I-35 from the not-yet-proclaimed "Live Music Capital of the World."

Ultra was playing what was apparently their finale. Sid Vicious strolled about occasionally speaking to someone. But when band equipment was loaded off stage, he became pensive and his mood visibly heavied. Johnny Rotten walked to and fro at a more quickened pace.

It seemed the guys were psyching up for their show. Steve Jones pointed out it was Elvis Presley's birthday and that got a few laughs. Elvis had OD'd just six months before. But it was time to move on.

Out of the blue, Rotten spouted, "Fuck these cowboys."

Leaning against the wall, lanky Sid Vicious, wearing an opened black leather jacket with no shirt, had the look of a narcotized mercenary waiting to strike.

The four boys walked out nonchalantly as if the place were empty. They plugged in and right away hit the crowd with a blast of their anthem: "God Save the Queen." The volume was intense.

Rotten strutted to the edge of the stage and spit on people while Vicious snarled to live up to his name. Their aggressive presentation was more like a pro boxer going for a knockout than like rock idols.

What caught my ears were Paul Cook's drums. Incessant rhythm, several beats past heavy metal. Like blasts from a Gatling gun.

Lead guitar Steve Jones supported Cook with power chords playing to his beat and both seemed to be ignoring the bass licks. Sid Vicious would often break time and play unmusical riffs on his bass or just swing it at the crowd, then jump back into the rhythm.

The music was fast and exciting. Johnny Rotten sang and screamed and shouted through the lyrics, stopping and starting at will. It took a couple of songs for the Randy's audience to get loose.

I was expecting total chaos.

At first, the crowd was self-conscious because everyone knew that, in other concert towns, people threw drinks and spit at the band. It was expected. Was there anyone here loose enough to do it? When the second tune started, teams of slam dancers pogoed around the packed hall.

Along with spit-wads, someone finally threw a can of beer. Soon flying cans hit the stage. I was surprised Randy's was selling cans. The stage was not protected, unlike many Texas country dancehalls which enclosed their stages with a net or chicken wire to protect the bands.

Up front people cussed and traded verbal insults with Vicious. He dipped his bass and swung it at the stage-hugging taunters. Could have injured someone but didn't. The crowd got pretty crazy as the Sex Pistols ended the night with their anthem "Anarchy in the UK."

But no problems.

Randy's Rodeo was a seasoned veteran of rowdy audiences.

* * *

AS IT TURNED OUT, the Sex Pistols concert was one my life's most memorable rock music experiences. It was fresh, irreverent, and musically game-changing. Like seeing the untamed Elvis or young Beatles.

And this new sound of the Sex Pistols came from the most basic instruments for rock music, playing the simplest of melodies to support unsophisticated lyrics shouted in cadence as often as sung. WTF! Here was a British band with the identical configuration as Led Zeppelin, yet...

Keeping it all in perspective, Johnny Rotten was twenty and Sid Vicious nineteen.

I remember walking back to my car thinking: I just saw rock 'n' roll's future... and its name isn't Bruce Springsteen.

13

Punks End the Hippie Era

For the punks, 1977 was Year Zero. Global prosperity had peaked and U.S. interest rates were pushing toward 20% with President Carter at the helm. Disco dandies and urban cowboys were all the rage. But just two weeks after the consciousness-wrecking experience at Randy's Rodeo came Austin's punk inauguration of Raul's on The Drag.

It had been a Latino music club. Jessie Sublettt approached the manager, Joe Gonzales, and told him a night of punk rock would attract UT students. Gonzales decided to take a chance.

Club history was made. Sublettt played bass for the Violators and then with his own Skunks. That night the bands threw open the doors to Raul's and gave a new generation their own Austin music culture hangout.

Eight months later, the club was baptized in the Sex Pistols' tradition. The Huns were on stage, jibing back and forth in typical punk fashion with the audience, when a free-for-all broke out. Police interpreted the out-of-control event as a riot-in-action!

In the end, head bashing and broken chairs resulted in several arrests. TV news covered the altercation and the *Statesman* printed the story. To the youth, it validated the Huns' music and proved their hometown nightclub was the real thing. Raul's was the "in" club in Austin.

Keep in mind this was also the year when *Saturday Night Fever* promoted a lifestyle change that had already occurred in the Texas capital and reduced students' appeal for the Armadillo and older live music clubs. It took the illustrious album, *Never Mind the Bollocks, Here's the Sex Pistols*, from 1977 until 1991 to sell a million copies. It didn't even break the Top 100 chart.

But the soundtrack for *Saturday Night Fever*, also released in late '77, topped *Billboard*'s 1978 charts from January to July and eventually sold 25 million copies! It set a new all-time high for single album sales, one that would last four years until Michael Jackson released *Thriller*. Forty-plus years later heading toward 2020, *SNF* remains the best-selling original soundtrack ever.

However, the short-lived Sex Pistols definitely made an indelible mark in the annals of rock music. Forty years after the punk quartet released their single of "God Save the Queen," a 45 rpm copy sold for $15,822!

On my first trip to Raul's I realized my appearance was as out of place there as it was in a disco. Both Yuppies and Punks of the Me Generation rejected my shoulder length blond hair drawn back into a ponytail, and my blue jeans with Adidas running shoes. But I liked both punk and disco music.

And I regarded the hairstyles and clothing of the women in both cultures as equally sexy. It fascinated me that a disco and a punk revolution could occur at the same time and come from opposite poles of the pop culture's fashion, dance, and social manners. Both were hormone-driven expressions of youth in their courting years. They parodied internal belief systems, not unlike the jazz-age flappers or psychedelic-era hippies.

Joe Gonzales made Raul's into the punk rock equivalent of Clifford Antone's blues club or James White's Broken Spoke country dancehall. Yet, by presenting this edgy soul of a new community-based music, Raul's had also inherited the spiritual lineage of the Vulcan Gas Company and Armadillo World Headquarters. Its communal undertones influenced how bands, audiences, and staff related.

Though bands often played out a public rivalry, musicians, artists, and club regulars helped each other in tough times. The nation's most infamous punk club south of CBGB's and east of The Mab only made it a little over three years. In the end, like the Vulcan (which also lasted three short years) and the Armadillo (ten years), folks in the Raul's scene left their mark on Austin. They were the core of the new counterculture.

Bands like Big Boys and Standing Waves toured successfully, showing their fans that Austin was still a leader in cutting-edge music; a lineage from the 13th Floor Elevators to Willie Nelson to the Butthole Surfers.

Meanwhile in the void between *The Austin Sun* and *The Austin Chronicle* floated *SLUGGO!*, a punk culture 'zine. Wikipedia describes it:

"In 1979, *SLUGGO!* departed from the typical music fanzine with the introduction of its thematic issues. Topics were Violence, Unco, and culminated with its 'Industrial Collapse' issue. *SLUGGO!* also created the

Instant Review, publishing critiques of local performances overnight with free distribution on the streets the very next day. Their press was used not only for printing the fanzine but was also made available to local bands for printing band posters and record covers, and to other raconteurs for printing various handbills and broadsides. *SLUGGO!* House became one of the centers of the exploding Austin scene and drew considerable local and national attention as a hotbed of musical and artistic action."

Nick West was at the Sex Pistols concert when he told Debra X-it of Austin his dream to start a punk culture 'zine in the state capital. In San Antonio he had already published a crude prototype issue of *SLUGGO!* in tabloid newsprint, but the San Antonio printers had refused to print the full run, calling the eight-page newspaper "un-American."

X-it and Drastik Graphics art partner Rick Turner teamed up with West and former editor of the *Daily Texan*, Kelly Cash, to publish the popular punk zine. The staff put out five issues in Austin, and two in San Francisco, each a work of art. Individual covers for their 30- to 50-page hand-stapled books were printed and then hand-collaged or painted over in production parties.

West and his *SLUGGO!* cohorts were surprised to learn that people in Paris, Boston, Amsterdam, Berlin, and New York were reading it. Andy Warhol ordered every issue in triplicate!

As usual, in the early '80s, two critical factors for the creative scene's growth in Austin were cheap rental housing and abundant part-time work. Hippies had their Ghetto, but the post-hippies had Palaces. These dwellings were low-rent Victorian-era and 1920s bungalows on both sides of 6th Street and scattered around historic Clarksville, owned by a landlord who well knew he was helping support the arts. I asked Debra X-it to give a brief description of the kind of community living in those bungalows...

"All three creators of the Guadalupe & 24th Street Mural at the Renaissance Market lived there. Several of the Uranium Savages. The chefs who cooked at the first real non-steak gourmet restaurant in Austin, Fonda San Miguel. The Chickadiesels, the Reversible Chords. *SLUGGO!* Magazine crew. Gaslight X-it Theatre Project, the red-fez-wearing Shrovinovers of the Uranium Savages' guerilla theatre, and The Insect Party people started an annual costume festival loosely inspired by the Beaux Art Ball in Paris. Everyone lived either in the Insect House or in the three Palaces: Corn Palace, Bean Palace, Crystal Palace."

This was in Austin's first wave of punk culture, launching bands such as the Dicks. Then something unexpected happened: progressive country artist Joe Ely partied with the Clash in England and befriended the guys. The band phoned him while putting together a Texas tour and they booked into Lubbock and Austin with Ely's band opening.

The Armadillo World Headquarters show with the Skunks, Ely, and the Clash took on the label of legendary. That mix signaled a coming post-punk scene with a more polished new wave sound that pulled emerging rock bands away from the garage. It was a perfect closeout event for the '70s decade in Austin. The Clash album, *London Calling*, featured a cover photo from their 'Dillo standing ovation.

It was a year and a half after the 'Dillo had been razed when Clash returned to Austin. The guys had two days off so they produced a video for "Rock the Casbah." They honored the famous concert hall by having an armadillo scoot through scenes. Not only is this one of the best rock videos ever, but it was also the first music video filmed in Austin.

That's when the Clash discovered the hip music scene in the capital city of Texas. And it's when Joe Ely's singing hardened from the clean West Texas country voice I first heard the time Hank Alrich played an early 1975 demo tape. His voice became more gravelly, almost shouting, bordering on the edge of punk rock. And on stage he projected a Springsteen presence.

Joe Ely's country roots made his hard rock band stand out from a cluster dominated by hard-core punks. The other local group that fit in, yet stood apart from all the other punks, was Joe King Carrasco and the Crowns. His was a new Tex-Mex sound like a jazzy mix of the old Sir Douglas Quintet and the not yet arrived Texas Tornados.

Joe King called it Border Wave. Both of these punk-influenced Joes released their albums on the MCA Records label. Three for Joe King, and from 1977 to 1998 ten for Joe Ely, a longer MCA run than Jerry Jeff Walker.

14

Sailing the
Christopher Cross Anomaly

The music of Christopher Cross was not country, folk, blues, or punk. Christopher Cross wanted to make soft-rock pop hits. Perhaps that's why his historic musical accomplishment—that eclipsed all other albums by Austin musicians—caused so little stir among the hometown music reviewers.

Cross had moved from the Alamo City to the Capital City. The man had a unique attitude toward his music. He told me his focus was songwriting and recording and he was only performing the live gigs to support his studio taping expenses.

He'd met his recording engineer, Chet Himes, when they attended Alamo Heights High School just up the street in my old neighborhood. Both guys played in local bands. Chet was in Homer and Chris had Flash. Homer was the superior band. At KTSA we played and charted Homer's hard rock version of Willie Nelson's "I Never Cared for You," a great arrangement.

Relocating in Austin, the guys worked together on studio recordings. One day Michael Brovsky, who represented Jerry Jeff Walker, Guy Clark, and Carole

King—three great singer-songwriters—noticed Cross at Pecan Street Studio. His company, Free Flow Productions, had brought Carole King to Austin to record three studio albums at Pecan Street. Later his own South Coast Records would sign Joe Ely and Houston folk rockers, the Shake Russell/Dana Cooper Band. Chet Himes got to engineer many of the sessions.

It was Brovsky who scored a Warner Bros. Records contract for the unknown Christopher Cross. He set up a showcase performance on the outskirts of town at the Alamo Roadhouse.

Michael Ostin sat at a table that night, nurturing a cold longneck and listening. He had just finished his college education and was looking to get his feet wet in the music business. His dad was Mo Ostin, a first-magnitude industry heavyweight serving as the president of Warner Bros. Records.

Mo was loved by many and respected not just for his business savvy but also for his personal relationships with musicians. Decades before, Frank Sinatra had hired the man to run the Reprise label that WB financed as an outlet for Sinatra. Mo had gone to Monterey Pop; Jimi Hendrix's mind-blowing performance spurred Mo to sign the guitar genius to Reprise.

So it was that Michael Ostin grew up among the movers and shakers working in the highest strata of the record business. He was now well connected in the L.A. scene and himself a musician. That night at the Alamo Roadhouse, young Ostin instinctively recognized the pop hit potential hidden in the vocals and songs of Cross.

Warner Bros. opened its doors wide for the son of Mo Ostin. Using the goodwill of his dad's friends, he put together a dream session for the *Christopher Cross* album. Michael Omartian signed on as co-arranger, horn and strings arranger, producer, and piano player. Backup singers included the Eagles founder Don Henley, Doobie Brothers lead singer Michael McDonald, J. D. Souther, and Nicolette Larson.

Andy Salmon, who used to play surf rock with the Pipelines at my Lake McQueeney dances, played bass at Omartian's session and San Antonio keyboard ace Rob Meurer was on synthesizer. Former Electromagnets' guitar wiz Eric Johnson and Jazzmanian Devils' saxman Tomás Ramirez provided jazzy solo tracks, recorded at Pecan Street Studio and added to the mix.

Cross was smart and kept his personal manager, Tim Neece, while his engineer had to be Chet Himes. Chet in 1980 would engineer the Van Wilks master-work, *Bombay Tears*, for Mercury Records.

This Warner Bros. album would be a Free Flow Production and it was young Michael Ostin's first recording project, the start of his stellar career. In 1981 *Christopher Cross* won five Grammys and went 5X-platinum!

It was a work of brilliance. Cross became the only 20th-century artist to simultaneously grand slam the "Big Four" Grammy Awards: Best Record, Song of the Year, Best Album, and Best New Artist. He even won a Grammy for Best Background Vocals.

Chet Himes was nominated for the best recording engineer award because of the album's quality and texture, but Pink Floyd's tour de force, *The Wall*, inched him out. Fair enough.

But it had to be a coin flip, and the fact is, Himes in 1979 had digitally recorded the Cross album. Long before Pro Tools. Most likely the Grammy board was reluctant to hand another category award to *Christopher Cross.*

At that same ceremony, Chris Cross and Michael Brovsky watched their neighbor, Willie Nelson, win the coveted Grammy for Best Country Song: "On the Road Again."

Wow, this was a stupendous way to start the decade: Song of the Year and Best Country Song of the Year. A head-snapping national victory for Austin music!

Austin's cadre of hipper-than-thou music columnists ignored the *Christopher Cross* album. Local musicians snickered. Punks let it be known they couldn't stand Cross and mentioned his name with the same disgust they held for progressive country and blues.

If the Grammy-quaking *Christopher Cross* album had any musical shortcomings, it was that his band could not duplicate the sound on tour. And on stage, Cross himself was not a pop-star-looking kind of guy. Some of the band members had argued for Chris to capture the Fleetwood Mac audience, but he wanted Barry Manilow's.

The year following his sweep of the Grammys, something else incredible happened. Christopher Cross won an Oscar! He got it for performing and co-writing another pop standard, "Arthur's Theme (Best That You Can Do)."

It would be pretty easy to get a big ego if your first album is a super smash, with a single that goes to #1 and becomes a standard, and your first song used in a motion picture receives an Oscar. Back home in Austin, punk, rock, country, blues musicians all threw up. Who plays this kind of music?

Chris did. During the three years following the

release of his first album, Cross placed seven tunes in the Top 20! Four of those songs got into the Top 10, and two of those records went all the way to first place.

Had the same thing happened to another local singer-songwriter, such as Joe Ely or Steve Fromholz, the music community would have exploded with admiration and joy. But praise wasn't there for the soft-rock singer.

It should be a source of great local pride that two of the greatest ballads from the 1970s were composed in Austin: "Muskrat Love" and "Sailing." Both have endearing melodies still heard on the radio, in elevators, and from phone ringtones.

But hard-core rock music critics regularly list those songs among the worst of all time. Austin never cheered Christopher Cross or acknowledged his record-breaking accomplishment. It would be forty more years before singer Billie Eilish matched his 'Big Four' Grammy sweep. It's no wonder Cross moved to L.A. He eventually returned to Austin, but not in the 20th century.

FYI, the Grammy was originally named the Gramophone Award.

15

The Explosive Eighties

Club Foot, operated by John Bird, was my favorite concert venue of the '80s. It was known for presenting the city's top punk-oriented bands, such as the avant-garde Butthole Surfers, formed in 1981. These guys were a musical contradiction in a city known for country musicians and blues-rockers.

As the initial punk scene wound down, Austin bands surfed the new wave, incorporating more sophisticated rhythms and instrumental bridges into their music. And they did a better job of supporting the insightful lyrics for which Austin songwriters were famous.

Jesse Sublett of the punk Skunks had christened this sound New Sincerity. Yet it was noise band Scratch Acid, with their screaming vocalist David Yow, who had my ear. Much to their credit, the group's touring performances and local recordings for Rabid Cat Records directly influenced Kurt Cobain when he started Nirvana. Scratch Acid made it five years before their breakup. Yow and bassist David Sims formed Jesus Lizard and moved to Chicago to initiate a successful alt-rock career lasting more than a decade.

The eighties were the Austin years when I sought out groups with names like True Believers, Glass Eye, Wild

Seeds, and my New Sincerity favorite, Zeitgeist, which later renamed itself The Reivers. That name honored William Faulkner's last published novel. Vocals came from songwriter John Croslin and crowd-pleasing singer Kim Longacre, who often used her voice as a melodic instrument.

The quartet almost made it big. Four albums, with two on Capitol Records—*Saturday* is a classic—allowed The Reivers to go seven years before throwing in their towels as the '90s began.

With the punk era at its peak and the blues rock era coming to the fore, Willie Nelson released his second-biggest-selling album: *Always on My Mind*. Ten years earlier, Elvis had released its title song, which then became a touring staple for The King.

Willie's version topped *Billboard*'s Hot Country Singles and made #5 on its Top 100 pop charts. Elvis hadn't even made the Top 100, and he only reached #16 on the country list. Willie thus brought more Grammys back to Austin: Song of the Year, Best Country Song and Best Male Country Vocal Performance! His single was certified platinum while the album was certified quadruple-platinum, and in 2008 *Always on My Mind* was inducted into the Grammy Hall of Fame.

An era of national labels recognizing Austin's female singer-songwriters began in 1986 and carried on throughout the '90s. In '86, Reprise issued the album, *Rosie Flores*, by a San Antonio rockabilly master singer-guitarist who, like myself, Doug Sahm, Margaret Moser,

Robert Rodríguez, and others had migrated eighty miles north to embrace the wildly creative Austin scene. That same year, MCA stepped up and released a classic by Nanci Griffith called *Lone Star State of Mind*. Its title song reached #36 on the national country charts. This rising Americana star recorded four more albums for MCA before jumping to Electra Records in 1993 and creating *Other Voices, Other Rooms*. In 2002 she moved to Rounder for three albums, the last being *The Loving Kind* in 2009. Many of the new Americana folky voices were on independent labels, yet they hit the charts.

The phenomenal Lucinda Williams, compared by some to Stevie Nicks both in voice and physical appearance, released her self-titled album to rave acclaim in 1988. It held the song "Passionate Kisses" that in 1994 won two Grammys for country singer Mary Chapin Carpenter. *Lucinda Williams* was reissued in 1998, and the Americana classic was again released in 2014 to celebrate the album's 25th anniversary.

But it was in 1998 for Mercury Records when her masterpiece, *Car Wheels on a Gravel Road*, won the open praise of folk, rock, country, and jazz critics from coast to coast. The album was originally recorded in Austin in 1995 and burned up two producers, including Steve Earle, before being re-recorded in Nashville. Mercury let her go, and Lost Highway Records picked up the singer-songwriter. They did an incredible job of promoting five—five!—of her albums into the top thirty: *Essence* #28; *World Without Tears* #18; *West* #14; *Little Honey* #9; *Blessed* #15.

Reportedly a hard-to-deal-with artist, Lucinda started her own label in 2014, cleverly still using the

Highway brand for *Down Where the Spirit Meets the Bone* released on Highway 20 Records. It reached #15. This fine musician has earned 3 Grammy Awards from 15 nominations, and received 2 Americana Awards out of 12 nominations. In 2002 *Time* magazine named Lucinda Williams "America's Best Songwriter."

Lost Highway focused on country artists and was a Universal Music Group subsidiary label that gave Austin's Hayes Carl two albums, with his *KMAG YOYO* in 2011 charting #12 country and #67 in Top 100.

Tish Hinojosa is another San Antonio expat. The lady self-released *Taos to Tennessee* also in 1987, and it was good enough for A&M Records to give her an album in '89 called *Homeland*. After that, she went onto Rounder for six notable albums throughout the '90s, and then Warner Bros. distributed three of her eclectic sessions. Many of Tish Hinojosa's albums contained songs in both English and Spanish.

But not every great female talent ended up on a large national label. For example, Eliza Gilkyson started her recordings with small local companies in 1969 and by the 21st century, her musical artistry primarily appeared on Red House Records, ten albums through 2015! Red House also did four albums with Austin's truck-driving country music king, Dale Watson.

But the biggest surprise of the 1980s came out of the aptly named Hole In The Wall, a neighborhood bar situated on The Drag. In 1986, two of the little club's regular performers, Pat and Barbara K. MacDonald, calling themselves Timbuk3, released the I.R.S. Records album *Greetings From Timbuck3*.

To achieve their distinctive new wave sound, this husband and wife duo used a drum machine! Their CD contained an MTV-launched *Billboard* Top 20 hit: "The Future's So Bright, I Gotta Wear Shades."

The duo became local counterculture stars and toured the nation, releasing five more albums in the following decade, but never scored another charting song.

Also playing in and out of the Hole during the '80s were my favorite Austin singer-songwriters: Townes Van Zandt, Daniel Johnston, and Blaze Foley. These three guys represented a pinnacle of intelligent lyricism in the still-not-recognized Live Music Capital.

Meanwhile, a new creative Austin neighborhood had emerged, the Wilson Street Cottages. This compound held a dozen small bungalows, an old house, and a two-story apartment. As it was in the '60s Ghetto and the '70s Corn Palaces, rent for the Cottages was cheap, and its artistic residents were musicians such as Ronnie Lane, Miss Lavelle White, J. D. Foster, Blaze Foley, Susanna Van Tassel, and Carolyn Wonderland.

Neighborhood bands such as the Wagoneers in the late '80s had two albums on A&M Records; and in the mid-'90s when the Gourds formed their progressive bluegrass band, they too lived on Wilson Street. No relation to Eddie Wilson.

16

Buttholes in the Ritz

I'd first seen the Butthole Surfers in San Antonio when they were Trinity University students. In the mid-'80s they had a gig at the Ritz Theater with Roky Erickson and the Explosives. The Buttholes' album, *Rembrandt Pussyhorse,* was fresh in the record shop bins and Roky's acclaimed *Don't Slander Me* had just been released.

For me, this concert was a one-of-a-kind event. Had the producers booked local art band Ed Hall to start the night, it would have been avant-rock perfection.

I had seen Roky Erickson perform only twice since the 13th Floor Elevators dissolved and that was back in the 1970s with his group, the Aliens. Instead of Tommy Hall's electric jug, that band featured Bill Miller playing a home-devised electric autoharp, sometimes played through a fuzz box with a butter knife. Miller, too, had been an Austin pioneer of psychedelic rock with his 1960s group, Cold Sun.

Roky was in excellent form, and the Aliens had an alt-rock sound much like platinum album stars White Stripes of thirty years later.

These '70s shows happened about the time Doug Sahm brought me a red vinyl 45 by Roky called "Starry Eyes." The unforgettable melody with its simple love song lyrics immediately became one my favorite pop-rock singles. Its effect on me was like the first time as a boy I heard the Penguins singing "Earth Angel."

Doug produced, financed, and even played guitar on this minimalist sounding record, as a goodwill project to help Roky. Flip side was the excellent horror rock classic, "Two Headed Dog."

A few years later, he would convince his friends, Doug Clifford and Stu Cook of Creedence Clearwater Revival, to get Roky into a studio. Those recordings became the classic Roky Erickson albums: *I Think of Demons* and *The Evil One*. *Demons* is the British title. The 1980 U.S. LP was released by Columbia as *Roky Erickson and the Aliens*.

This is Roky's finest. I would go so far as to say it stands among the greatest rock albums of the 20th century. Ten original horror rock songs. Who creates such lyrics? A resurrected Lovecraft. This collection is the work of a mature Roky, age 33, still in strong voice. Stu Cook produced, and that may account for its mesmerizing pace, a power-chord-led blend of CCR merged with the Silver Bullet Band. Editing these songs together would create a horror rock opera.

And tonight someone at the Ritz Theater has the city's most controversial musician on a bill with this town's most controversial band. I am looking forward to a night with Roky and the Buttholes.

* * *

MY EVENING STARTS when I go to a movie and have a head-snapping surprise. Realizing I was going to end up at an eclectic concert motivated me to attend a late matinee at the Dobie Theatre, known for showing art films. This one was a black-and-white, low-budget indie called *Down by Law*, starring Tom Waits. I had seen him on stage at the Armadillo and only knew of Waits as a distinctive low-growl singer-pianist mostly respected as a songwriter's songwriter, like Randy Newman. Now he was an actor.

In this film, Waits played a New Orleans deejay named … Lee "Baby" Sims! I almost fell out of my seat. Maybe the writer-director Jim Jarmusch or Tom Waits heard The Baby's radio show in New Orleans, or San Diego, or Los Angeles, or somewhere… Likely they found this one-of-a-kind radio personality unforgettable, as had many others.

By the close of his spectacular 40-year career, my dear friend Lee "Baby" Simms had been a deejay in 22 different cities. Memories flooded in. We hadn't talked since a cross-country trip a decade before. KONO in San Antonio is where I suggested Lee Simms use Baby with his name.

In 1999 Salman Rushdie wrote *The Ground Beneath Her Feet*, his alternative history of rock music, and named a character Lee Baby Simms. Not to mention, a guitarist out of Portland called himself Lee Baby Simms, while a Lawrence, Kansas, delta blues rock band called itself The Lee Baby Sims Show, and the New Jersey band Steel Train titled an album track "The Lee Baby Simms Show." Plus a popular nightclub DJ in Europe used the handle Lee Baby Sims.

When I got to the Ritz, its audience was fully charged with live music excitement. I saw the *Statesman*'s music reviewer, Casey Monahan, heading for backstage. Meanwhile, a hesitant Roky Erickson was ushered out to stand in front of the mic. I couldn't help but note how Gibby Haynes and King Coffey of the Buttholes stood mesmerized with eyes fixed on Roky as if recalling their roots. Sadly, his performance that night was a huge nonmusical disappointment. It was painfully awful. It seems that Roky had earlier decided he wasn't going to sing anymore, ever. He didn't even want to go to the Ritz. The promoters commandeered him. So there he stood on stage with arms folded like a wooden cigar store Indian. Occasionally he turned his back to the audience.

I was reminded of the 13th Floor Elevators playing at HemisFair in May of 1968 when Roky flipped out and started talking in tongues, giving his audience a rapid nonstop stream of glossolalia. The singer was rushed to Houston where a hospital staff administered shock treatments.

That happened only six months after I'd seen the guys do their terrific show at the Vulcan Gas Company. Fortunately that night at the Ritz, now rundown and shabby with Jim Franklin's wonderful murals painted over, the Butthole Surfers made up for Roky's paralysis and the crowd went away more than satisfied. Most were young punks, and to them, Roky Erickson was a dinosaur curio. Too bad Ed Hall didn't play.

* * *

SEVEN YEARS LATER, King Coffey would help Roky record *All That May Do My Rhyme* to the raves of pop music reviewers. Speedy Sparks, Doug Sahm's longtime compadre, produced it and released it on King Coffey's own Trance Syndicate Records. A label that began and ended its legacy in one decade.

This excellent hometown record company produced nine years of Austin's punk alt-rock scene and released seventy records, including the bands Sixteen Deluxe and Ed Hall. Trance in 1998 also introduced the first album by exceptional alt-rock band, And You Will Know Us by the Trail of Dead. The band, headed by Conrad Keely and Jason Reece, followed up in 1999 with an album on Merge and then with three on Interscope Records.

Once upon a 1981 phone call, I told Chesley Millikin that his new company, Classic Management, needed to check out a hot San Antonio group called the Butthole Surfers. His response came back as a squealing rush of Irish laugher followed by his famous, "Carry on!"

17

Janis Not Welcome at Maggie Mae's

Last time I saw Janis Joplin perform was in San Antonio, October 1969, in the HemisFair Arena. She hadn't had a hit record in what seemed a long time and her single "Kozmic Blues" had not been that well received. To pack a large arena a musician needs a hit song; big album sales alone will not do the job.

Traveling with Janis was her three-horn band that had more of a blues element than Big Brother. When introduced to Janis backstage, her pre-show nervousness surprised me. She was upset that her show opener, an unknown ZZ Top, had their sound unplugged in the middle of a song after they sang "…need a girl who will treat me right, I need a girl who can fuck all night." My record promoter friend Bill Ham was backstage and told Janis about the incident. Just last week Ham had brought KTSA a Scat Records 45 by ZZ Top called "Salt Lick" and told me he was going to manage this new Houston trio. He was excited his band would open for the famous singer. "They're off to a great start." As a favor, I put his record on the nighttime playlist.

Janis was now moving about the room and overly

talkative. Rolled buds of Maui and Southern Comfort waited on a table, but she wasn't smoking or drinking.

That night, before her set began, the lady blurted out a bombardment of F-words to chastise arena management. Then Janis delivered a high-energy performance rivaling Mick Jagger or Jim Morrison. Musically top-notch blues rock.

Place was half-full, 7,500.

Jimi Hendrix had a similar career dilemma. Last time I saw him, it was in that same facility, again half full. We spoke briefly in his backstage holding room. It had been a year and a half since he'd placed a single into the Top 50.

Hendrix was traveling with the Band of Gypsies and had changed record labels, moving from Reprise to Capitol. And, like Janis, had changed his music. His evolving repertoire now featured a jazz-flavored blues-rock and less hard rock. The quality of his guitar artistry was more elegant than ever.

I first met *Rolling Stone*'s Greatest Guitarist of All Time in 1968 when The Jimi Hendrix Experience played the Municipal Auditorium, sponsored by KTSA. Unfortunately, midway through their show Hendrix blew out several of the Sunn amps lining the stage, noticeably reducing the band's audio.

Then, during a wee hours party in his Austin Highway motel suite, tucked away from the downtown tourist area, a half-dozen of us smoked heavy Colombian bud and did some rails of coke. The man was friendly, unpretentious, and easy to laugh with. He liked that in 1962 I worked in Seattle radio with Pat O'Day and MC'd shows at the Spanish Castle, a venue he magically honored in his album *Axis: Bold as Love*. Pat O'Day was now the head of Concerts West and in charge of his tour. Hendrix returned to the Auditorium in August and made up for the poor audio of their previous show with a great thirty-minute performance.

Afterwards I saw the rock star and his drummer Mitch Mitchell downtown at The Love Street Light Circus where they decided to jam with local band Sweet Smoke. I felt privileged to see him close up playing on that small stage.

In 1970 four years had passed since Jimi and Janis first burst on the scene. Each desperately needed to boost their income with a smash hit. Those big hits came, but too late. In the fall of that year both rock superstars died, two weeks apart, each at the young age of 27, each due to drug overdose.

Posthumously, Jimi Hendrix charted #3 with his album, *The Cry of Love*. Janis Joplin got her #1 single with "Me and Bobby McGee."

Had they lived, I believe both stars would have found their way to manageable sobriety. And I like to imagine, had she lived, Janis would have eventually hung out with Willie at his Pedernales Country Club and recorded a platinum-selling country album. I'd love to hear her version of "Jambalaya" or "Crazy."

* * *

KENNETH THREADGILL, after his wife died, shuttered his famous musical barroom and went off to play county fairs. Threadgill's former gas station on North Lamar sat deserted and ready to collapse on itself. The city wanted it torn down. A music lover had spray painted big red letters on the side of the dilapidated structure: "Janis Sang Here."

Eddie Wilson's decision to resurrect the old filling

station as a restaurant attracted national food reviewers to sample its Southern cooking, especially the delicious chicken fried steak that previously had been considered truck stop eatin'. Plus, fans of 1960s rock music were making a pilgrimage out North Lamar to see the place where Janis Joplin got her start.

However, in the 1980s, there were still many people who intensely disliked the singer because of her foul language and notoriety for overindulgence. A spinoff of this disfavor occurred when it was decided to place stars honoring Kenneth and Janis into the sidewalk on 6th Street. The silver haired yodeler had died in 1987.

Bill Narum selected the location for our ceremony at the intersection of 6th and Trinity. Across the street from Steamboat 1874 and in front of Maggie Mae's, a popular watering hole with UT students. It was a shot bar noted for the largest beer selection in Austin and nightly cover bands playing popular hits. They had not yet opened the rooftop patio that became a big attraction.

Music photographer Burton Wilson and chilihead artist Gordon Fowler showed up for the event, as did Threadgill's daughter, Becky. Eddie Wilson was the master of ceremonies. A bunch of us gathered outside Maggie Mae's. I had alerted press media so all the TV stations and newspaper photographers were there.

We were about to lay their stars when Bill Shea, an owner, charged out the front door and shouted, "Stop!"

We stopped.

"I will not allow Janis Joplin's star in front of my door. She represents everything that's wrong with America. You can put Kenneth here but not Janis."

At which point Becky Threadgill said, "Well, if Janis can't be here, Daddy wouldn't want to be here."

The manager of the Driskill Hotel, a big Swede,

stepped forward. "You can put Janis in front of the Driskill. Kenneth Threadgill and Janis Joplin are both welcome at our hotel."

When we finally put their stars in the sidewalk at the historic 6th Street hotel, a nice crowd showed up again. Rip Torn even left a movie set to come and kiss the star of Janis. By the fates, her star ended up on a corner directly across from where Clifford Antone once proudly stood in front of his nightclub.

Maybe Janis was looking down from blues rocker heaven and wanted it that way.

18

Tornados in Austin

For my ears, the Grammy-winning Texas Tornados ruled the 1990s.

Their name came from Doug Sahm, who in 1973 released his Atlantic album, *Texas Tornado*, with its title song. In '76 it was Dot Records with *Texas Rock for Country Rollers* by Sir Doug and the Texas Tornados. The late '70s finds him calling his band Texas Tornados while playing a benefit at Soap Creek Saloon to reelect Sheriff Raymond Frank. In 1983, Takoma Records issued *Live Texas Tornado*.

Doug's new Tornado lineup issued its first CD—with English and Spanish versions—for Reprise, *Los Texas Tornados*. The musicians with Doug were Texas legends: Augie Meyers, Freddy Fender, and Flaco Jimenez. Their drummer was longtime San Antonio friend Ernie Durawa.

These guys were the first Tex-Mex supergroup and played diverse gigs such as Bill Clinton's presidential inauguration and the Montreux Jazz Festival. They even made it into the Top 30 on the *Billboard* country music chart. Doug told me that receiving the 1991 Grammy for "Soy de San Luis" as the Best Mexican-American Performance was a lifetime-proud moment.

Everyone knew that Doug admired his fellow band members. I also knew he played an influential role in Huey Meaux's decision to produce Freddy Fender's hit "Before the Last Teardrop Falls," and rerecord "Wasted Days and Wasted Nights."

Flaco Jimenez is a superb accordionist and one of the seminal Tejano musicians. Doug grew up listening to the Jimenez family's conjunto music, and in January 1973 with his *Doug Sahm and Band* album he launched Flaco nationally. The accordionist later performed with superstars such as Bob Dylan, George Harrison, Buck Owens, and the Rolling Stones.

Flaco is the older brother of Santiago Jimenez, Jr. Unlike Flaco, who plays a three-row accordion, Santiago, Jr., mastered a traditional two-row button instrument like their conjunto-pioneering father, Santiago. In 2000 Santiago Jimenez, Jr., along with Austin yodeler Don Walser and Austin piano maestro Pinetop Perkins, received National Endowment of the Arts lifetime honors: National Heritage Fellowships.

That is a mouthful of a title. But it is the U.S.A.'s highest award for traditional and folk arts. Twelve years later, the NEA similarly honored Flaco.

Very few people get to have the experience of knowing they and their brother are official living national treasures.

In the 1970s and '80s, Augie Meyers had already scored with two popular Tejano polkas. They were on his personal label, White Boy Records. The upbeat tune,

"Down in Mexico," was selling well until its radio play stopped when LULAC claimed the singer's enunciation of "Mexican" sounded like "Messkin" and was racist.

That was a pile of crap, but station owners didn't challenge, didn't want the FCC hassle, so they killed a hit. Ten years later, Augie sang "Hey Baby *Qué Pasó*" and jumped into the Top 100 at #76 with a bullet and immediately was picked up by Atlantic Records. They dropped the ball by waiting to paste their label on the disc and the sales died.

Once a song or album starts to sell, the worst thing that can happen is holding up distribution. The buyer is fickle and quickly moves on to other favorites, so all pop music sales come and go within weeks.

"Hey Baby *Qué Pasó*" went on to be translated into fourteen different languages, with the many versions selling over six million records! But not for Atlantic. The song has become a kind of anthem in San Antonio.

Doug Sahm picked La Zona Rosa as the site for the first Texas Tornados music video. Owners Gordon Fowler and his wife Marcia Ball were happy to host the filming party for their friend. La Zona was the city's hip new venue for lunch, drinks, and live music.

Gordo had decorated their Austin restaurant club like a cheap but chic bar in Juarez, with its menu Tex-Mex. A dozen local artists contributed unique paintings installed on its tabletops. Bill Narum painted his table lilac and stamped on a red pair of bare feet, dancing the salsa. Jim Franklin painted a large wall mural of Mexican food surrounded by strange-looking tropical snakes.

This is before the larger La Zona music hall opened.

You might find Governor Ann Richards and her capitol crowd at lunch or the latest Austin culture makers enjoying a band at night. A great place to hang out.

La Zona Rosa was packed to the rafters for the Texas Tornados' video event. It was the place to be. A few commanding downbeats from Ernie Durawa and the crowd went silent in anticipation.

Here was a once-in-a-lifetime treat. On an intimate nightclub stage were Augie, Flaco, and Doug groovin' with his boyhood idol, Freddy Fender. The award-winning Texas Tornadoes never sounded better. The bar sold out of tequila during that memorable night of South Texas music. A hint of marijuana fragrance drifted in the air around La Zona from dusk 'til long after closing.

This was indeed a groover's paradise.

19

Toward the 21st Century

Across town from the Tornados' video party was Doug Sahm's youngest son, Shandon, at the Backroom. In appearance, Shandon, like his older brother Shawn, had that long-faced Germanic skull of their father. The Backroom was the heart of Austin's hard rock music scene; a celebrated venue with a trunk full of backstage stories. I hope someone will tell all one day.

Shandon Sahm was drumming behind his pals, Kyle and Sims Ellison, in the metal-edged quintet Pariah. The guys were high school friends from San Antonio who'd relocated to Austin, where they quickly scored a contract with Geffen Records. This dynamic group played loud hard rock, and the five guys looked the part of touring stars. Geffen Records thought so, too.

In 1993 Pariah released *To Mock A Killingbird*. The album fizzled. Many blamed the label for not fully promoting it. But really, it just wasn't the sound of the moment. Metal was the eighties.

In reality, the alt rockers of the nineties were an initial expression of the death rattle for the reign of rock music, a phenomenon that exploded in 1964 with the arrival of the incomparable Beatles. Three-chord-driven guitar, bass, and drums would no longer dominate pop music sales. Over the next fifteen years, the genre's appeal went into decline. It was 2017 when hip hop first outsold rock.

But for the moment, alt rock was hot. And David Geffen was busy looking for a band with grungy roots like Nirvana.

Also to the disadvantage of Pariah, the label had signed Austin pros, the Arc Angels. This older band often played Antone's but never the Backroom. Geffen's overloading of their promotion department with two new Texas bands to break, just as alt rock was flying high, didn't help either's chance for success.

In less than two years after their album, the Pariah guys became discouraged and called it quits. Next, the Arc Angels called it quits. The mighty Geffen Records had struck out twice in a row with Austin rockers.

Bass player Sims Ellison, who during Pariah's touring days was dating actress Renée Zellweger, made a brief appearance in Madonna's "Deeper and Deeper" video. He and Renee broke up and she began dating guitarist Doyle Bramhall II.

Then in a fit of post band, post Renee, and post dreams, a mood of heavy depression set in and Sims picked up a gun and suicided. Soon afterward his father established a free mental health service for Austin musicians, naming it the SIMS Foundation.

I would say Pariah, during its fleeting moment in the sun, was the best rock band in Texas.

Shandon Sahm moved on to drum for the Meat Puppets, who had been playing fifteen years and had a big fan in Kurt Cobain. The band had just released their gold album, *Too High to Die,* produced by Buttholes guitarist Paul Leary on London Records. It contained the charting single "Backwater." Fifteen years later, Shandon was still playing with the Puppets.

Another of my favorite hard rock bands in that last decade of the 20th century was Dangerous Toys, with their dynamic singer, Jason Masters. Columbia signed the quintet in '89 and for two records marketed them alongside Judas Priest. Their self-titled album, *Dangerous Toys*, went gold.

The guys also recorded albums for DOS and DMZ Records before saying goodbye to their fans, along with the old millennium, and leaving four albums in their wake.

* * *

UP TO NOW, I've mostly described the live music scene, but for the next three chapters I'm going to change horses and focus on Austin's national recordings. Their importance cannot be overstated.

Nationally distributed albums promote the artist's music and build a fan base for live shows. To survive, musicians have to tour, sell merchandise, and collect publishing revenue from recorded songs. Sometimes a song will get picked up for a movie soundtrack or a TV series and provide a bonus of extra royalties. For a musician, one hit record equals a lifetime of income.

As these local artists become noted, or even popular, music lovers discover they hail from Austin. Today's musicians and their road crews are modern-day traveling minstrels playing their music while promoting their hometown roots.

From the 13th Floor Elevators to Gary Clark Jr., whether playing small clubs or big festivals, touring musicians splash Austin's reputation around the globe. The Live Music Capital is dependent on a never-ending supply of recording stars.

* * *

THE MULTI-TALENTED Arc Angels were a superior band who received top-notch critical acclaim from music reviewers. A year after Stevie Ray Vaughan's helicopter crashed into a Wisconsin hillside, the famous Double Trouble rhythm section, Tommy Shannon and Chris Layton, aka Whipper, knew it was essential to keep working. They needed to get back on the road and replace their lost income. And they had to find a national record label.

The bass and drums duo joined with acclaimed guitarists Doyle Bramhall II and Charlie Sexton to form an Austin supergroup, the Arc Angels. The guitarists were singers, too, with the good looks needed for music videos. Bramhall's daddy grew up in Dallas drumming in bands with the Vaughan brothers and later co-wrote songs with Stevie. The guys named their quartet after the Austin Rehearsal Complex where they first jammed together.

The band's music couldn't have technically sounded any better. Theirs was a clean-driving, blues-rock that appealed to music aficionados as well as fans of Gun N' Roses. How could it miss? In 1992 Geffen Records quickly snatched the guys up.

Later that year, the label released their self-titled *Arc Angels*, produced by Steven Van Zandt. In my opinion, a mistake. Little Steven was too much of a Jersey/Miami guitarist to understand the roots of modern Texas blues-rock and bring out that heritage in a studio. No grit. Nevertheless, before you knew it, the quartet had twice performed on national TV for David Letterman. Yet the album wasn't selling, and behind the scenes, the brand new band was already falling apart.

Even with drug-wise Tommy Shannon and Chris Layton doing their best to help Doyle II manage his heroin addiction, usage increased. Soon he stayed too high too long and became undependable. Along with other Austin fans, I sadly watched as the starward-bound Arc Angels fell to Earth. They broke up in 1993.

In less than a year, Shannon and Layton found two more excellent guitarists and a first-class, soul-rock vocalist in Malfred Milligan. Their band was Storyville and it launched in 1994 and was soon in negotiations with Atlantic Records. It was the label's return to Austin blues-rock following their Lou Ann Barton album fourteen years before. Atlantic released two albums, *Piece of Your Soul* in '96 and *Dog Years* in '98. Storyville at its end didn't officially break up, they just kinda dissolved.

Also in 1994, Epic Records, seeing a slowdown in SRV sales, released the first of two fine albums by brother, Jimmie Vaughan. Musically, for my listening, I've always preferred Jimmie's laid-back style over Stevie's virtuoso hot-dogging. But laid-back is not a commercial pop sound.

Epic issued *Strange Pleasure* in '94 and four years later *Out There*. Those albums didn't chart and the label dropped the artist.

Next, Jimmie organized a live tribute extravaganza in Austin for his younger brother: B. B. King, Dr. John,

Robert Cray, Buddy Guy, Clapton, and others played their hearts out in a blues-rock salute. Epic released *A Tribute to Stevie Ray Vaughan* and a tune written by Jimmie, "SRV Shuffle," won a Grammy for best Rock Instrumental Performance.

Jimmie Vaughan was picked up by indie label Artimes, and in 2001 his *Do You Get the Blues*, was awarded the Grammy for best Traditional Blues Album. Combined, the Vaughan brothers garnered nine such trophies from the National Academy of Recording Arts and Sciences. A unique accomplishment, family style.

* * *

AUSTIN IN THE EARLY NINETIES introduced our city's expanded, now multigenre, music scene to the music industry. Tex-Mex and hard rock got its attention.

It was time Austin showed off its jazzy side of life. Guitar virtuoso Eric Johnson was signed by Capitol Records and opened the decade by releasing *Ah Via Musicom* and to great acclaim it broke into the Top 100 chart. This album held the single "Cliffs of Dover" that won a Grammy for Best Rock Instrumental Performance and was ranked by *Guitar World Magazine* at #17 on their list of 100 Greatest Guitar Solos.

He followed it with *Venus Isle* that made it to #59 on the charts. And in 1997 Sony Records released *G3: Live in Concert* with Eric Johnson, Steve Vai, and Joe Satriani.

Meanwhile, as both Eric and the Texas Tornadoes received their deserved awards, saxophone and flute master Tony Campise was nominated for a jazz Grammy for the Heart Records album, *Once in a Blue Moon*. Heart released a Campise album each year from 1990 to 1995.

1997: That's the year Arista-Austin opened its doors in a brief attempt to use the city as a farm team to complement their Nashville product. At last a national label had come to our musical town.

But strangely enough, Arista's most successful releases were two rock albums by Sister 7 with lead singer Patrice Pike: *This the Trip* and in 2000, *Wrestling Over Tiny Matters*. Soon after the label closed their Austin office and slunk back to Nashville.

20

After Stevie

Following the untimely death of Stevie Ray Vaughan, the guitarist who best captured the Austin ears of his fans was Ian Moore. He embraced blues-rock with licks sounding like Greg Allman mixed with Muddy Waters.

Maybe that's why Capricorn Records offered him a contract. They were once the hub of Southern rock.

I remember when Eddie Wilson and I flew to a Capricorn Records party in Athens, Georgia. Big turnout of musicians and music executives. Promoting the Headquarters, we gifted armadillo cast silver pendants. Eddie flagged down Bette Midler and presented her with a silver 'dillo. She gushed over it and presented him with a kiss.

I got to meet Alex Hodges, the primary booking agent for Capricorn's musicians, who decades later would be Stevie Ray Vaughan's manager.

The first of Ian's three albums for Waldon's revised label was *Ian Moore* in 1993. The following year the company put out an EP: *Live from Austin*, recorded at Steamboat 1874 on 6th Street. His final, in 1995, was *Modernday Folklore*. A few years after, Capricorn Records folded. And the discouraged Ian Moore decided to change his music and move home base to Seattle, where he added a tasty jazz-pop feel to his still bluesy licks.

This was 1996, the year Patty Griffin's career hit liftoff. Signed by A&M Records, she recorded three albums with them before she moved to indie label ATO—founded by singer/guitarist superstar Dave Matthews—that placed two of Patty's efforts in the Top 40, hitting #34 with *Children Running Through*. Then on to Nashville labels Credential for #38 *Downtown Church* and New West for #36 *American Kid* in 2013.

Locals took note when Robert Plant moved to Austin to live with Patty for a couple of years. She and Plant could be seen late night in clubs around town, and the Zeppelin frontman would take the little stage in the Continental Club to sing a song or two. She even toured with Robert Plant and the Band of Joy, providing him backup vocals and guitar. Patty Griffin's next two records charted in the 60s on *Billboard*'s Top 100 pop albums.

This is about the time when another star moved into the Live Music Capital. Dennis Quaid had married a local gal, a Texas real estate agent. His mother, too, was a Texas real estate agent.

I felt a distant affinity with the actor because we had both attended Bellaire High School and the University of Houston. Turned out, this movie actor fronted a band! Perfect.

Dennis Quaid and The Sharks would soon be performing on the historic stage at the Continental. It took ten years before the happy couple divorced and the actor, singer, rhythm guitarist returned to LA.

My favorite Austin club band in the mid-'90s was Spoon. They had a laid-back, almost psychedelic sound with great original songs from Britt Daniel. The quartet got signed to Matador Records and released *Telephono*. Two years later for Electra Records out came *A Series of Sneaks*.

Now the city's rock scene was heating up. In 1992, Bill Ham had moved Lone Wolf Management and Hamstein Music from Houston to Austin. He decided to manage local hard rockers, Pushmonkey, and got their self-titled album released on Arista with some radio play on its track "Handshake."

Also that year The Music Company Records—newly started by Lars Ulrich, drummer for Metallica—signed Goudie, headed by Johnny Goudie. Johnny Goudie is on my list of talented Austin musicians who should have been international stars: Bob Schneider, Jason McMaster, Alejandro Escovedo, and Charlie Sexton.

The band, Goudie, released *Peep Show* in 2000, their only shot and it missed. Meanwhile, Sony records came to town and signed the Vallejo brothers—A.J., Alejandro, and Omar—to a one album deal and in 2000 released the rock band's *Into the New*. It, too, missed. Then in 2001, Electra/Asylum, in a major cost-cutting move, dumped Ulrich's label and so after years of hard work it was all over. Goudie called it quits. Vallejo continued by releasing albums via their own record company, VMG.

* * *

DURING THE LAST CENTURY'S final decade, Texas' newly proclaimed "Live Music Capital of the World" scored two national rock hits. First, in the spring of '96, aging punks, the Butthole Surfers, released their only gold album, *Electriclarryland*, on Capitol Records. Incredibly the notorious band had a hit single—more rap than punk—with the track, "Pepper." Its sales went Top 20.

Nevertheless their career-long problem gaining radio play continued with many deejays refusing to say their name.

Two years later, from out of nowhere came Fastball. The Austin trio scored platinum with their second rock album for Hollywood Records, *All the Pain Money Can Buy*. Nominated for two Grammy Awards, that 1998 album held three charting songs! And "The Way" went all the way to #4 on the coveted *Billboard* list.

Fastball's follow-up album fizzled. The album's title should have been a warning signal, *The Harsh Light of Day*. Its lack of sales caused the discouraged musicians to dismantle their band. Fortunately, they had placed songs in movies and were on 11 soundtracks that augmented their royalty checks. Later, the guys tried a Fastball comeback, but it was too late for the trio to recover that lost magic.

Through the decades, I've watched Austin claim its share of one-hit wonders. It was the Bubble Puppy redux.

Attracted by the noise of all of this rock music, Houston quintet Blue October quietly moved toward Austin. Band leader Justin Furstenfeld followed his drummer brother Jeremy to settle in San Marcos and a few years later the guys scored a contract with Universal Music. Their arrangement with Universal gave the band four well-distributed albums and some great music videos to promote their singles.

In spring of 2007, the guys struck platinum pay dirt with their album, *Foiled,* which contained two platinum singles, "Hate Me" and "Into the Ocean." In 2014 Justin built the Up/Down recording studio near Wimberley. He wanted a secluded place where the band could produce and mix their music. Top 20 album *Home* was recorded there.

Austin band Okkervil River also charted in 2007 when their album, *The Stage Names*, reached #62 on the pop hit list and the next two albums went Top 50: *The Stand Ins* made #42 and *I Am Very Far* in 2011 reached #32. Both for Indiana's indie label Jagjaguwar.

And it's very cool that in 2010 Roky Erickson chose Okkervil to back him on his first release of newly written songs in fourteen years: *True Love Cast Out All Evil.* His final album. Roky singing love songs? Wow.

By 2001, Spoon had moved to Merge Records. Merge is where the guys had their first of five consecutive Top 100 chart successes, and their 2005 album, *Gimme Fiction*, made it to #44. It held a single that reached #31 called "I Turn My Camera On."

But a couple of years later came their double whammy as *Ga Ga Ga Ga Ga* hit #10 and its single "Don't You Evah" topped out at #1 in the nation! The next Merge release in 2010 bettered the previous sales by taking *Transference* to #4 and pulling two hit singles: "Got Niffin" again hitting #1 and "Written in Reverse" going to #30.

I was proud that Austin had launched one of the best of high-quality rock bands in the U.S.A.

21

A Star Is Born...
in San Marcos

By the mid-'90s, country music had elevated Willie Nelson to permanent stardom and legendary status. The country music industry had altered its style because of Willie. He was no longer expected to turn out platinum albums, yet the man was more prolific than ever and recording some of his best music.

Filmmakers got a new movie set when Willie built a Luckenbach-ish western town named Luck, using the Hondo Crouch-ish slogan: "You're either in Luck or out of Luck." His town was used in 1986 to film *Red Headed Stranger*. Perhaps one day Luck will be opened by Willie for tourism, like Enchanted Springs Ranch in Boerne or the former Happy Shahan's Alamo Village in Bracketville. It too was a movie set, used in 1959 for John Wayne epic *The Alamo*.

And just as the musician's Austin Opera House venue had emulated the Armadillo World Headquarters, he further honored the 'Dillo's memory by naming his new operation, Willie Nelson World Headquarters.

His Fourth of July Picnics, which haven't really been picnics for decades, still drew fifteen thousand or more people, rain or shine. And his Farm Aid events became more frequent as young millennial families began wanting locally grown produce.

His never-ending national tours maintained good audience turnouts with fans young and old. Willie's lifetime of touring was almost nonstop. To many, it seemed the musician lived in his bus. And in a large way, he did.

Larry Trader once said, "Woody, the man has got to tour. He's not like Kenny Rogers. Willie's got a band to feed."

The Texas Hill Country nurtured other country musicians. And they were selling lots of albums.

Most notable is George Strait, who eventually moved from San Marcos to San Antonio. The singer was consistently atop *Billboard*'s country music sales charts. In 1990 he even made a singing cowboy movie, *Pure Country* and, though it tanked at the box office, the soundtrack went 6X-platinum!

George Strait and his Ace in the Hole Band started their career in 1975 by playing at the Cheatham Street Warehouse, thirty miles south of Austin. This was smack dab in the middle of the outlaw country revolution. But Strait was definitely, and perhaps defiantly, not outlaw. He was a real cowboy and worked a day job managing his family's ranch.

In the period when Willie Nelson released two multi-platinum recordings, *Somewhere Over the Rainbow* and *Always on My Mind*, and starred in *Barbarosa*, George Strait was packing crowds into the Warehouse. It would be six years before he took his first steps up the ladder to mega success.

"Unwound" in 1981 was his first single for MCA Records and it went Top 10 on the country hit list. Then his second record "If You're Thinking You Want a Stranger (There's One Coming Home)" made it to #3. His next release, "Fool Hearted Memory," hit #1. Every year until the end of the century, George Strait released a #1 country single. And during that time he sold over 66 million albums! Closing in on 2020, he was officially the 11th best-selling artist of all time, ahead of the Stones, Madonna, and Springsteen. The singer was listed as the 5th richest country music star, worth $300 million. Willie tied Bryan Kelley for 33rd with a net worth of $25 million.

This star was a hat act. In 2001, the man had changed from a white to black hat, matching the look of the younger Nashville stars branded as "New Country."

It must have worked, because in 2010 George Strait was named Artist of the Decade by the Academy of Country Music while the Country Music Association proclaimed him Entertainer of the Year. The singer had received more awards than any other artist in any genre. And he set the record for the most #1 hits on the *Billboard* Hot Country Songs chart... 45 singles that shot to the top. His concerts packed football stadiums.

The strange thing is, Austin music fans and writers in *The Chronicle* and *The Statesman* generally ignored the Central Texas hit maker. His music wasn't in Willie's bag. Not hip enough. Strait was too straight.

Yet, like the outlaw musicians before him, this singer came to Nashville as someone outside the box. The mainstay product of Nashville studios was country-pop and this new fellow was a traditionalist. Like the *Shotgun Willie* album in 1973, the *Strait Country* album in 1981 smashed the Nashville hit-factory mold.

And, like Willie Nelson, through years of thick and thin, George Strait kept his band together and toured with four original members of Ace in the Hole on his bus.

Strait celebrated his sixtieth birthday in 2012 by releasing his 59th MCA chart-topping single. And then he announced his retirement from the concert circuit with a final grand tour named "The Cowboy Rides Away."

I was amused that country superstars Garth Brooks and George Strait had both retired from touring while elderly Willie Nelson was still actively bussing from gig to gig through his eighth decade. I guess that's the difference between a country star and a folk hero.

22

Sons of the Cosmic Cowboys

During the 1990s, fans all around the country wanted to hear the music of Central Texas musicians. From San Antonio, singer Moe Bandy still drew big rodeo crowds while Johnny Bush continued to pack dance halls. The region was fortunate to have singer-songwriter brothers Charlie Robison in San Antonio and Bruce Robison in Austin, both raised in Bandera. Bruce married Austin singer-songwriter, Kelly Willis. Charlie married a Dixie Chick, Emily Erwin.

Also launched from Austin was the career of Rick Trevino, who recorded his country records in the Nashville style but sang in both English and Spanish. His dad was a Tejano musician and had encouraged his son's country leanings.

Rick signed with Columbia Records in 1993 and released "Just Enough Rope," the first mainstream country music single from Nashville to offer both English- and Spanish-language versions. The following year his album, *Rick Trevino*, earned gold. His records kept selling and in '97, "Running Out of Reasons to Run" hit #1 in country music.

Next, Trevino borrowed a page from the Doug Sahm songbook. He and Ruben Ramos joined forces to form and record the Grammy-winning album, *Los Super Seven*, for RCA Records. That band included, among other musicians, Freddy Fender and Flaco Jimenez, with Doug Sahm joining on vocals.

Twenty-five years earlier, the first Mexican-American country music star, Johnny Rodriguez, had sung English-Spanish verses. Three years after Johnny first hit with "Pass Me By," Freddy Fender went country and recorded a 1975 bilingual-style crossover that charted #1 on the *Billboard* Top 100! "Before the Next Teardrop Falls."

Both men grew up in small towns in the Rio Grande Valley. Rodriguez was a South Texan who, during the cosmic cowboy heyday, recorded 20 national albums and charted 46 singles. Even with a half a dozen #1 country hits such as "You Always Come Back To Hurting Me," "Riding My Thumb To Mexico," and "Just Get Up And Close The Door," Austin venues ignored him.

To see Johnny Rodriguez, you had to go to San Antonio. The capital city of Texas was definitely Willie country.

Also in the 1990s, Lyle Lovett, Steve Earle, and Robert Earl Keen drifted through Austin with performances linking that decade's Americana music with the 1970s' progressive country era. Kelly Willis started the '90s with MCA and her *Well Traveled Love* reached #64 on the country charts. Six albums later, she ended that decade with her Rykodisk Top 30 country album, *What I Deserve*.

This was a period when Columbia Records folk-country artist Shawn Colvin moved to Austin. Her 1996 platinum album, *A Few Small Repairs*, held a poignant self-written Top 10 pop hit, "Sunny Came Home." That single in 1997 assured her of a profitable lifetime career by going up to #7 and winning two 1998 Grammys: Song of the Year and Record of the Year.

The lady had previously won the 1991 Grammy for Best Contemporary Folk Album of the Year, *Steady On*. Throughout the '90s Shawn Colvin managed to release four albums and rack up seven other Grammy nominations.

It was in 1998 during the 25th anniversary of Willie's Fourth of July Picnics, this one held in Luckenbach, that an unknown country singer was brought on stage and endorsed by the outlaw legend himself. The lucky man's name was Pat Green.

Green was born in San Antonio and living in Waco when he began his rise to financial success. During the first decade of the next century, six of Pat Green's albums for Universal Music Group and BNA Records made the country Top 10, three of those reaching #2.

Meanwhile, we had the Dixie Chicks hanging out in Austin where Natalie's multi-instrumentalist daddy, Lloyd Maines, was a session producer. He recorded the girls at Cedar Creek studio.

Lloyd became a centerpiece for the city's music scene. It was during the mid-'90s when Sony Music decided to revive the defunct Monument Records label and sign the female trio. By the end of the '90s, the talented Chicks had broken out nationally with alternative country hits and exploded to international superstar brightness.

Backing up their music, the trio had chosen a great name and on stage looked the part. In 1998 their debut album, *Wide Open Spaces*, turned out to be a 12X-platinum smash! Holy cow.

Lloyd Maines convinced Sony to record its title song that

soon became the girls' signature tune at their huge sold-out concerts. The following year *Fly* went 10X-platinum! Both records were certified diamond by the RIAA. These sales were unheard of for a country music artist.

Then in 2002, the women released *Home* and brought home additional multiplatinum awards for Open Wide Records, their Columbia sublabel. The CD contained a Top 10 crossover pop single with "Long Time Gone," a Top 10 gold record "Landslide," and a Top 30 hit "Traveling Soldier." Lloyd Maines had produced their marvelous album at Cedar Creek.

In 2004 and 2005, Facebook and YouTube were born and the Chicks immediately picked up thousands of new friends. It was the first time fans and viewers from around the globe could see clips of the girls in concert.

The three Chicks' phenomenal roll of smash hits continued into 2007, when they won Grammys for both the Song of the Year and Record of the Year with a platinum single, "Not Ready to Make Nice," that hit Top 5 pop charts. At that same ceremony their CD, *Taking the Long Way*, won Grammy Album of the Year.

It had been three decades since the Austin scene had claimed those multi-Grammys via *Christopher Cross*. Getting awarded the prestigious Album of the Year and Song of the Year is like winning a Super Bowl.

The Dixie Chicks were happening as three Lubbock boys, Jimmie Dale Gilmore, Joe Ely, and Butch Hancock were reforming The Flatlanders. The guys took up with New West Records, an independent that had opened an office in Austin. Don't know why it was called New West since it came out of Athens, Georgia, and Nashville. Their Flatlanders inaugural album, *Now Again*, went to #19 on the *Billboard* country listing and three of their next four charted in country's Top 40.

A lot of people associate Austin's country music heyday with the Armadillo era of cosmic cowboys and outlaws. In actuality, during the 1990s, country musicians from Central Texas made a lot of money touring and sold *millions* of country records, far more than any past decade.

MCA had started the decade with their first Jerry Jeff Walker album since 1977, *Great Gonzos*. That same year MCA returned with a more country-oriented Joe Ely and placed at #57 on the charts with *Live at Liberty Lunch*.

Electra Records signed Joe's Lubbock running buddy and fellow Flatlander, Jimmy Dale Gilmore, for three albums. *Spinning Round the Sun* in 1993 made it to #62 country. It would be the next century before Rounder and Red Eye returned Jimmy Dale to the *Billboard* top country listings.

Even the Geezinslaw Brothers, who started way back in the mid-'50s, had a hit. The comedic duo received the "Indie Best Seller Award" for their 1992 album, *Feelin' Good, Gittin' Up, Gittin' Down*, and its novelty single, "Help, I'm White and I Can't Get Down," climbed halfway up the *Billboard* Hot 100 Country chart.

Ely came back in '95 with *Letter to Laredo*. Two years later, Ray Wylie Hubbard, who had sobered and detoxed himself, thanks to the guidance of Stevie Ray Vaughan, returned to the record stores on the Rounder label with *Dangerous Spirits*, followed by four more albums for the Nashville-based company. Ely was back again in '98 on the charts with *Twistin' in the Wind* at #55, his last for MCA.

In 2000 Ely started the new century on Antone's

Records and for Clifford's label he charted at #66 country with *Live @ Antone's*. In '03, with *Streets of Sin* on Rounder Records, he hit #51, and by 2015 he'd placed two more in the top 50. In his notable career, Joe Ely released over two dozen albums.

Throughout this Austin decade of great musical growth, although his singles had slowed way down, Willie Nelson continued selling albums. From the *Red Headed Stranger* LP in 1975 through 2003 and *The Essential Willie Nelson*, the singer had collected 25 Gold or Platinum Awards, either as a solo or in duet. He started the '90s with *Born for Trouble* at #31 and in 1993 ended his awe-inspiring eighteen years on Columbia Records at #15 with *Across the Borderline*.

Over those years, Columbia-Sony-CBS financed and distributed forty-six different Willie albums. In 1995 Capitol Records picked him up for *Healing Hands of Time* reaching #17; and then our folk hero went on to Island Records for *Spirit* and *Teatro* scoring at #20 and #17 in '95 and '98.

It was another successful charting decade for Willie. And the next ten years would top it.

In 2002, he signed with Lost Highway Records and his first release, *The Great Divide*, went to #5 country and crossed over to hit #43 on the pop charts. *Countryman* in 2005 did #6 and he closed out Lost Highway in 2008 with *Moments of Forever* that reached #8 for country music's Top 10 selling albums.

Willie Nelson started the next decade with Rounder Records. Fellow Texan T Bone Burnett, whose creds include an Oscar and a dozen Grammys, produced the album, *Country Music.*

Willie's comment after the studio session: "We ventured into all kinds of music, but this is country music. No one would argue the fact that these are country songs."

Strangely, the album was Grammy nominated, not for a country award, but Americana. *Country Music* reached #4 in the country listings and hit #20 on the *Billboard* Top 100.

Not bad for a seventy-seven-year-old singer.

But then in 2019 at age eighty-six, the singer returned to Sony (previously Columbia and CBS) for a studio album: *Ride Me Back Home.* Amazing.

* * *

PERHAPS THE MOST culturally notable 1990s occurrence was the emergence of middle-class musicians. The city was home to several artists who never produced a hit or signed with a national label, yet made a good living playing music in Austin and on the national club and festival circuit, much of it performing their own compositions. These hard-working performers bought homes and raised families, sent their kids to college.

Equally surprising, the city now had a few people who earned a living writing about these musicians!

23

The Lance Armstrong Decade

In the mid-1990s, Lance Armstrong moved to Austin. The young man rode into town already well established as a world-class triathlete. Lance trained by running and biking Hill Country trails and swimming in area lakes.

Then a personal disaster occurred. The twenty-five-year-old athlete was diagnosed with testicular cancer and underwent major surgery and chemotherapy in 1996.

While still in recovery, he established the nonprofit Lance Armstrong Foundation, stating its mission was to "to inspire and empower" cancer sufferers and those who love them. His chosen slogan: "Unity is strength, knowledge is power, and attitude is everything."

Later the Lance Armstrong Foundation would form LIVESTRONG for health education and create an outreach promotion using yellow plastic wristbands. Yellow being the winner's color at Tour de France.

Here was a gimmick that changed the face of charitable fundraising. Everywhere it became fashionable to wear a yellow wristband, even with your formal wear and Rolex.

It was in 1999 that Lance Armstrong first stunned the world. The former testicular cancer patient won the Tour de France!

ABC's *Wide World of Sports* proclaimed the Austin cyclist their Athlete of the Year. The following year the world gasped again when the man won the Tour a second time!

When Lance won the prestigious race a third consecutive time, I quickly assembled a video crew to record a live music homecoming celebration on the shores of Town Lake. I especially wanted to capture blues-rock guitar master Kenny Wayne Shepherd with Double Trouble.

Charlie Jones, who had produced the city's A2K event on Millennium Eve, was in charge of the giant "Viva Lance!" concert and the victory parade down Congress Avenue that would lead folks to a day of free concerts on Auditorium Shores. Governor Rick Perry and Mayor Kirk Watson were on stage to shake the champion's hand. Lance was in top form and rumor was his singer girlfriend, Sheryl Crow, was backstage.

Austin was thrilled and enthralled by Lance's phenomenal Tour accomplishment of three wins in a row. The following year the cyclist did it again! And again the year after, and again, and again. The man won seven straight Tour de France victories!

To the benefit of community health Austinites were inspired to step outside and embrace cycling. City Council established the beautiful Lance Armstrong Bikeway providing the riders safe access to downtown and Lady Bird Lake.

Bill Stapleton represented Lance Armstrong for corporate sponsorships beginning in 1995. He also marketed an excellent Austin musician, Shawn Colvin. Stapleton then branched out from management and agent work to produce events. He founded Capital Sports & Entertainment, which led to forming C3 Presents with three Charlies: Jones, Attal, and Walker. This is the group who created the nationally popular Austin City Limits Festival and transformed a dying Lollapalooza into an annual tourism destination for Chicago. Those successes led to forming C3 Management and representing a roster of musicians, including jam band rockers Blues Traveler and Texas Hill Country singer-folk guitarist Robert Earl Keen.

All of this growth was possible because Lance Armstrong had created enough spinoff events and corporate sponsorships to provide financial stability to the fledgling C3 Presents. There would be no C3 or Austin City Limits Festival were it not for Lance Armstrong.

All went beautifully for over a decade. But in 2013, the world of Lance Armstrong experienced a pole flip... an extinction-level event. The man confessed to using performance-enhancing drugs to win his races.

Media went crazy. I had never seen anything like it.

Within a few days, the champion's seven Tour de France victories were pulled from the record books. Immediately Nike, Budweiser, Radio Shack, and other sponsors jumped ship. So it was goodbye to $50 million in endorsement money.

I knew Capital Sports & Entertainment had just seen their primary cash flow smash into the proverbial wall.

For the first time, Bill Stapelton and company would be heavily dependent on producing music events rather than sports star marketing.

For over a decade, Lance Armstrong had an incredibly positive influence on Austin, a healthy influence. Here was a man who could have earned the hometown stature of Coach Darrell Royal or Willie Nelson, but instead got snarled in the most famous cheating-in-a-race drug bust in history.

No one was surprised when *Forbes* magazine proclaimed the former bicycle hero: Most Disliked Athlete of the Year.

tevie Ray Vaughan had ended with the heart attack of
Joug Sahm. Both musicians died in the mountains.

last saw Doug in late September at Threadgill's on
North Lamar. His usual table by the window had been
taken so he took a seat in the diner, waiting for early
lunch. He sat in the same booth where I used to see
Madalyn Murray O'Hair. Madalyn and I met when
KTSA became the first station outside of Austin to
broadcast her weekly radio program: *What On Earth Is
An Atheist?* I had put her on Sunday mornings along
with a half-dozen Christian preachers. She presented
me with her autographed book of the same title.

Doug waved me over. "Man, you know what I love?"

I shrugged.

"Being on the open road between towns in my Cadillac.
I just sit back, flip on cruise control, light a fat doobie,
and turn up the music. It's a groove driving through Big
Sur. I was in Oregon and northern California last week.
Beautiful."

"Sounds good to me."

"Oh, man." Hand to the side of his mouth, Doug
whispered, "I've got the big-taste in my car." He looked
around to see if anyone could overhear. "Augie gave it to
me."

I raised my eyebrows and nodded, knowing it must be
quality bud. Then he said, "Did I tell you the new CD is
finished? Back to my country roots. It'll blow your mind."

"Country? Nice switch. Most folks don't know your
boyhood love was country music."

I asked if he ever got to see Charlie Walker from
the old days. Walker was around when Little Doug sat

24

Doug Sahm Drives Away

The '90s began with a sense of sadness that lingered from Stevie Ray Vaughan's tragic ending. Ten years later, the decade ended with more sadness.

It started in April. When the Electric Lounge put the key in the lock and shut its door forever. A strange mix of One Knight funk, *SLUGGO!* living art, and Raul's camaraderie. Poetry slams and Nashville Pussy. Joan Jett, Link Wray, and The Gourds. No other club in the Live Music Capital like it. The wake lasted a full week as regulars and the curious paid their last respects and said goodbye. Music reviewers typed out words of praise to honor the six-year-old little venue. The last band on their stage was Spoon.

On a sweltering July night in 1999, I went to the closing of the beloved Liberty Lunch that Joe Ely had saluted to start the decade. The venue was suffering the same fate as the original Soap Creek Salon, original Antone's, and famous Armadillo. The word *redevelopment* always meant the wrecking ball.

The soulful funky Lunch had been serving up a tasty mix of great live music for over twenty years. And during its last ten years was voted Best Club in *The Austin Chronicle* Reader's Poll.

Too crowded, couldn't get in. I saw people crying.

Two months later, I saw a packed house closing down Steamboat 1874, on 6th Street. The club where Stevie Vaughan and Chesley Millikin shook hands and ignited their magic flame. The club where fifteen years later Chesley would elbow his way through the door by pushing down owner Danny Crooks and knocking out four of his teeth.

After twenty-three years on 6th Street, the city's number one music nightclub was getting evicted. It had to make way for an urban cowboy shot bar run by Houston wheeler-dealers, whom the locals referred to as The Carpetbaggers.

On that final night of Steamboat, Bob Schneider's first band, Joe Rockhead, circa 1990, regrouped to funk-rock headline for a crowd flowing out the door and to the sidewalk and down the street. Inside, Schneider's girlfriend, actress Sandra Bullock, and pals attended the festive wake from the heart of a jammed dance floor. David Cotton was guarding the 'Boat's door.

Rumor was that another Austin resident film star, Matthew McConaughey, was trapped in that crowd outside where lit joints were passed in Austin tradition. Later that year, the popular actor was charged with resisting arrest when the noise cops burst into his home to stop him from playing bongo drums too loud and found McConaughey nude.

They were keeping our city safe. Could have knocked.

Danny Crooks, the 'Boat's beloved operator, had

prided himself on launching musicians into su
careers. That night he appeared, and was,
hearted. He always gave the bands one hundred
of the door and the 'Boat lived off the bar; som
Danny gave musicians-in-need money from his pe
earnings. His assistant, David Cotton, would see
the newest bands of promise.

Appropriately that night, the always-irrev
Uranium Savages performed. The zany band
claimed the dubious honor of playing the closing
night for both Liberty Lunch and Steamboat 1874.

Nightclubs come and nightclubs go and indeed the '9
suffered its losses, as the Austin Opera House also ende
its fifteen-year run.

But there were also startups of lasting importance
The first Emo's on 6th Street, The Back Yard on Bee
Cave, Stubb's Waller Creek Amphitheater on Red River,
Threadgill's World Headquarters on Riverside, and
north of the UT campus Spider House welcomed its first
live music fans. Each of those 1990s Austin venues went
on to earn their live music gold spurs.

* * *

SO IT WAS that Austin closed out the century by losing
several of its best clubs. But worst of all that November,
just two weeks after his 58th birthday, Doug Sahm died.

The musical genius was found peacefully at rest in
the king-sized bed of a Taos, New Mexico, motel room.
At an elevation of 7,000 feet, you could say the man died
high. A decade that started with the helicopter crash of

on Hank Williams' lap. Legend says that incident took place just up the road from Threadgill's in the Skyline Club during Hank Williams' final performance before his untimely death.

The Skyline was also the last place Johnny Horton performed before his demise by automobile. Doug told me Charlie Walker had moved to Nashville and he last saw him during a Texas Tornados gig.

We joked about going to hear bands at the Farmer's Daughter, famous for parking lot brawls. He asked me about our San Antonio friend, Joe Mansfield, who was now the marketing power behind the phenomenal record sales of Garth Brooks. Garth ranks number two in total albums, right behind the Beatles. We talked about how much Doug liked the Lyle Lovett big band sound and Ray Benson's swing music, but he was most interested in Rick Trevino's style of country western.

Doug felt the end of the century was the perfect time to go back to his 1950 roots. He would start his own label, Tornado Records, and call this one *The Return of Wayne Douglas*.

But as it turned out, this return was also his departure. Full circle. Doug Sahm would leave The Stage playing the same kind of music that kicked off his remarkable career.

The Threadgill's waitress arrived. She carefully set out Doug's meatloaf with mashed potatoes and brown gravy, ranch dressing salad on the side. Iced tea. I remember thinking, same thing Clifford Antone would order. I also noticed Doug had put on weight.

After lunch, we stepped outside and got into his shiny new Caddy for a parking lot toke.

I waved goodbye as Doug Sahm drove away.

MOVIES AND GAMES
AUSTIN STYLE

I see no line between the imaginary and the real.

Frederico Fellini

1

Movie Makers in Austin?

While attending the national Underground Press Syndicate's conference at the Armadillo World Headquarters in the early 1970s, I saw a guy dressed like a wagon train scout with shoulder-length hair and wearing knee-high rough-out boots topped with fringe.

"Who's that?"

Eddie Wilson chuckled. "Kit Carson."

In conversation with the wagon train scout, I learned he worked at the Texas Commission on the Arts and made movies. As it happened, Kit Carson had worked with playwright Horton Foote, who received an Academy Award for his film adaptation of *To Kill a Mockingbird*. The movie starred a young Robert Duvall, whose 1980s portrayals of latter-day Texas cowboys in Larry McMurtry classics *Lonesome Dove* and *Tender Mercies* would epitomize realism in the new breed of Hollywood westerns. Kit was one of the men trying to make Austin into a movie production town.

Another man trying to sell Austin to Hollywood was Warren Skaaren. I knew of Warren from Urban Development at the Governor's office. I had phoned him when broadcasting my KTSA editorials spotlighting

Mexican-Americans living in a below-poverty-level housing project in San Antonio. No plumbing in many homes, plus dangerous electrical wiring.

I learned then Warren was also fronting a lobbying effort to involve state government in promoting big-time moviemaking. I decided to run editorials in support of Texas filmmaking and mailed a letter of KTSA endorsement to Governor Preston Smith.

It was only natural that San Antonio's leading radio station favored this industry. In 1927, *Wings* became the first movie to win an Academy Award for Best Picture. They filmed that feature at the now dissolved Kelly Air Force Base and it premiered in the city's newly opened Texas Theater.

This new lobbying effort mostly came from Dallas and Austin filmmakers. The effort culminated in 1971 when Governor Smith created our Texas Film Commission and appointed its first director, Warren Skaaren. He served three start-up years in that office before moving on to a successful career in the motion picture business.

Warren always had an interest in filmmaking. One of his pre-Film Commission projects was the documentary *A Special Place*. It was about the historic fight to save the San Antonio River from the Chamber of Commerce and Corps of Engineers who planned to pave it, giving consumers easy downtown shopping access. Now the documentary itself has become historic.

So the years went speeding by and one day in 1989, I looked up at the silver screen to see Warren Skaaren credited as co-writer for the superhero hit of the year, *Batman*.

* * *

I WENT TO the Austin film business planning session. Mike Tolleson was the only person I knew in the room. L. M. "Kit" Carson arrived wearing his fringe-top boots. I met UT instructor Richard Kooris and he talked about creating a "Third Coast" for moviemakers. First time I'd heard that expression. Next, I met Tobe Hooper and complimented him on his experimental feature, *Eggshells*, with its soundtrack by Shiva's Head Band.

In 1972, Tobe had documented our Central Texas music scene with his film, *Hill Country Happening*, which featured Rod Kennedy's inaugural Kerrville Folk Festival. He was now working on something called *Leatherface*, a movie in the low-budget horror tradition of Gordon McLendon's Dallas film, *The Killer Shrews*. As with *Eggshells*, he was co-writing with Kim Henkel.

Warren Skaaren suggested they change the title to *Texas Chainsaw Massacre*. He invested in it and helped with distribution.

Good grief! Who could have guessed the Austin-made horror movie would pull in $30 million to be the twentieth century's top money-making independent!

That film evolved into a lifetime franchise, spawning a comic book series and video game, plus a half-dozen sequels, all using *Leatherface* and his family as slashing antagonists. Tobe Hooper's movie far outgrossed—both financially and in bloody content—McLendon's horror flicks of the 1950s.

2

Peter Fonda, Willie Nelson, and Meat Loaf

Major Hollywood studios between 1977 and 1984 gave moviegoers a quartet of entertaining musicals filmed in the "Live Music Capital of the World." Their playbill reads like a Joe Bob Briggs' drive-in theater festival: *Outlaw Blues, Roadie, Honeysuckle Rose*, and *Songwriter*. Joe Bob might open his music movie memorabilia night with a documentary:

John Szalapski had arrived in the capital with his camera in 1975 to interview Townes Van Zandt, Guy Clark, Rodney Crowell, and Steve Earle, along with local music fans. He was making the first outlaw music documentary by filming in Nashville and Austin.

Today *Heartworn Highways* remains a definitive 90-minute glimpse documenting the birth of a new stylistic transition among country music performers.

And that is when Hollywood discovered Austin.

In 1977 the Warner Bros.-backed *Outlaw Blues*, promoting Nashville's renegades, was filmed inside Austin nightclubs. It was during the making of *Outlaw*

Blues that Austin's hip music community got their first taste of feature moviemaking and they liked it.

Peter Fonda was the star and my big surprise came when I learned he actually sang in the film, six tunes. Susan Saint James and John Crawford were involved and frequently the stars would be seen off stage in Austin's clubs listening to live bands. Soap Creek Saloon was used as a set. Steven Fromholz, Greezy Wheels, singer Natalie Zoe, and the staff at the *The Austin Sun* got on-screen parts. Our hip mayor, Jeff Friedman, played a newsman.

Two years later Warner Bros. returned with *Honeysuckle Rose*. Once again Austin's hippies, punkers, and disco dandies got jobs as movie extras; they dressed up like ranchers and farmers.

Mad Dog author Bill Wittliff, who had met Willie at the Armadillo, was hired to help write the screenplay. He had already created another Rose for a made-for-TV movie script, *Thaddeus Rose and Eddie*, starring Johnny Cash.

Honeysuckle Rose is the story of a cowboy singer and his touring band. The soundtrack gave Willie Nelson another hit LP, and most importantly, his newest signature song: "On the Road Again," a song he wrote.

But, of course, he still opened his shows with the Johnny Bush anthem, "Whiskey River." Willie asked Kenneth Threadgill to be in the film and perform two songs: "Singing the Yodeling Blues" and "Coming Back to Texas." Kenneth was included on the double-platinum selling album, and I'm sure the aged Mr. Threadgill was grateful for the royalty checks.

Locally verified rumors of Willie seen naked, meandering between the location trailers at night and having an affair with leading lady Amy Irving got *Honeysuckle Rose* promoted on the covers of national tabloids. Upon the film's debut in theatres, critics panned the movie, but it had paid off at the box office and the industry wanted more.

Willie had shown the world that a Hollywood-quality movie could be made using Austin talent. He even filmed inside the historic Skyline Club, at that time home to the second version of Soap Creek Saloon. He brought the movie, *Barbarosa*, to town in 1981, and this time Bill Wittliff was the sole screenwriter. It was a first rate shoot-'em-up western. I think it holds Willie's best acting—if he was acting—and Wittliff's best original script, not taken from a story or book. And yes, that animal Barbarosa dined on was an armadillo. It was a common South Texas food during the great depression and dubbed the Hoover hog.

Then, when he made *Songwriter* in 1984, Willie called on another Mad Dog, Bud Shrake. Shrake was one of the nation's most successful sports writers. His popular *Harvey Penick's Little Red Book: Lessons and Teachings from a Lifetime of Golf* made history as the bestselling sports hardback ever published. And his penning of the screenplay for *Songwriter* was part of a natural progression for Shrake, who had written the Dennis Hopper western, *Kid Blue*, in 1973. To a certain extent, *Songwriter* played off Willie's pre-stardom career.

In *Songwriter*, Willie plays a country music composer using tricks to get out of his contract with a Nashville manager, Kris Kristofferson, who raked off all the profits from his songs.

The story has it that in real life, a struggling Willie Nelson had to sell his 1961 song, "Night Life," for $150 and through the years he watched it recorded by more than 70 artists and sell over 30 million copies. Reality is: he copied its melody and lyrical theme from Brownie McGhee, who at age fifteen penned "Sporting Life Blues."

Okay, there may be minor differences, and I prefer Willie Nelson's lyrics. However, if George Harrison could be charged with plagiarizing the Chiffons' biggest hit, "He's So Fine," for his song, "My Sweet Lord," then to my ears, Willie lifted "Night Life."

Maybe a case of Cryptomnesia?

As a matter of fact, in 1960 Pappy Daily of D Records would not release Willie's "Night Life" because it didn't sound like a country song. Brownie McGhee's original version is in the Smithsonian archives; check it out.

Two years after *Songwriter*, in 1986, filmmaker Willie brought his *Red Headed Stranger* back to life on the silver screen. Again he called on Bill Wittliff to write the script and, this time, serve as the film's director. Willie and Wittliff would also be the producers.

Again, most of the movie was filmed on the outskirts of Austin. But this time folks such as Bud Shrake and Darrell Royal financed the film independently. Historically, this feature is Austin's first indie film to go national since *Chainsaw Massacre*, but in the long run, the Redhead wasn't as popular with theatergoers as Leatherface.

The following year Bill and his wife Sally founded The Wittliff Collections, focusing on writing and photography, at Texas State University in San Marcos. Ending that decade, Wittliff was hired as the screenwriter for the six-part TV adaptation of Larry McMurtry's *Lonesome Dove*.

An accomplished photographer, Wittliff documented the weeks of production. All his materials are stored in the University's archive along with those of friends Billy Brammer, Jap Cartwright, Bud Shrake, and recent additions such as Austin novelist Sarah Bird and populist commentator Jim Hightower. Even a bit of our TYNA TACI Longneck campaign for Lone Star Beer is preserved at TSU, thanks to Jerry Retzloff's donating his personal beer memorabilia.

While film crews in 1979 made *Honeysuckle Rose*, another musicians-on-tour movie was in the works. This one from United Artists was shot from the perspective of the grunts: *Roadie*.

Released in 1980, the movie was built on a fun-filled screenplay by *The Austin Sun* alumni Big Boy Medlin and Michael Ventura. Former publisher Jeff Nightbyrd was their location scout. *Roadie*'s lead character, Travis Redfish, had been a frequent *Sun* "contributor" as Big Boy's alter ego.

Their chosen star was Dallas-bred rock singer Meat Loaf, a huge man who allegedly weighed 245 pounds in seventh grade. He was already an international cult film hero on the midnight movie college circuit for his portrayal of the motorcycle rocker, Little Eddie, in the punk horror musical, *Rocky Horror Picture Show*. Meat Loaf's multiplatinum album, *Bat Out of Hell*, produced by Todd Rundgren, was famous and its hit song was

"Paradise by the Dashboard Light." Thirty years later, his *Bat* album was still shipping a couple hundred thousand copies annually and had racked up total sales of 43 million.

Chase scenes for *Roadie* were filmed in downtown Austin on barricaded streets. Club Foot was used as a set. Manor Downs was home for the outdoor concert scenes, but a painted backdrop was used to make close-ups look as if the band was playing in a big city. Austin country bands Alvin Crow and the Pleasant Valley Boys and Asleep at the Wheel got parts in *Roadie,* along with the already legendary Roy Orbison.

My favorite Austin band at the time, Standing Waves, had their moment in the film. Many felt this was the act to break the typecasting jinx of Austin as a progressive country town. Instead, it would turn out to be Christopher Cross, followed by Stevie Ray Vaughan.

The filming of musicians, such as Blondie, drew hundreds of punks to Manor Downs for the first and last time. The horse track was in no way a punk scene.

Plus, listening to live music performed for a fictional movie is not entertaining, even for the most devoted fans. Musicians replay the same part of a song endlessly. Over and over and over...

After all, this was a movie set and they were performing for the director's cameras and not the audience. Hours went by as the band loudly performed the chorus to "Ring of Fire" from the paddock stage. The band's speakers had been aimed away from the horse stalls and toward the little town of Manor two miles away, where rumors were flying rampant.

Elderly citizens were horrified. It was the Downs that brought the Grateful Dead with their dancing skeletons, and now they're hosting a movie with a man named Alice who looks like a zombie and a woman named Blondie noted for her black lace brassiere.

Lordy, what next?

Roadie was released two months before *Honeysuckle Rose* in 1980 and was also given a rousing thumbs-down by critics. Yet through the years, that crazy, low-budget musical comedy has earned cult status and raves from B-movie fans.

And even today, I'll occasionally spot an old bumper sticker with the film's perfect slogan: "Bands make it rock… Roadies make it roll."

3

Definitely Not Gene Autry

During the 1970s, *Outlaw Blues* and *Honeysuckle Rose* were radical for western movies. These outlaw-themed features updated the archetype of the singing cowboy to modern times. Roy Orbison had tried a similar approach in 1967 when he starred in *The Fastest Guitar Alive*, but it was a dud. Willie Nelson's singing cowboys had paid off.

And during the 1980s, Willie continued to star in westerns. Shortly after his *Red Headed Stranger* galloped into theaters accross the country a series of made-for-television movies followed. A superb 1986 remake of *Stagecoach* brought executive producer/actor Willie together with friends Kris Kristofferson, Johnny Cash, and Waylon Jennings. The film showed off the acting talents of hit maker quartet The Highwaymen and won a Western Heritage Wrangler Award for Fictional Television Drama. Then on a Sunday night in January of 1988, CBS showed ex-con Willie out to rob a train in *Once Upon a Texas Train* to 21 million viewers ... and in November featured our Texas outlaw in *Where the Hell's That Gold?!!?*.

In 1989, Willie Nelson formed Pedernales Productions to co-partner in another made-for-TV western, *Pair of*

Aces. It starred Willie and Kris and Rip Torn and had roles for locals Sammy Allred and Turk Pipkin. Two old Maddogs, Bud Shrake and Gary Cartwright, were the writers for this Austin-made film. The show garnered great TV ratings, and so in 1991 the guys returned to play *Another Pair of Aces*.

Tell me, who else could match this sensational Willie decade? Twenty-three albums, twenty-eight singles, six hundred thirty-two concerts, five Fourth of July Picnics, four Farm Aids, one autobiography, and ten movies.

Wow!

The point I'm making is this: Willie Nelson, in his prime, was the central force in the emergence of Austin as a filmmaking city. From his catbird seat, Willie directed the good ship Austin to sail within landing distance of the Third Coast.

4

Todd Rundgren or Michael Dell

Billboard *Magazine* held its first International Video Music Conference in Los Angeles, mid-November of 1979. This was the introductory year for the instantly popular Walkman and its big brother, the boom box.

At this conference I saw Karen Darvin, the redhead I'd last seen with Bruce Springsteen at the Armadillo. She accompanied Todd Rundgren, whom I'd also met at the 'Dillo.

Todd reported he used an Apple II computer for video graphics to produce an RCA SelectaVision disc. His images would accompany Tomita's version of Holst's *The Planets*.

Then Michael Nesmith told me about his new company, Pacific Arts, that was creating a video music film called *Elephant Parts*. Later, it won the first Grammy ever awarded for Video of the Year. Nesmith thought it cool I was from San Antonio and asked me about his former hometown.

I wondered about his artist mother, who reportedly was in poor health. She had just sold her invention, Liquid Paper, for $47.5 million plus royalties. Everyone with a typewriter used her product to cover their mistakes. It was a few months later when the entrepreneur died in Richardson, Texas. Her will made the former Monkee a rich man.

* * *

BY DECEMBER 1983, I was finally ready to purchase my first home computer. The Internet was one year old, and newly introduced hard drives meant no more swapping floppy discs to load programs and save data. My time had come.

I almost bought an Apple III Plus because Todd Rundgren had upgraded to those machines for his Bearsville studio. But hey, I'm no artist. My priorities were a modem and a word processor.

In days before personal computers, businesses paid $14,000 to buy a stand-alone Lanier or Wang document processing machine. My far less expensive and far more versatile home system would send a document to a Diablo wheel printer for business letters or an Epson nine-pin dot matrix for research charts.

I favored the idea of the graphical interface on a new kind of computer from Steve Jobs called the Macintosh. Tiny black-and-white screen, minimal software, and memory topped out at 128 KB. Still, I liked using a mouse.

Microsoft had introduced Word for DOS that used a mouse, along with their communications program called Access, which also used one. The Bellevue, Washington, boys were experimenting with something they called Windows. I still have my 5¼-inch floppies holding my 1984 copy of Windows 0.1 for DOS. Antique software.

Looking through *Byte* magazine I spotted a mail order company selling exceptionally low priced IBM computers. The company was PC's Unlimited, based in Austin. A local store! I called to order my system on the phone and drove to Duval Street. PC's Unlimited had a new storefront in an old shoebox of a building. They were still moving in.

The newly constructed plywood service counter and white plasterboard walls were not yet painted. A young and sort of pudgy fellow wearing horned-rimmed glasses, white dress shirt with sleeves rolled up, stood behind the counter. Likely, a college kid with a part-time job. He took my order number and disappeared into the back room. I had ordered an IBM XT and increased its onboard RAM to the whopping-big max of 640 KB. My unit was customized with a 640 x 350 pixels EGA color graphics card. I would add the math co-processor later.

The young man returned lugging a bulky IBM box down the hall and around the plywood wall to place it on a table. A smaller box held my special-order 20MB hard drive set in an external case with its own built-in power supply, which had to be turned on separately from the XT. Also external from the unit was my blazing 1200-baud modem.

I introduced myself. He dabbed the perspiration from his forehead and said his name was Michael Dell.

"Is there some kind of scrape or dent on the XT case?"

"No. The box has never been opened."

I was puzzled. PC's Unlimited was a new company built on selling a highly discounted IBM PC. These units cost hundreds of dollars less than identical machines at local stores. "How can you sell brand new IBM computers for so much less than Computerland?"

"Woody, these are called gray market. To get bulk discounts from IBM, authorized stores have to buy more PCs than they can sell. I buy their surplus at cost or less. Legal, brand new, but not authorized for IBM factory warranty."

"I just saved fifteen hundred bucks. How do you make a profit?"

"Computer markup is outrageous." Michael Dell smiled. "It's like the jewelry business."

I later found out he really *was* a college kid. He quit school at the end of that semester and devoted his full energy to running his growing company.

Already, this kid Michael Dell had totally changed the marketing of "genuine" PCs via his direct phone sales and not having chain store overhead. His company soon drew large numbers of high tech engineers into Austin. Computer hardware manufacturers followed these engineers, and software programmers followed them. Dell's student-to-riches success story inspired countless high-tech startup ventures in Austin. When he took his company public as Dell Computers in 1988, a share of stock could be had for $8.50.

Wish I had bought some.

5

Raided by the SS

Before there was a Web... local Bulletin Board Systems were running on home computers. You dialed their BBS with your line phone and could upload and download small files, you could post a message, and two-way text chat was available. A visitor logged out of a "board" by disconnecting and then dialed up another. Since it cost a lot of money to phone out of town, most people visited local boards.

When I entered the 1984 online scene, Austin had dozens of sites in operation, many in dorm rooms and just up for one semester. My pre-web Austin favorites included *Black Ice* and the sci-fi board, *Deep Thought*, along with the *Klingon Empire* that featured uncensored discussions, plus... the mysterious *Illuminati* run by the astonishing Steve Jackson.

I first heard about Steve Jackson via his smash hit role-playing board game: *Car Wars*. This game was released while board leader *Dungeons and Dragons* still had a significant cult following. His title was in the Austin tradition of evoking a smile. First published in 1980, *Car Wars* came in a Ziploc bag. The gaming industry voted it Best Science Fiction Board Game. Steve Jackson was planting seeds for the growth of the game creation business in Austin.

A decade later, Steve Jackson hosted the *Illuminati*. His BBS developed a worldwide following of hardcore gamers who communicated by relaying FidoNet data packets from one local hub to another. These role players were into sci-fi and sending cryptic messages back and forth. They drove the government snoops crazy.

The feds were mainly concerned with his universal sci-fi sourcebook, *GURPS Cyberpunk*, written by former *Legion of Doom* member Loyd Blankenship. Might this be a coded terrorist manual? Time for a raid!

On March 1st, 1990, the USSS swooped into the Texas capital to confiscate the suspicious *Illuminati* computers. It was one of the first raids of its kind and they grabbed 300 floppies, 5 hard drives, and 3 computers. The infamous BBS was offline until Steve Jackson pulled out of retirement his decade-old Apple II+. By the time his equipment was returned, the man had been driven to the edge of bankruptcy.

Soon after this raid, the gaming hero decided to file a lawsuit against America's version of the German Stasi. Years went by. Much to everyone's surprise, in 1993 he won!

The international gaming community applauded when the court fined the U. S. federal government. That spook raid had cost Steve Jackson a lot of business, but the publicity only added to the mystique of his games.

In the end, it was the fledgling San Francisco-based Electronic Frontier Foundation, with their noble purpose of protecting Internet liberty, who successfully prosecuted this outrageous assault on a small Austin BBS. John Perry Barlow, a lyricist for the Grateful Dead, was a co-founder.

6

Lord British

The quiet arrival of Richard Garriott, aka Lord British, in Austin, foreshadowed an international reputation. I recall seeing comments about his games on the Internet services called The Source and CompuServe. They were the first online platforms.

Science fiction icon Isaac Asimov in 1979 endorsed The Source by saying it was the birth of the Information Age: "It's not hardware. It's not software. But it can take your personal computer anywhere in the world."

You could subscribe for $100 and pay $2.75 an hour to log in for access.

Garriott's company was Origin Systems and in 1983 he opened its new headquarters in Austin. Origin was built around his successful text-based series called *Ultima*. They were role-playing games, such as Steve Jackson's *Car Wars*, but these were coded onto 5.25" floppy disks. They were interactive text-based games that ran on Apple II and Commodore 64 home computers. A new form of entertainment!

I was instantly a fan and for a few years the games *Ultima* and *Zork* replaced mystery novels in my life. During many a stoned late-night, their interactive scenarios responded to my actions with messages that passed my Turing Test. They seemingly came from a living person.

In the mid-eighties, Origin used *Car Wars* as a model for their video game, *Autoduel*, and by the end of the 1980s, a video game industry emerged in the Live Music Capital.

It came to bloom in 1992 when Electronic Arts bought the profitable Origin Systems. Their 1990 smash hit, *Wing Commander*, was the stuff of franchises and EA wanted it. Origin had employed artist Danny Garrett, who helped bring aboard fellow 'Dillo artists Bill Narum, Micael Priest, Jim Franklin, and Guy Juke, so EA had inherited the Armadillo Art Squad.

Creating a modern video game is a team-intensive production needing talented writers for script and code, artists, filmmakers, actors, and musicians. It is like making a movie.

Much to his credit, Richard Garriott stayed true to our local philosophy of Keep Austin Weird by maintaining his stance as Lord British. He dubbed his home Britannia Manor and opened it up each Halloween.

This imaginative gamester and amateur magician fit perfectly into a town noted for decades of hosting a pantheon of folks playing out eccentric character roles: Captain Armadillo, the Guacamole Queen, the Royal Hawaiian Prince, Catman, Scout Stormcloud, Rock 'n' Roll Randy, Artly Snuff, Bicycle Annie, Doc Neon, Roger & Roddy One Knite, Summerdog, the Texas Blondes, Mr. Biscuit, Bob Daddy-O Wade, Karry Awn, Blackie White, Crazy Carl Hickerson, Le Beast, Xalapeño Charlie, the Zig-Zag Man, the King of 6th Street, Casino, Matt the

Electrician, Handsome Joel, Niz, and thong-wearing, street corner cross-dresser Leslie Cochran. Upon Cochran's death, March 8 was officially designated annual Leslie Day in Austin.

Our weird city's musical heritage includes Ramon, Ramon & the Four Daddyo's, Lee Ann and the Bizarros, Rotel & the Hot Tomatoes, the Austin Lounge Lizards, and the Uranium Savages. Spamarama, honoring the canned meat, had its beginnings at Soap Creek Saloon in 1976 and turned into an annual event.

Not to mention the city's wildly celebrated birthday party for Eeyore. No, this big yearly party for the melancholy donkey from *Winnie the Pooh* wasn't started in 1963 by a crazed proto-hippie. It was the brainchild of a crazy UT professor.

Lord British was right at home in Austin.

7

Sheauxnough— It's The Austin Chronicle

It was 1981 and local bumper stickers proclaimed: "Remember the Armadillo." The little city of 350,000 people was buzzing over the success of Doug Hanners' first Austin Record Convention as digital CDs began arriving in shops to replace 12" vinyl albums.

Eddie Wilson had reopened Kenneth Threadgill's historic service station as a wonderful restaurant that saluted the birthplace of Austin's music scene. And it was the year a disastrous Memorial Day flood caused Shoal Creek to spill over its banks and onto Lamar Boulevard and into a three-years-old Whole Foods Market. The building was severely damaged. The owners didn't have flood insurance, but thanks to hardworking volunteers, their store was rebuilt.

Whoda guessed that thirty-six years later they would sell Whole Foods Markets to online retailer Amazon for $13.7 billion. The volunteers should be proud of their role in this accomplishment.

I was in Austin to discuss radio C-101 poster art with Micael Priest at Sheauxnough Studios, the arts collective he had co-founded with fellow artist Sam Yeates.

Micael and friends were on the second floor of an empty state laundry building that was easily identified by its 16-foot-tall smokestack. Half Price Books had space in that building and Austin's jazz label, Fable Records, was downstairs. Across the street from Sheauxnough was Schlotzsky's bakery. Both were names I could never spell.

Scout Stormcloud was leaving as I climbed the stairs and walked into a high-ceiling warehouse loft. The art collective's huge studio accommodated desks and large, adjustable-tilt drafting tables. I saw an overhead projector and copy camera. A very down home-scene, but professional.

Across the room, stood Bill Narum, head bent over his tilted artist's table where he was creating a delicate graphics layout. I watched him use a scalpel-like X-Acto knife to cut around an image and then after dipping a small brush into a jar of glue he lifted the cutout to its desired location to paste.

"Lookey here," Micael Priest said.

With theatrical aplomb, he pulled open a ceiling-to-floor black drape. Behind that curtain were even more office desks and tables along with telephones and typewriters.

"This is our brand new newspaper, *The Austin Chronicle*," he said with pride.

There stood Margaret Moser from *The Austin Sun* and Ramsey Wiggins from Armadillo World Headquarters. The un-air-conditioned *Chronicle* office was hot and this new enterprise owned a typesetter with a large camera that required a cool room. So the *Chronicle* gang hastily constructed an enclosed space for their equipment and installed a window air conditioner.

Everyone in the office was sweating, but at least the machine stayed cool.

Priest introduced me to *Chronicle* publisher Nick Barbaro and the editor, Louis Black. I wished them well in their new business. They had yet to publish their first issue. It was almost named *The Austin Eye.*

Four decades later, it's safe to say their tabloid has lived up to its name, and then some. Barbaro and Black not only gave Austin a priceless chronicle of its cultural arts, but these two men also greatly enhanced those arts.

As Micael Priest would say, "Mighty fine."

* * *

THE CHRONICLE TEAM'S first contribution to the city was the Austin Music Awards. *The Austin Sun* had tried something similar. This time it took.

The inaugural ceremony was staged at Club Foot. The club was operated by John Bird and remains my favorite concert venue of the '80s. Their bookings were eclectic in the Armadillo and Liberty Lunch tradition. And likewise, many of the Foot's shows are high-profile.

The multitiered hall could hold a thousand people, so its general seating offered excellent close-range views of the stage. Club Foot was far more intimate than the 'Dillo or Liberty Lunch. Can you imagine seeing REM, U2, or King Sunny Ade playing in such a small place?

Because of these diverse bookings, Club Foot used several poster artists, including my favorite '80's music artist, JAGMO. In the 1980s the Foot had commissioned the Art Maggots and others to produce that decade's best collection of live concert poster art.

I recall a 1984 ride into Austin from Manor Downs with Chesley Millikin to meet up with Stevie Ray Vaughan, who was performing and receiving a Music Award. Both guys were excited.

Margaret Moser had taken over production of the event and moved it into the much larger Austin Opera House still being managed by Tim O'Connor and owned by Willie Nelson. Stevie was genuinely proud of his hometown music award.

Rightly so.

Austin is a town chock full of top-notch guitar players. In time, the Austin Music Awards became a strengthening force of self-esteem for the local music community. I've been with award winners days later and seen how pleased they are by their honor. Sometimes, when the money's not there, the recognition and exposure make all the difference to the artist's confidence, and to their promo kit.

It was ultra-cool when in 2012 Moser, celebrating thirty years of Austin Music Awards, headlined her ceremony with two artists who were prominent at that first event in Club Foot. The old-timers were Joe Ely, who had won the first Musician of the Year citation... and Alejandro Escovedo, who, as part of the post-punk roots rock quartet, Rank and File, beat out Willie Nelson to be named Country Band of the Year. Huh?

At this 30th anniversary show, SXSW keynote speaker Bruce Springsteen was called up from the audience to jam on stage. I noted The Boss still wore a leather jacket, although it was more like a sport coat, and brown, not black. The affable musician had become a superstar's superstar, and he looked great.

8

This Business of Music

The '80s saw the beginnings of the Austin City Council's recognition of live nightclub music as an economic resource. It started with a survey taken by a UT student.

One hot afternoon I was on my way from Pecan Street Studio to the Alamo Hotel's step-down restaurant when I saw a small woman in knee-length khaki shorts crossing 6th Street. Phyllis Krantzman. We had met at the Armadillo where she frequented shows.

She waved. "Hey, Woody, I'm doing a survey of people around the music business for my master's degree. Can I interview you?"

The project suited Phyllis Krantzman perfectly. She was a true live music fan, one who appreciated the live music scene and saw its growth potential. Her completed report, "Impact of the Music Entertainment Industry on Austin," was the first economic study to place a cash value on the Austin live music scene.

It caught the attention of Ernie Gammage, a blues guitarist and a founder of the newly formed Texas Music Association. Mike Tolleson was president of the Austin chapter, as was Pleas McNeel for San Antonio. The idea of music as business was still new to the city, but many were now promoting it.

Randy McCall had been a dedicated booster of the local music economy since his Armadillo days and had become president of the Austin Federation of Musicians. Eddie Wilson of Threadgill's restaurant presented a tasty accolade to the beginnings of Austin's music scene. Clifford Antone's blues club was attracting national music press, and *Austin City Limits* was a favorite TV show on PBS.

It was in this cultural milieu that guitarist-songwriter Ernie Gammage presented young Krantzman's accredited research to David Lord, the man in charge of the tourism branch of the Greater Austin Chamber of Commerce. Lord recognized in her economic impact report the potential to boost Austin's economy as well as attract visitors.

People mainly visited the city to see the State Capitol and LBJ Library. Marketing the local music scene could broaden the city's appeal. Here was a clean industry that paid its own way.

Lord took the report to Chamber president, Lee Cooke. Cooke also saw the value in what Phyllis Krantzman had brought to the fore and he financed another music survey. The result, called the White Paper, demonstrated Austin was home to a stable and thriving music community. This indicated the potential for economic growth, including additional hotel business.

Lee Cooke was the first to direct the Austin Chamber to help develop that growth and to use the Austin Tourism Bureau to market live music. And by 1986 the Chamber and David Lord in its tourism department were promoting Austin's music scene to attract visitors and new businesses. Historically, it's appropriate that Cooke's five-year term as head of the CoC started with the rise of Stevie Ray Vaughan and concluded with the rise of South by Southwest.

9

Four Men + Four Months = SXSW

This wouldn't be Austin's first music conference nor was it the first time a local music festival for non-Austin bands had been suggested. In the mid-seventies, Mike Tolleson at Armadillo World Headquarters wanted to hold local music industry conferences.

The event he put together had the legal sounding mouthful name of the BMI Seminar on Performing Rights for Publishers and Songwriters. It was held in the Armadillo with about 50 music people attending. Meeting were panelists Roger Sovine and Frances Preston of BMI and local band managers, club owners, musicians Doug Sahm, Willie Nelson (with his wife Connie), drummer Paul English, Rusty Weir, and fiddler Alvin Crow.

Shortly after *The Austin Chronicle* was first published, the *SLUGGO!* magazine staff, along with the fem-punk band Chickadiesels, drove to San Francisco for West Fest. They came back inspired. Why not do an Austin festival for punk bands and new music? Progressive country and blues-rockers not invited.

Nick West, and Debra X-it, KUT deejay Neil X (first

to play the punk bands on Texas radio), and Richard Dorsett of Inner Sanctum Records made two *Chronicle* pitches. In true punk fashion, their meetings turned into shouting matches with the explosive Louis Black shouting the loudest. Nick Barbaro thought a festival had possibilities. Like the fabled meeting of the psychedelic tribes in the '60s, this could be a national gathering of the punks. But the idea died, or at least went into hibernation.

It was November of 1986 when former Standing Waves punk band manager and *Chronicle* employee Roland Swenson and Liberty Lunch booking agent Louis Jay Meyers met with Nick Barbaro and Louis Black. Earlier that year, Swenson and Meyers had been part of an effort with Chamber of Commerce president Lee Cooke to bring a sanctioned version of New York City's successful New Music Seminar to Austin.

The guys had participated in a group that set up a table at the Seminar to play cassettes of Austin's best musicians and hand out Chamber pamphlets. An ad was placed in *Billboard Magazine* touting Austin's musicians and using the phrase, "Live Music Capital of the World."

Thanks to Cooke, the city for the first time spent money to promote live music.

"Would the New Music Seminar promoters like to do an event in Austin?"

The answer was no.

Swenson and Meyers wanted to push on. With the Chamber's encouragement, they envisioned creating a national conference showcasing all kinds of musicians. The duo proposed changing their profitable Austin

Battle of the Bands into a music industry festival. Louis Black was skeptical but he went along with Barbaro's decision. They would co-found the South by Southwest music festival and conference. The four would form a corporation and put *Chronicle* resources behind their event. The Austin Music Awards show would kick it all off. Swenson, Meyers, Barbaro, and Black set their new event's date for March, during Spring Break, when the clubs would be empty.

In those days, Austin's college-aged nightclub customers departed en masse for Gulf Coast beaches or parties in Mexican border towns. The local club business was dead. Bands who got paid from a cover charge suffered most. Everyone was hoping that SXSW would bring some out-of-town customers and new groups to the ailing clubs. For only $10, music fans could buy a wristband to get them into all the showcase performances. Clubs needed the bar sales.

After four months of continuous hard work and countless meetings, the day had come and people were arriving. The four guys sprang into action. Their inaugural event was underway. No time to stop and rest.

But before they knew it, the last attendees were heading for the airport. Their conference was over. Much to everyone's surprise, the first SXSW had been a giant success. Bigger than anyone expected!

They had featured almost 200 bands and hosted 700 paid registrants. Wow.

Next year might even be larger... Besides, the speed limit would again be 65 mph, so musicians driving to Texas could travel long distances in less time. Lee Cooke at the Chamber was excited.

Six years after that inaugural event, Louis Meyers,

believing the festival had run its course, decided to cash out and leave the founding group. It was then SXSW expanded into a three-part conference by adding Film and Multimedia—later renamed, Interactive—to the Music festival.

By the turn of the century, their event was considered Austin tourism's most important conference. The 2011 event was held a quarter of a century after its founding. By then, your $10 local wristband cost $175. And to celebrate the anniversary, South by Southwest used 3,000 volunteers to showcase 1,500 bands and service 10,000 registrants.

This use of volunteers to produce commercial events has a long tradition in Austin that goes back to Willie's first Picnic. I suspect one of these days the IRS is going to want payroll taxes from the production companies even if their "volunteers" don't get paid in cash.

Roots? Have no doubt, the SXSW money tree grew from punk culture seeds.

10

ACTV to AMN

Ifirst realized my focus was shifting when, instead of joining Pleas McNeel and others to lobby for the creation of a San Antonio cable access center, my efforts went to Austin. In 1971 cable was the new kid on the media distribution block. Cable meant, instead of four TV channels, there would be dozens with a few held for public use.

I joined a visionary Austin group pledged to assure community access to cable TV's facilities. Mike Tolleson, Bill Narum, and Randy McCall were among these cohorts. In the spring of 1973, Tolleson, with a cadre of video activists and Narum carrying his videotape deck, climbed up Mt. Larson to the cable system's head end, a small unstaffed building where Austin's Capital Cable received and broadcast its network programs. Narum plugged in his deck and the group cablecast the first public access show in Texas. It was on channel 10.

Austin was to be second in the nation, after New York City, to have a cable access center for the public!

Randy McCall and I ended up on the first Austin Community Television board of directors. We liked to imagine the day when our new access channel would have its own production studio and portable video equipment to record musicians in the clubs.

Jump forward to 1994 when the nation's most visionary economic development project was approved: *a public cable channel dedicated to local music.*

Engineer Ronny Mack, music videographer Hank Sinatra, and veejay Tim Hamblin led the charge to establish The Austin Music Network cable TV channel. A prototype broadcast that year covered SXSW where the keynote speaker was Johnny Cash.

At that conference, the Network recorded a seminal event, which since has become punk rock lore. It happened at the 6th Street alt-rock club, Emo's, when the sixty-two-year-old Man in Black stepped up to its stage mic. Performing with only an acoustic guitar, he started with "Let the Train Blow the Whistle."

The packed crowd, mixed with punks, cowboys, and music executives, went nuts. They loved him! Like fellow highwayman Willie Nelson, whose career was reborn in front of hippies at the Armadillo World Headquarters, Johnny Cash almost overnight found himself respected by young punks and rock musicians. He'd been reborn at Emo's.

Johnny Cash named his first post-Emo's album *Unchained*, to reflect his awareness of this new audience. He selected Tom Petty's band, the Heartbreakers, to back his session at Sound City, the LA studio where Nirvana recorded. The singer won the Grammy for Best Country Album. The country star had returned to his roots. He went back to the 1950s when his music was rockabilly in the vein of Eddie Cochran and his co-artists at Sun Records: Carl Perkins, Jerry Lee Lewis, and Elvis Presley.

However, this star-studded Austin concert was not

the first important Central Texas event in the career of Johnny Cash. Forty years earlier at a roller skating rink in San Antonio, the young military airman fell hopelessly in love with a beautiful girl. He courted her on the River Walk and carved their initials in a bench. After their marriage in St. Ann's Catholic Church, the unknown musician was inspired to write a song for his new bride, "I Walk the Line."

Sun Records sold two million copies.

* * *

IN THE 1990S, establishment-Austin finally embraced live music as a cultural resource and tourism attractor. It was Community Access Television president and city IT genius Ronny Mack, who in 1988 introduced a slogan for a proposed city channel to serve the music community: "Television for the Live Music Capital of the World."

On their proposal's letterhead was the first City of Austin use of the "Live Music Capital" phrase. A great Texas brag!

It caught fire when Austin's mayor pro tem Max Nofziger, himself a musician and sporting a flamboyant mustache with shoulder-length hair, stepped up to champion the cause. A music commission was formed to advise the city council on establishing this unprecedented TV channel.

Not long after, Mayor Lee Cooke pushed to make the inspired brag the official city slogan. As a former head of the Chamber of Commerce, he understood its value to increase tourism, remembering it was his 1986 *Billboard Magazine* ad that first used the slogan. It came to be that on August 29, 1991, the City Council officially proclaimed Austin, Texas: "Live Music Capital of the World."

Wow.

Now the city *had* to live up to it.

To help kick off this new title and demonstrate its appropriateness, KUT deejay Larry Monroe pledged to see a different live music performance every night for one whole year. And he did it!

By the year 2000, the City Council had outsourced the Austin Music Network project to a contractor, Rick Melkier. He soon ran out of capital and was losing his downtown studio. The man wasn't alone; the dot-com boom was going bust and several high tech dreams were financially collapsing in Austin.

In the middle of the night, an idea came to me. I had convinced Time Warner Cable to put a high-band fiber optic connection into Threadgill's on North Lamar. It was a fiber connection same as the Erwin Center's and would let the restaurant produce live cablecasts from its stage. This meant the wayward Network could use Threadgill's for its real-time live programming.

I phoned the embattled manager, who said, "I'll move the *whole channel* to Threadgill's."

Eddie Wilson agreed.

AMN, the five-year-old music network, was right at home with the older generation of diners at Threadgill's. You might find City Council members Robert Barnstone and Daryl Slusher or *American-Statesman* writers Brad Buchholtz and John Kelso in the same room as KXAN-TV commentator Jim Swift and web-famous movie pundit Harry Knowles or country piano master Earl Poole Ball.

Sadly, it wasn't long before the notorious Y2K dot-com business implosion took Rick Melkier's cable TV venture all the way down. I suggested the nonprofit Kenneth Threadgill Music Project might help keep the dilapidated channel alive.

Eddie made an offer to City Council members who, seeing a disaster on the horizon, awarded the Austin Music Network contract to our little charity designed to give needy kids music lessons. I agreed to function as volunteer hands-on consultant and temporary network manager. It was a total wreck, old equipment falling apart, no cameras, the staff impoverished and picking at each other, total demoralization.

I remembered the dreams of decades ago at the beginnings of Austin Community Television and noted many of those dreams had blossomed in the 1990s. Both Richard Linklater and Robert Rodriguez had used ACTV to produce their first movies; political commentator Alex Jones used it to start his international alt-news network. Videographers Hank Sinatra and Dave Pruett rigorously documented the local music scene; both men are Austin music culture heroes and their archives are priceless treasures. Jerry Avila produced *Primetime Tejano*, and the dream of a local music channel had become a reality with the birth of AMN.

Question:

What are the odds that a TV channel for Austin music would end up at the birthplace of the modern music scene—now owned by a founder of Armadillo World Headquarters?

I sensed the approving smile of St. Cecilia.

11

Video in the Lomax Spirit

Six months went by quickly. Seasons changed. There were dewberries, baby birds chirping in budding oaks, and new calves in the fields near my rural home outside Austin. But you wouldn't know it from inside an old construction site trailer with a hole in its roof set at the rear of a busy parking lot.

Eddie said, "Woody, if you don't go on the payroll and manage this project, I'm not going to do this either. We'll give it back to the city."

I was doing this as a goodwill community project and hadn't asked for a penny. I was filling in until an experienced manager could be found. I really didn't want to be paid. "Okay. I want $75,000 a year to build the network."

"You got it."

I dedicated my AMN stay to my childhood heroes John Lomax and his son, Alan, with a nod to the broadcasts and live music club recordings of Bill and Bill, Jr., Josey. In the 1930s the Lomax men made the first systematic field recordings of American folk musicians by loading a 300-pound disc recorder in their car trunk. Both had attended UT Austin and maintained ties with friends such as historian and folklorist J. Frank Dobie.

Thus dedicated to field recording, I set out to document the spirit of live music in Austin and festivals at the turn of the century. I would use a variety of Austin filmmakers using their own equipment as producer-directors.

This would be my third and last immersion in Austin's live music scene. I wanted to capture the clubs as well as musicians. My wish list for nightclub tapings included: the Backroom, Hole in the Wall, Emo's on 6th, Threadgill's World Headquarters, Art's Rib House, Ego's, Red Eyed Fly, Beerland, Speakeasy, Headhunters, The Continental Club, Texacalli Grille, Flamingo Cantena, Momo's, the Saxon Pub, and the short-lived Hard Rock Cafe.

The musicians I wanted: Britt Daniel and Spoon, And You Will Know Us by the Trail of Dead, Eliza Gilkyson, Bobby Doyle, Groupo Fantasma, Texana Dames, Ruben Ramos, Stephen Bruton, Patrice Pike, Manuel "Cowboy" Donley, Blue October, Push Monkey, W. C. Clark, and the Bells of Joy.

In 2002 when Lewis Black of *The Chronicle* and Evan Smith held the first Texas Film Hall of Fame Awards show, I was excited. Good move.

I drove to an old Mueller airplane hangar used by filmmakers and now called Austin Studios. Parking lot was full, big turnout. Ann Richards gave a fine speech, Asleep at the Wheel performed, and I dreamed of a time when there would be an awards show that included music videos. That's the category where the groundbreaking desktop cinematography was happening.

When my time at the channel was up, our AMN producers had recorded three hundred musicians performing in dozens of venues. We sent hundreds of hours of field recordings to the Austin History Center, far more than all other AMN staffs combined. Three of the best captures came from iconic Antone's, by then on West 5th. I got Double Trouble, Bob Schneider, and keyboard artist Marcia Ball's spectacular invention, the Pianorama, where half a dozen pianos allowed super-pianists Floyd Domino, Riley Osborne, Johnny Nicholas, and others to jump in and out of her nonstop jam.

At the Mercury we caught the 2002 Roky Erickson birthday party and Spoon doing "Starry Eyes." Then we scored a surprise performance by The Legends: Freddie Martinez (of Freddie Records in Corpus Christi), Augustin Ramirez, Carlos Guzman, and... Sunny Ozuna. We recorded Bobby Doyle singing and tickling the ivories of the glass-top piano bar in the historic Driskill Hotel. At the Continental, I videoed Raúl Salinas, the "cockroach poet," backed by an L.A. jazz band.

After the 9/11 terror attacks in 2001, I sent a team into Lucy's Retired Surfer Bar (Dick Dale often played there) where they recorded nonstop bands from 2 p.m. to 2 a.m. to raise money for the survivors. It was a benefit called United We Jam.

And, thank the fates, under a blue moon on Halloween we shot Flametrick Subs at the Black Cat before it burned down. And then we recorded a classical guitar-led trio in the Texas Governor's Mansion, before an arsonist set it on fire.

AMN even helped champion a future star in seventeen-year-old Gary Clark, Jr. I wanted to shoot inside the musically historic Victory Grill, one of the founding Eastside blues clubs. A pickup band of old pros calling themselves the Eastside Kings had caused positive talk among local musicians. And there was this seventeen-year-old kid who was supposed to be pretty good.

I sent a video team to the Grill. I always made it a point to attend these shoots. That night I saw a young guitarist laying down licks like he was Jimmie Vaughan. Gary Clark didn't sing or use electronic feedback, just tasteful straight-ahead blues. He didn't yet call himself Jr.

I asked the video editor to break out his performances and we put them in high rotation on the Network. Soon viewers were asking where to see him, and music writers got interested. During a City Council break, Mayor Kirk Watson asked me about the Gary Clark video. Then one day I saw he was booked at Antone's.

Once again the years rolled by and suddenly it was 2012 and Gary Clark Jr.'s Warner Bros. album, *Black and Blu,* was #6 on the charts, 2015 saw *The Story of Sunny Boy Slim* at at #8, and in 2019 he scored #6 with *This Land.* Clark Jr. became a touring star, and, like Stevie Ray Vaughan, the guitarist turned himself into a three-name hat act. This grownup Victory Grill kid is music history still in the making.

* * *

FILMMAKER CLAUDE MATHEWS, who donated an Ikegami video camera to get our control room veejays on the tube—and also produced the excellent Kenneth Threadgill documentary, *Singin' the Yodeling Blues*—turned me on to Tom Herod. As a young film student, Herod produced a short documentary, *An Evening At*

Threadgill's. During the fall of 1971, along with his UT instructor, Richard Kooris, he shot inside Threadgill's using 16-millimeter color film.

This early Threadgill's performance footage is historically the oldest visual recording of the Austin live music scene. Bill Neely picks and sings a rousing version of "Alabama Jubilee" with Sweet Mary Egan from Greezy Wheels playing fiddle, while Kenneth Threadgill, wearing his white bartender apron, dances a jig. The mix of ages and lifestyles in the fun-loving, beer-drinking, cigarette-smoking audience is priceless. Herod reported that several UT professors cleared out the instant they saw his camera.

Mathews said he nearly fainted when he found that students in UT film school were using Tom Herod's historic film to test projectors! Running the rare 25-year-old celluloid strip back and forth. Eddie Wilson, Claude Mathews, and I started a film restoration process funded by a grant from Threadgill's restaurant.

Tom Herod now has both a fully repaired 16mm film master and a digitized high-band beta tape copy. *An Evening At Threadgill's* is archived in the Austin History Center. His film is one bookend of the two documentaries that visually portray Austin's musical ascendance in 1970s. The other was produced by Richard Gaylord and Mark Hanna for KTBC TV channel 7. It was made during Hank Alrich's grand closing of Armadillo on New Year's Eve 1980.

For the big finale the USA Network flew in to create a Feature Presentation for their Night Flight program and called it *Last Dance at the 'Dillo*. Comander Cody and the Lost Planet Airmen, Maria Muldaur, Asleep at the Wheel, and Kenneth Threadgill were introduced one last time by Jim Franklin aka Captain Armadillo, also by hosts Fletcher Clark and Turk Pipkin. Charlie Daniels, Jerry Jeff Walker, Joe Ely and Steve Fromholz arrived to salute the doomed icon. Micael Priest drew the last poster.

Richard Gaylord recognized the importance of the event and came to focus his camera on everyone's still fresh memories and record a classic keepsake: *The Rise and Fall of the Armadillo World Headquarters.* It too is preserved in the Austin History Center.

* * *

LIKE ALL THE Austin Music Network managers, I left under fire. Michael Corcoran, aka Corky, in his *Statesman* column and Sammy Allred with Bob Cole on KVET 98.1-FM said I was making too much money. Ken Leak in *The Austin Chronicle* claimed I had embezzled $85,000. The gossip list of complaints ranged from selling dope to harassing the women and being incompetent and hard to work with. It got crazier by the day.

I had managed to get AMN on the San Marcos and San Antonio cable systems, and I started a 24/7 live web stream and secured a weekly two-hour show on an American music satellite channel, but it was time for the staff to fly the Network without me. The Austin Music Commission, headed by Kevin Conner, took over and he lasted two months. Lewis Myers then took command and made it a year. In the end, he was falsely charged with theft of music videos. They said he was selling them in Europe.

Within 18 months, everything I had done was undone or lost by the new managers. The new building, its trained staff with decent wages and health insurance, the one-of-a-kind, remote video package designed for small clubs, and the new custom-built studio with its sound stage: gone.

Once again the channel was leased out to become a commercial venture; they funded a new studio and changed its name to ME TV. After a few years, it failed.

Austin musicians lost a great and unique resource.

12

A Slacker Meets a Mariachi

It took Richard Linklater to kick it over the top for the Austin filmmakers, as Willie had for the musicians. Then Robert Rodriguez stepped in to solidify Austin's place in the film community, as Stevie Ray had for the music industry.

Linklater's inaugural film was a shaky-cam-style, seven-minute documentary: *Woodshock*. The nation's first all-punk festival.

The event was launched inside the city limits, but in 1983 moved to Dripping Springs and the notorious Hurlbut Ranch! Yes, the same ranch that had catapulted outlaw country music and Willie Nelson into the national spotlight.

The site hosted four consecutive years of the Woodshock Music Festival. These promoters set their stage closer to the creek with shade trees and swimming nearby. Thousands of punks would show up for the all-night revelries. Austin's top alt bands, from the Hickoids to Son of Sam to Glass Eye and the Reivers, played these concerts.

In 1985, Richard Linklater and his cinematographer

buddy, Lee Daniel, captured its Texas-style punk ambiance on Super 8 film in homemade movie style. That same year, Linklater founded the Austin Film Society. In 1991 Linklater and Daniel created the art film, *Slacker*. It altered everything. The feature was nominated for the Grand Jury Prize-Dramatic at the prestigious Sundance Film festival.

Here was a hit movie, locally written and made by an Austin crew that embedded local musicians such as the Butthole Surfers, Poi Dog Pondering, Glass Eye and Daniel Johnston in the production. *Slacker* cost its investors just $23,000 to produce; for comparison, Tobe Hooper's 1969 indie, *Eggshells*, had twice that budget.

But Linklater delivered a box-office gross of more than $1.2 million. From St. Martin's Press came *Slacker* the book with Linklater's script and notes. And nationwide sales of the *Slacker* movie poster followed!

To be sure, other great moments in Austin filmmaking had occurred before. But what made *Slacker* so different was its star was Austin. Though, definitely not the slick marketing image the Chamber of Commerce or Tourism Bureau promoted.

Much was shot in the Les Amis Cafe neighborhood off The Drag. It could have been set in the '60s at the Ghetto or the Corn Palaces of the '70s. These keep-Austin-weird slackers that cinematographer Lee Daniel filmed are driven by superior intellects, no matter how misguided. Its focus on Austin's hip subculture attitude resulted in a general head twist and community-wide readjustment of self-image.

National media feedback altered the public culture in the capital city, as once had *The Gay Place* and *Austin City Limits*. Like those old novels about Greenwich

Village bohos in the pre-beatnik '50s, *Slacker* convinced artists, writers, filmmakers, and techies: Austin is the creative place to live.

The local film community's other tipping-point came from Robert Rodriguez. His *El Mariachi* won the 1992 Audience Award at Sundance. The movie was Spanish-language and had been made for $7,000. It was a violent film with English subtitles, and on my first viewing it somehow reminded me of Jodorowsky's *El Topo*. Columbia put up two hundred thousand to do a reshoot and released the English version to great success. It was such a success that it led to a *Mexico Trilogy*.

Four years later, a book by Robert Rodriguez, *Rebel without a Crew: Or How a 23-Year-Old Filmmaker with $7000 Became a Hollywood Player*, was published. And in 2012, *El Mariachi* was selected for preservation in the National Film Registry to be housed alongside major studios classics such as *2001: A Space Odyssey* and *Forrest Gump*. In the next year, the NFR added *Slacker* to the prestigious list.

Rodriguez became famous for his action films while Linklater became a renowned auteur.

At last, Austin had emerged as moviemaking's Third Coast, thanks to a slacker and a mariachi.

MANOR DOWNS AND STEVIE RAY VAUGHAN

History remembers only the brilliant failures and the brilliant successes.

Randolph S. Bourne

1

Together Again

By the end of December 1976, I was still licking the wounds from my failed attempt to launch the Armadillo brand and spirit nationally. Lee Baby Simms had taken a high-salary deejay gig in Cleveland. He was now recognized as the nation's most idiosyncratic Top 40 radio personality. Everywhere he went, the man pulled top ratings, be it San Antonio or Los Angeles.

Lee phoned. Would I ride north with him? There was no reason not to leave town, so unannounced to anyone, I just up and split.

Our road trip in his new Buick Riviera turned into a Kerouac-style Hunter S. Thompson adventure. The two of us overimbibed in controlled substances as we laughed and hooted our way across the U.S.A. And since Lee Baby's new Riv had a great sound system, over and over again we played a cassette of Stevie Wonder's *Songs in Key of Life.*

New Year's Eve found us in a rowboat adrift on an underground lake in a Kentucky cavern and firing a midnight shotgun blast. We stopped to cut hickory walking sticks in Tennessee and plowed through snowdrifts on the Appalachian highways. Cleveland welcomed us with a roaring blizzard as we checked into a large hotel suite provided by the Lee Baby's new employer.

Next morning, waiting for room service breakfast, the phone rings and Lee answers. "Woody, it's for you."

"Me? But no one knows I'm here and I'm not registered..."

Bill Seale had left a callback number in Corpus Christi. I had met Seale three years before when he was hanging out backstage at the Armadillo with his friend, Texas oilman Bruce B. Baxter, III. It was the Jerry Garcia and Merl Saunders concert.

The guys were friends with Garcia and his road manager. Bruce was Frances Carr's older brother and she, having organized past Dead tours, was there with her partner, Sam Cutler. The couple operated a horse track called Manor Downs.

It was a few days before Christmas 1974 and the mood was high. I still recall Doug Sahm smoking a delicious-smelling joint with Garcia and sax master Martin Fierro.

Five months later, I again saw Seale with Bruce at the 'Dillo for Garcia; this time his band was Legion of Mary. But how could Bill Seale, or anyone, know I was in Cleveland in this hotel? Many times over the years I asked how he knew. The man would just grin.

When I returned his call, Seale explained Bruce had turned thirty-five and was expected to move back home from Marin County and manage his oil business. It was the end of his walkabout. He could no longer wander the country as an eccentric playboy and hang with the Hells Angels, who had dubbed him Loose Bruce.

To gain respect from the conservative business community and have cultural influence in his hometown, and especially to hear the Grateful Dead on the radio, he bought a radio station, KNCN 101.3-FM. He signed on playing "Truckin' ", a song recognized decades later by the Library of Congress as a national treasure. Family accountants and lawyers thought this was a horrible investment, mostly because it wasn't their idea.

Seale told me outside advice was needed. They would pay for a visit and analysis.

"Lee, I don't want to do radio again. I've left that behind."

"Woody-row. Get your ass back to Texas and help these guys."

2

Loose Bruce and
the English Professor

Early the next morning I grabbed a flight out of Cleveland that connected into Corpus Christi. Bill Seale had silver-white hair, and a presented a broad smile. He was a former English professor.

Loose Bruce was a smaller man with dark hair, tortoiseshell glasses, a well-trimmed beard, and wearing a navy blazer. I couldn't help notice he carried a wooden cane with a brass skull handle. Both men wore skull rings with ruby eyes.

These guys were unlike any other station operators I'd met. Though I was nervous about them at first, they quickly put me at ease and in time became my dear friends. To keep me in Corpus for extended stays, Bruce and Bill supplied me with a car and a furnished apartment, complete with an attractive live-in housekeeper.

I named their station C-101. The spoken word "C" had additional meanings in this Spanish-named town on the Texas coast; it stood for Corpus Christi, the sea, see, and *sí*.

Next, I created their logo, a seashell with antenna. Then drove my Saab Turbo to Austin to have Micael Priest oversee its art design and production. Thirty years later the logo was still in use. Besides window stickers, I wanted a poster showing a blonde mermaid holding to her ear a lightning whelk shell with a long silver antenna.

Bruce was newly married to a photogenic San Francisco model named Tonya. She suggested our C-shell be the official Texas State Shell, a lightning whelk. It would reference the Grateful Dead's emblematic lightning bolt.

I told Micael Priest that Sam Yeates was my artist of choice. The man's beautifully rendered women had graced music posters for the Armadillo, quality equal to the famous Vargas girls. Priest grinned and nodded, "Mighty fine."

Sam Yeates painted one of the finest mermaids the world has seen. We turned his art into a giant display-sized billboard, placed where the main highway entered the city to dead-end at the bay. You couldn't miss seeing it. Since the lovely mermaid was a mythical creature, we hadn't bothered covering her breasts.

Wrong! Police said, "No way, boys."

So we had to comply by repainting the mermaid's long blonde hair to blow across her nipples.

Popular Austin musicians regularly performed in Corpus. Willie Nelson did a show and the next day Bruce, Seale, and I ended up in his bus. He played a rough mix of his next album, *Stardust*, and right away, I sensed platinum. These were not outlaw country songs; they were mostly pop standards pre-1950, like "Blue Skies" and "Georgia on my Mind."

Radio programming genius Buzz Bennett asked me to write an article on radio formatting to be published in a book sent to leading U.S.A. hit-music program directors. I figured I could help Willie by writing about him instead of my views on programming. The book would come out a month before his album release, which would make Joe Mansfield, recently promoted to VP of marketing at Columbia in New York, very happy.

I intended to present Willie as an essential act-to-watch for a Top 10 hit. To my surprise, the man was reluctant. I got the impression he didn't understand I was about to do him a big favor and he thought he was doing me a favor. Not so. These heavyweight national programmers couldn't have cared less about a country-western singer named Willie Nelson.

However, I pressed him and thus we met at the Villa Capri Motel in Austin for the interview and soon my story about Willie's "modern sounds in country western music" was in the hands of top radio people for cities large and small. In 1978, the *Stardust* LP went platinum; in 2002 it was awarded quintuple-platinum! Willie Nelson's biggest hit. It stayed on the charts 551 weeks.

* * *

ONE SUMMER, C-101 erected a stage on Mustang Island and produced a concert featuring Marcia Ball and Augie Meyers. Its success inspired Tonya Baxter and she wanted C-101 to sponsor a night of entertainment at the city's inaugural Bay Shore Festival. She thought

Doug Sahm would be perfect.

Doug playing Corpus Christi? No way.

Twelve years before, Doug had left Texas because of his pot bust in Corpus. It would take mucho coaxing to lure the musical genius from the safety of Austin.

But somehow Bruce and Seale did it. Doug Saldaña would return to Corpus Christi! C-101 quickly spread the word that Sir Douglas would be on the outdoor stage at the first Bay Shore Festival.

Night of the show, by 10 p.m. a huge crowd had gathered. When the band took the stage, from out of the audience came a unified shout, "Welcome back, Sir Douglas!"

The singer waved his black Stetson. High on Humboldt County's finest, and his own personal adrenaline, Doug moved his fans through a high-energy set with two long encores before officials flashed the lights. He left the stage with the crowd shouting for more.

Thanks to Doug Sahm, C-101 was now ingrained in the C-city's arts culture.

3

For Sale: Manor Downs

I met Bruce's sister, Frances Carr, in the fall of '73 when she and her partner, Sam Cutler, moved to Austin. Eddie Wilson offered his guest room while they searched for a local residence. We became acquainted while sitting around the dining room table.

Frances Carr, age twenty-three, was a beautiful woman with long, dark-blonde hair. Sam was about thirty, wore a mustache, and fronted himself with a strong British accent. The couple wasn't sure what they wanted to do in Austin.

Back in California, they had been business partners in a company called Out of Town Tours. Exclusive agents for the Grateful Dead, they also handled tours for New Riders of the Purple Sage, Rowan Brothers, Doug Sahm, Mike Bloomfield, Sons of Champlin, and Ramblin' Jack Elliot.

Frances was browsing *The Austin American-Statesman* classified ads for a house when she spotted a horse track. Manor Downs. In total disrepair and now used for dirt bikes, it sat outside the city limits near the little impoverished town of Manor, population, 700.

"Hmm," she said. "Having a horse track could be fun, and profitable."

The couple drove out to see… liked what they saw and decided to open a racetrack. To manage their start-up, they moved into a modest wooden home on-site. Sam would supervise the construction of an events center, designed to look like a county fairground.

Manor Downs had lots of open space, not just for the horse track and long rows of horse stalls, but also for a rodeo arena and a large outdoor concert facility. Big parking field.

Their plan: generate enough income from ancillary events to finance American Quarter Horse races until Texas allowed pari-mutuel wagering. They were betting the legalization of track gambling would happen within the next few years. Turned out to be thirteen years.

Not long after the couple moved into their new home, local farm and ranch folks noticed strange comings and goings at odd hours. People such as Doug Sahm, Gary P. Nunn, Micael Priest, Bill Narum, Ken Featherston, Big Rikke, Peter "Craze" Sheridan, Robert Ellsworth of the Ellsworth Air Force Base family, Richard King IV, Dr. John Luker, Jimmy Borglum, descendant of Gutzon Borglum who sculpted Mt. Rushmore, and George and Jimmy Farenthold, whose mom was running for governor.

And that's not to mention the party-loving staffs of Armadillo World Headquarters and Soap Creek Saloon, who'd drive to Manor from Austin for the Downs' BBQ and hospitality.

Incredible as it seems to me now, for exercise in

1974, I would pull my hair back to a ponytail and pedal my 10-speed bicycle from the Armadillo to I-35's access road and then onto Highway 290 East and the eight-mile stretch leading to Manor Downs. That route today would be suicide. Much of it is an 85-mph toll road.

Back then, all of us did our best to be down-home polite with the Manor locals. Sam Cutler trimmed his mustache, cut his long hair, and switched to wearing a western hat and a rodeo belt buckle with cowboy boots.

Even the Hells Angels took off their colors. Nice try.

Just the arrival of this eclectic counterculture parade was enough to alter daily conversations. In the Café 290, I overheard, "Well, least those weirdo newcomers are spendin' money and hirin' people."

4

From Altamont Speedway to Manor Downs Horse Track

Sam Cutler was notorious in the rock 'n' roll business. He was road-managing the Rolling Stones when the band played their disastrous free gig at the Altamont Speedway.

In early December of 1969, Cutler had helped organize the free event that featured the cream of the Bay Area bands, including the Jefferson Airplane; Crosby, Stills, Nash & Young; Santana; and the Grateful Dead. The Altamont Free Concert promoted by KFRC 610-AM should have been a most glorious day for those 300,000 people who came in the spirit of peace, love, dope, and music.

Instead, the megaconcert became the antithesis of Woodstock. It signaled the official end for the Summer of Love that was birthed two years before at Monterey Pop.

It was a glorious day for a concert. The crowd was much larger than anticipated and extra help was needed. The Hells Angels came to party at Altamont, not to work backstage security. However, when asked to do so, they did. Drunken or not, the guys would rise to the occasion.

No doubt, they were heavy-handed. Fights broke out. While the band was on stage, a Hells Angel punched out Marty Balin of the Jefferson Airplane. The Grateful Dead refused to play.

The disaster started as the Rolling Stones performed "Sympathy for the Devil." Mick Jagger was singing its dark lyrics and a black man in the crowd felt his gun. As the band segued into "Under My Thumb," the man drew his pistol and charged the stage. A Hells Angel grabbed him and stabbed him to death.

Can life get more symbolic than that?

They called it murder.

The guy had pulled a gun, but the press didn't mention this small detail. Fortunately, someone filmed the killing. It shows the man was going to shoot Jagger!

To have the Hells Angels providing security at the concert was not the bad idea it may now seem. After all, they often did it for the Grateful Dead, and just a few months before in central London, the HAs had been in charge of security at the smooth-running Hyde Park Free Concert that played to over a quarter-million people. At that event, Sam Cutler was the stage manager and, after seeing his organizational abilities, Jagger decided this was the man to road-manage the Rolling Stones' U.S.A. tour.

After the San Francisco debacle, Cutler and the Hells Angels took all the heat in the press for the brutal killing and near-riot. Not reported was that Sam Cutler had opposed the last-minute decision to move the concert from Magic Mountain to Altamont. The Grateful Dead's manager, Rock Scully, had chosen the site from a helicopter flyover.

Cutler had pointed out the speedway's flaws, that it was too flat and its stage too low, that people in the back would push forward, trying to see the bands. It was precisely what happened.

The Rolling Stones' free concert had been ruined and the British rock stars left town without Sam Cutler. He stayed behind to co-manage the Grateful Dead and did it long enough to get the musicians into a studio and record their classics, *Workingman's Dead* and *American Beauty Rose*. Those two albums relaunched the band's career.

Cutler meanwhile found a business partner in Frances Carr and left the management job. They became the Dead's touring company, Out of Town Tours, with its slogan, "Here Today, Gone Tomorrow."

He and Frances coordinated the 1972 European tour, which led to the band's triple record live album that went double-platinum, *Europe '72*. It was the band's last circuit with co-founder Pigpen, who died a year later, age twenty-seven.

* * *

BILL SEALE maintained that Sam Cutler wholly redeemed himself from the Stone's Altamont tragedy at when the Grateful Dead played another speedway. It was the humongous 1973 Summer Jam at Watkins Glen.

"They had a thousand portable toilets and several thousand one-gallon water jugs from the National Guard. When people arrived, a great wall of boxes filled with these jugs greeted them and everyone knew things were in good hands."

Seale also used to say, with a twinkle in his eye, "If the Dead only had a singer, they would be famous."

Optimistic promoters had printed 150,000 tickets for the day at Watkins Glen Grand Prix Raceway and were holding their breath. They hired only three bands to perform: The Allman Brothers, The Band, and The Grateful Dead.

Sound checks started while the crowd was still arriving. They reached back to the horizon. Day-of-show estimates claimed over 600,000 people! It broke the Woodstock record as the nation's biggest outdoor concert and by the end of the century still held the record for most tickets sold. The bands were great and the outdoor sound perfect. Bill Graham, who staged the event, had contributed 12 ultra-high-powered amplifiers so that even if all that vast audience could see was a tiny stage, they still could hear the music.

The Grateful Dead's five-hour sound check warmed up this enormous party. It was the largest concert ever and, thanks to rain, the world's biggest mosh pit.

5

Friends of the Dead in Texas

Of the five Grateful Dead concerts at Manor Downs, my favorite was the Fourth of July in 1981. There had been an agonizing meeting about the price of tickets; dare we charge all of $10.00?

Chesley proclaimed the high price disgraceful. But it was done.

The weather could not have been better, as the first of 14,000 fans arrived to celebrate their independence. As usual at the vanguard were the Deadheads, coming days early in their colorfully painted VW vans, VW Beetles, 30-year-old pickup trucks, plus a few who traveled by thumb.

The hip community raised colorful flags and pitched camping tents in the spacious fields adjacent to the racetrack. I thought it was highly appropriate that, upon entering the narrow bumpy asphalt road directing visitors to the horse track, concertgoers were greeted by an official Travis County sign: Dead End.

Bob Weir, Phil Lesh, Bill Kreutzmann, Mickey Hart, and keyboard player Brent Mydland arrived a day early and spent time hanging out with Frances and Chesley. Some of the guys stayed overnight in guest homes at the Downs. Jerry Garcia wouldn't be in Austin until the morning of the show and then would take a chopper from the hotel to the gig. The musicians were relaxed and in a good mood from having a day off after their last show in Houston. The day after the Downs concert, the band would be playing in Oklahoma City.

By late afternoon on day-of-show, SH 290 East traffic was backed up five miles from the Manor stoplight towards Austin. I could monitor its pitifully slow progress from the racetrack's video tower.

The Grateful Dead patiently waited off stage until the last of their fans' cars finally snaked from the highway into the parking fields. By then the sun was sinking below the horizon. Firecrackers popped and balloons were set adrift as beautiful girls whirled about in brightly colored silks. Tables were set up in front of VW vans to sell everything from stickers and T-shirts to roach clips and mushrooms.

The mixed sweet and heavy aromas of marijuana with patchouli oil and sandalwood incense laced the air while concert aficionados in the know dropped acid. The track infield was filling nicely. No hassles. No patting down or checking for camera or audio recorder; the Dead allowed taping and the Deadheads traded event tapes: "Hey, I'll trade you Red Rocks for Alpine Valley."

Unannounced, and almost unnoticed, the band walked onto the stage and plugged in. Fans perked up at the sound of Jerry tuning his guitar, just picking and noodling... his strings rippling lightly in the quiet field and fading twilight. Slowly the melody for "Jack Straw" became recognizable and loud cheers arose from the crowd.

Their concert was underway.

The Dead's second set was dreamlike. The band came back to the stage from their half-time break at Frances' home. The big Texas sky had turned deep black velvet, holding more bright stars than a city resident can fathom.

The band started their set with "Feel Like a Stranger," and in the audience, folks on LSD were starting to peak. People twirled and spun with arms held high. A few more songs poured from their one-of-a-kind wall of sound speaker system. Then, during "Playing in the Band," a jam began and their music slid from a heptatonic to an octatonic scale; from there the sounds dissolved into waving tones and syncopated percussions accented by the tinkling of triangles and the soft rushing of cymbals. The crowd knew the Dead were sauntering into their answer to a traditional drum solo with a performance known as "Drums."

Kreutzmann and Hart methodically set about working their percussive magic. What the crowd did not know was that Frances had set up a first-class fireworks display.

As the two drummers worked out and played off each other, rockets began streaming into the sky and bursting into kaleidoscopic fountains leaving behind a twinkling veil of neon sparkles. Kreutzmmann and Hart had a perfect view of the stunning aerial display and synchronized their beats to incorporate the explosive bursts and pops into their drumming.

The audience was wholly thrilled and the large cadre of LSD trippers melted into total ecstasy when the heavens themselves sent a bright green shooting star arcing across the Milky Way.

The drums with fireworks performance impercep-tibly morphed into a spacy version of "Space," extending the surprise mini-event to an amazing fifteen minutes. As the last few rockets burst and the night sky went black again, the mind-warping notes from Jerry's guitar morphed into a sparkling momentum as he tastefully lead the Grateful Dead into an extended version of "Not Fade Away."

Perfect!

They closed their performance with "One More Saturday Night."

The audience trailed out of the center of the race-track to hunt for their cars parked in the unlighted grassy fields and one by one they mooed.

"Moo!"

Imagine if you will, thousands of shadows faintly lit by starlight... a moving herd of mooing Deadheads. What fun.

6

The Wild Irishman

Five years after Frances and Sam Cutler arrived in Austin, they announced their breakup. Cutler was coming to see Bruce and Seale in Corpus and say goodbye.

We all liked Sam. When he arrived in Bruce's office, his usual boistrious exuberance had been muted. I volunteered the guest room in my apartment.

Over the next few days, he described his video plans for Manor Downs, how he laid it out for camera shots and production trucks. For Sam's goodbye weekend, Baxter and Seale hosted an open-ended "anything goes" party that lasted well into Monday.

Late afternoon, Sam Cutler borrowed a friend's Mercedes and waved as he rode into the sunset.

* * *

CHESLEY MILLIKAN phoned Bruce at his office. "Hey," he said, with his Irish brogue, "I may be coming your way. Frances wants me to be her managing director for Manor Downs." He giggled. "Never thought I'd be a Texan."

The man had been a partner in Out of Town Tours

with Sam and Frances.

"You'll look good in cowboy boots, Chesley," said Bill Seale.

"Yes, yes. Frances and I are working something out. I'll run Manor Downs for her, and she has agreed to start an artist management company with me."

After Chesley settled in at the Downs, he motored south to check out the Corpus scene. He stayed in my spare bedroom and late nights I would listen to Chesley's enthusiastic blabbering about Manor Downs becoming a state-of-the-art quarter horse training facility. His priority was to build the track's reputation among the equestrians.

He was also looking for a musician to manage. I told him I liked Automatic in Houston and Rudi Harst in San Antonio.

Chesley said he preferred Austin talent.

I suggested checking out the reggae-playing Lotions or punk rocker Joe "King" Carrasco.

7

Duke's Royal Coach

In the fall of '79, I stood with Chesley and Frances outside the punk venue, Duke's Royal Coach Inn, housed in the building of the former Vulcan Gas Company. They were there to see Joe "King" Carrasco and the Crowns. Joe King's roots were in the Tex-Mex jazz band, El Molino, that played regularly at Raul's in the days when it booked only Latino.

But in came the punks.

That explosion of punk music taking over his favorite club directly influenced Joe King. With new band, the Crowns, he again played on the Raul's stage.

The Crowns were not true punk or a garage band. Their performance was polished and used punk theatrics with their Tex-Mex-flavored, New Wave pop. He called it Border Wave.

Joe had adopted his Carrasco name from a modern Texas outlaw and when on stage he would don a crown *a la* Clifton Chenier and excite the crowd with James Brown knee-drops. The quartet's dynamite sets got everyone jumping and slam dancing as Joe King danced wildly across tabletops.

I knew ZZ Top's Billy Gibbons was hot on the Crowns but also knew ZZ manager Bill Ham was not.

After the first Joe King set, Frances, Chesley, and I lingered where I'd stood a decade before with a crowd of hippies waiting for the 13th Floor Elevators. Now there were punks.

Chesley said, "He's impressive, but not the kind of act we're looking for. Novelty act, too flashy."

They left before the second set.

At Duke's Royal Coach Inn, that night in 1979, I chatted with Joe Nick Patoski. He had picked up in Austin where Chet Flippo left off and had become a Texas music writer. The young man was appointed music editor for *Texas Monthly* magazine and years later became a highly regarded author of Texas musician biographies.

I learned that night Joe Nick had decided to manage Joe King. The two Joes were firming a deal. I told him I believed in the marketability of the band's pop melodies and Carrasco's visually dynamic stage act.

There was no argument that Joe King Carrasco was in good hands. I well knew what *Rolling Stone* writer Jon Landau had done for the career of Bruce Springsteen.

So to me, it wasn't a surprise when this unique Austin band and its Border Wave music got positive national reviews. Over the next 20 years, Joe King recorded nine albums for major record companies such as Hannibal, MCA, Stiff (Elvis Costello's label), and Big Beat.

Texas college kids made Joe King's song "Party Weekend" their new anthem. Billy Gibbons had financed the recording.

* * *

FIFTEEN YEARS LATER, Joe Nick Patoski became involved in one of the many estate controversies following Stevie Ray Vaughan's death.

August of 1990, Stevie's after-concert helicopter smashed into a fog-shrouded Wisconsin mountainside. Everyone who had ever been involved with the guitarist's carrier attended his funeral in Dallas. Fellow musicians such as Stevie Wonder, Billy Gibbons, Eric Clapton, Jackson Browne, and Nile Rodgers paid their respects. Frances and Chesley attended, likewise Charles Comer, Alex Hodges, and of course Tommy and Chris; those six were the nucleus of the team that launched the guitarist into stardom.

In the weeks following the funeral, things went sour. Most frequently reported was the haste of Jimmie Vaughan to evict Stevie's female partner from the guitarist's home in Dallas. Everyone knew that Stevie adored and loved Janna Lapidus, so these hostile actions were confusing. Perhaps Jimmie was afraid she would lay claim to the property.

His next project was to quickly assemble a collection of Stevie and Double Trouble outtakes from the past five years. Columbia records called it *The Sky is Crying* and in 1991 it sold two million copies.

Two years later French Smith, the godfather of Austin event promoters—Pecan Street Festival, T-Birds Riverfest, Freedom Fest at Zilker Park, Bat Fest—with other like-minded people decided to raise money for sculpting and casting a full-size bronze statue of Stevie Ray Vaughan with his guitar. City of Austin management didn't want this privately funded memorial placed in a public park and the Council had to be lobbied to override the Parks Department staff.

The statue was finally unveiled in late 1993 at a ceremony on the shores of Lady Bird Lake. That's when I learned the bad blood from that 1986 breakup of Stevie and Classic Management still flowed. It turned out Frances Carr was not formally invited to participate at the event until several music professionals found out and expressed their outrage.

At that same time, Joe Nick Patoski and Bill Crawford were doing extensive research and writing their acclaimed biography, *Caught in the Crossfire*. The writers were perplexed when the Vaughan family refused to cooperate with them. Jimmie Vaughan went so far as to try convincing Little, Brown and Company to drop this "unauthorized" biography for another book, one approved by him.

In the end, Joe Nick survived the Stevie-estate crossfire to lift his pen and write again. He authored two more definitive Texas music bio tomes, *Selena: Como la Flor* and *Willie Nelson: An Epic Life*.

8

David Bowie Left Hanging in the Moonlight

Frances and Chesley's startup, Classic Management, agreed to manage Stevie Vaughan in 1980. This was shortly after Chris Layton signed on as drummer. The band sounded good.

However, at the start of 1981, when Tommy Shannon added his bass line to the group, my belief in their success went up several notches. I was surprised when Stevie selected Chris Layton from progressive country band Greezy Wheels. But it was a tasty move and inserted a touch of jazz into Stevie's rhythm.

Stevie played Texas blues, which is a jazzy form of blues, as is progressive country for country music. Shannon, however, was a seasoned blues-rocker. I remembered his solid bass licks from the early trio days of Johnny Winter.

The only Austin bass player on par with Tommy Shannon was Keith Ferguson, a southpaw founder of the Fabulous Thunderbirds. Keith, a few years before Shannon, had also backed Johnny Winter. So with the addition of Shannon to his rhythm section, the SRV trio was tightened up and ready for the big time.

Chesley and I met for dinner at the Mad Dog and Beans restaurant across from the Pecan Street Studio where I was doing a project. After the meal, I gave him a tour of the Pecan facility and then walked a few steps to the Alamo Hotel Lounge at 6th and Guadalupe. Butch Hancock was playing.

From across their hundred-year-old mahogany bar, I ordered Shiner Bock. Chesley was off alcohol and drank another coffee.

With intensity he looked at me sipping my beer. "I can tell you this. Stevie Vaughan has a lot of potential. He represents quality musicianship and the right kind of music people like his work. Why don't you come to the Downs?"

Classic Management had by then represented Stevie for a year.

"What could I do?"

"I'm traveling and Frances is traveling. It's only going to get busier. We need another trustworthy person at the Downs while we're gone. You handle the marketing for Manor Downs and help me build Stevie and the management company."

"I have my own projects."

"You can work on them from the Downs."

A year passed. At Jerry Wexler's encouragement, Frances sent Chesley and the band to Switzerland and the Montreux Jazz Festival, where Stevie was introduced to David Bowie. He also met Jackson Browne, who offered a free recording studio. But still no record company deal.

Again, more top-notch music industry press.

I learned David Bowie hired Stevie to play the lead guitar licks for most of the songs on his next album.

Magic had struck!

Let's Dance became Bowie's first multiplatinum album. Eleven million copies! Produced by genius hit-maker Nile Rodgers, its three charting singles featured Bowie's haunting voice enhanced by the perfection of Stevie's crackling blues-inspired riffs. It was the song "China Girl," written by Iggy Pop and David Bowie, that created the initial SRV mystique. His guitar's commanding presence on a hit song associated with two mega-star, one-of-a-kind artists was his perfect introduction to uber-hip urban rock fans.

This blues-guitar wizard from Texas instantly spell-bound the faithful Ziggy Stardust cult that had followed the Thin White Duke through his many transforma-tions. They had already been primed by the buzz created over Mick Jagger asking Stevie to play at the Danceteria for a private Rolling Stones' party.

Important music press. A megastar's glitter can rub off to stick on other artists.

This Stones meeting was no accident. Chesley had orchestrated it. In point of fact, Mick Jagger even visited the Downs with his lover, Jerry Hall, and they stayed with Frances. Jerry, whose grandpa had been a Texas Ranger, was born in Gonzales and for a while boarded horses at Manor Downs. After two decades and four children, she and Mick called it quits. Later the fashion model wedded media billionaire Rupert Murdoch.

The fall of 1982, I visited Chesley in his track office and heard him finalizing three days of L.A. studio time with his friend Jackson Browne. The hope was this session would be the master recording for Stevie's first album.

Five months later, when *Let's Dance* had skyrocketed up the Top 100 charts, Bowie called and invited Stevie to be his featured guitarist on the eagerly anticipated Serious Moonlight Tour. It would be seven months on the road with 96 performances in front of 2 million or more fans. Rehearsals would be at Las Colinas near Dallas.

Wow. Stevie could visit his parents and hang with old friends Doyle Bramhall and Marc Benno.

He accepted. Here was the big time. Austin boxing trainer Richard Lord was brought in to teach Bowie some ring moves.

Weeks passed and one day I was sitting at my desk in the Musgrave-Roberts office when I got a strange call.

Chesley's gruff voice was shaking. "Stevie has just quit Bowie."

Through the phone came his labored breathing. I'd been told he suffered from asthma.

"What do you mean... 'quit'?"

"Quit the tour. Moonlight Tour is leaving for Brussels and Junior gets it in his head to back out."

"But he rehearsed."

"Stevie wants Bowie to let Double Trouble open for the entire tour. He wants more money. Bowie told me he couldn't do it, and Stevie says, 'Tell Bowie I quit.'"

"Sounds like attempted blackmail... and too much you-know-what."

"Always."

"Could be a breach of contract."

"Comer says Bowie has already found a new lead guitar player and plans to announce he fired Stevie to get a better musician."

"That's awful."

"It'll ruin his career. Comer and I are going to work this out. Any ideas?"

"I don't know, maybe, uh, Stevie gives up worldwide fame rather than leave bandmates behind... or something like that."

"Comer says if we don't beat Bowie to the punch, Junior is history."

The men worked on the story all night and before the daybreak, Charles Comer delivered their press release to New York media. It claimed Stevie had called David Bowie a cheapskate and quit his Serious Moonlight Tour. Stevie accused Bowie of paying his band members unfairly low wages.

A great chess move. Chesley and Comer had created a working-class hero myth. It sounded believable and caught the fancy of showbiz columnists. The story had people laughing while learning the name of that distinctive guitarist on "China Girl."

Bowie tried to counter by saying he let Stevie go because of drug use. Too late. Comer had commandeered a disaster into a publicity breakthrough. The guys had a PR victory.

I often wonder: if Stevie had been drug-free, would he have walked off the job?

It was Nile Rodgers who produced Stevie Ray Vaughan's international debut on David Bowie's *Let's Dance* album. Seven years later, Nile Rodgers returned and produced *Family Style*, Stevie's final album.

9

John Hammond and the Rolling Stones

Chesley had selected Alex Hodges of the Empire Agency to book Stevie's tours. Alex was perfect. He had booked major talent into Austin since Armadillo days and once represented the defining southern rock bands: the Allman Brothers and Lynyrd Skynyrd. He also booked crossover artists such as Charlie Daniels and Hank Williams, Jr.

Here was an ideal match, because Stevie and Double Trouble essentially focused on authentic southern blues-rock, accented with a taste of Texas. They could play many of the same venues and markets that had established Alex Hodges in the business.

In late 1982, after the band's Jackson Browne session, I got a call on my office phone. It was Chesley.

There was a calm excitement in his Irish voice. "My friend, John Hammond, is retiring from CBS Columbia. He's going to be their talent consultant. Hammond told me he wants his first project to be Stevie Ray Vaughan."

"Wow!"

That was when I decided on going to Manor Downs. I sensed a once-in-a-lifetime opportunity.

* * *

CLASSIC MANAGEMENT itself attracted me as much as Stevie's music. The company was not interested in just managing bands. Frances and Chesley wanted to build international stars.

They were off to a good start. In a world full of excellent unknown electric rock guitarists, Classic Management had made one man stand out from the crowd. Now, the wild Irishman had connected their Austin guitar slinger with his star-maker friend, John Hammond.

John Hammond had discovered Billie Holiday, Count Basie, Pete Seeger, Bob Dylan, Leonard Cohen, and Bruce Springsteen for Columbia Records. He even maintained a loose tie with Austin, having in 1935 discovered Austin-born jazz pianist Teddy Wilson.

Here was the most prestigious of living producers at a significant moment in his already historic career. He was leaving CBS. His payback from industry colleagues would never be more acknowledged than right now. What an incredible honor to be the first musician produced independently by the great John Hammond.

The man was seventy-two years old and Stevie might be his last significant find. It was. Hammond died four years later.

Gregg Geller, head of A&R for Epic Records, trusted Hammond's ear and committed his company to market a blues-rock record in an era dominated by new wave bands. Bill Bennett was an outstanding promotion man and Epic put him in charge of getting play on album rock stations.

Bennett was wholly committed to breaking the unknown Texas guitarist into the national scene. Classic and Stevie were in good hands.

It all sounds gutsy. However, keep in mind, ZZ Top was never more popular than during the SRV era.

* * *

I REMEMBER that day in early 1970 when Bill Ham stepped into my KTSA office and took me by surprise.

"Woody, I'm leaving the record business to manage ZZ Top."

"Bill, that's one hell of a chance to take. You have a good job and a wife. You might have a family."

Bill Ham always paused for emphasis; he was looking me in the eye. "I'd rather be working directly with musicians and not just promoting their records."

Ham was a musician himself; a decade before, he had sung for Nashville-based Dot Records, then hot with Pat Boone. As for ZZ Top's blues-rock, Johnny Winter of Houston also started his notable career with a trio and that led to seven albums for Columbia Records. This could work in Ham's favor when marketing their sound. In California the popular Steve Miller Blues Band had skirted with the genre, and Canned Heat was earning gold records playing boogie. Still...

He grinned. "My new company is Lone Wolf Management."

Bill Ham's employer H. W. "Pappy" Daily was a major record distributor and handled London Records. The man was also a music publisher, promoter and producer. He set the example Bill Ham would follow in his own career. Pappy financed *ZZ Top's First Album*.

When Ham brought it by KTSA, he told me ZZ was unhappy because he wouldn't let them play in Houston. "I don't want them categorized as a local band."

It could be said, Ham's first major achievement was getting his band signed to the Daily-distributed London Records where they would be in good company: the Rolling Stones. Then an important early stage image building event happened when Bill Ham negotiated ZZ Top to open for the Stones in Hawaii, at the height of the British rockers' popularity.

Finally came their first hit song. The band used a John Lee Hooker boogie rhythm as a hook to salute the hookers in the Best Little Whorehouse in Texas. "La Grange." And yes, this author in his Bellaire High School rite of passage did visit the notorious Chicken Ranch, founded in 1905. Five of us from the football team had a hand-drawn map that led us to Madam Milton's raised wooden buildings a short drive past the railroad tracks, three dollars a toss.

In his early management days, Bill Ham continued to work ZZ's records himself, by phone or visiting the key stores and radio stations. Five years and five albums went by when, during a 1979 San Antonio after-show party in the Hilton Placido Del Rio, Bill Ham said, "Woody, I've decided to leave London Records. 'La Grange' should have made Top 10." He was right. That record shot up the charts marked by red bullets, like a smash, but it peaked at 41. How could that be? Two albums later ZZ did get a hit with "Tush" making #20, but Ham knew it also should have gone Top 10. So Bill Ham moved ZZ Top to Warner Bros. Records.

The astute manager had shrewdly arranged for the band to own their recordings. That meant the London catalog of ZZ Top master tapes went along with them to WB. He was emulating Stones' manager Andrew Long Oldham, who, by owning their London masters, controlled

the Stones' destiny. Oldham himself had emulated Phil
Spector's path to financial success through product
ownership and publishing control. Ham also set up a
publishing company to manage the ZZ songs, Hamstein
Music. During the 1990s, his company expanded beyond
that Little Ol' Band From Texas to publish the majority
of Nashville's country music hits and made another cool
million for Bill Ham.

* * *

BUT IN 1983 and 1985, as Stevie and Double Trouble
was being launched, ZZ Top had their all-time best-
selling albums: *Eliminator* and *Afterburner*. Their 1983
Eliminator achieved diamond status, 10X-platinum!
More copies of this album were sold worldwide than the
entire catalog sales of Stevie Ray Vaughan and Double
Trouble.

Also in 1984 and '85 ZZ had their only Top 10 singles,
"Legs" and "Sleeping Bag." These hot Texas blues-rock
trios were driving each other's record sales.

Stevie Ray Vaughan tilted his guitar toward blues
roots while Billy Gibbons' blues licks embraced pop hits.
Big money investments from Warner Bros. and Epic
Records, promoting their bands, created the expanded
blues-rock market of the 1980s.

10

Deep Blue Roots

It is easy to hear, starting back in the '50s, the heavy influence of Texas blues-structured music on pop singers, beginning with the Slades, Sunny Ozuna, Doug Sahm, Roy Head, Janis Joplin, Roky Erickson, and Johnny Winter. White musicians then had to seek out that sound across town in black neighborhood clubs and hunt for it on AM radio.

Austin listeners in the afternoon heard black deejay Tony Von—"T.V. on the radio"—out of Taylor on KTAE 1260-AM, while in the nighttime hours it was Lavada Durst at KVET AM playing lesser-known rhythm-and-blues artists such as Wee Willie Wayne, first recorded in Houston.

In San Antonio, the black music came from Scratch Phillips on KCOR and white deejay Joe Anthony at KMAC. By the time doo-wop quintet, the Slades, hit it big in 1958, hometown pianists Robert Shaw had been playing on the Santa Fe circuit for decades, and Grey Ghost—the Thelonious Monk of Barrelhouse—had already become a Texas legend.

In 1963, the great American folklorist, Mack McCormick from Houston, recorded Shaw in Austin. This recording from Arhoolie Records was entitled *Texas*

Barrelhouse Piano. That label would later release Bill Neely's twenty-song country blues album, *Texas Law and Justice.* Smithsonian Folkways released an abbreviated twelve-song version of that album in 1974 and called it *Blackland Farm Boy.* Neely is considered the dean of Austin singer-songwriters and was a close friend of Texas rural blues songster Mance Lipscomb from Navasota, featured on Arhoolie's first album.

11

Stevie at Dirty's

At the end of the 1970s, my trips from San Antonio to Austin were only for special events such as the closing of the original Antone's on 6th Street and the original Soap Creek Saloon on Bee Caves Road and the beloved Armadillo World Headquarters. All three historic clubs were run off by high-dollar real estate deals.

I made the eighty-mile drive to Austin for 'Dillo performances by Sun Ra and his Arkestra, Talking Heads, Tubes, Parliament-Funkadelic, and—can you imagine—stadium-rockers Van Halen with lead guitar Eddie Van Halen jamming in a sold-out hall of 1,500 Texas hell raisers?

It was like a private party. One of the rare treats at Armadillo was seeing the foremost arena bands close up: Journey, Lynyrd Skynyrd, AC/DC, Bruce Springsteen, Rush, Police, Ted Nugent, Bad Company...

On the other end of the musical spectrum from blues and rock, a special delight for the ears is hearing the jazz saxophone of Phil Woods. Hank Alrich and his Onion Audio studio oversaw the recording of two Phil Woods Quartet concerts with Fletcher Clark mixing directly to a Studer two-track. From those performances Woods released two albums, *Live!* and *More Live,* and received a Grammy for Best Instrumental Jazz Performance, Individual or Group. Hank told me the cost of recording those sessions was a whopping $232. A beautiful compliment to Hank and his recording engineers.

Over a six-year period, Woods' alto-sax-led group won two more such Grammys. All three awards were for live recordings, two from his Austin gigs. This put Armadillo World Headquarters in the company of iconic jazz clubs such as Showboat in Baltimore and Village Vanguard in Greenwich Village.

The Phil Woods Quintet and the other nationally distributed albums recorded live at the 'Dillo highlight its unique musical diversity: Freddie King (twice), Commander Cody and the Lost Planet Airmen, Frank Zappa and the Mothers of Invention, Sir Douglas Quintet, New Riders of the Purple Sage, and McGuinn, Clark & Hillman taken from a live KUT broadcast.

Come December, I'd make it a point to visit the Armadillo Christmas Bazaar managed by Bruce Willenzik. The event was first held at the 'Dillo in 1976 and since has become an Austin tradition, attracting world class artisans to offer their wares. More than four decades later, it was still going strong.

In those days, before heading south on the I-35 superslab, I stopped at Dirty Martin's Place, on The Drag since 1926. Perfect for a big order of greasy fries and their famous Kum-Bak burger. Dirty's is considered a historic location, thanks to several generations of burger-hungry UT Exes.

One afternoon I spotted an old friend, Perry Patterson, sitting on a swivel stool at the lunch counter bar.

We first met when he ran the University Y on The

Drag. It had been under attack from the national YMCA for offering yoga classes and letting women participate. The home office considered yoga a non-Christian religion.

I broadcast editorials in support of Perry on KTSA, but the visionary lost his battle and left town. Six years had gone by since he moved to Berkeley. Perry sported a brightly flowered tail-out shirt and sat next to a man wearing a blue head wrap.

"Woody!" He jumped up and gave me a bear hug. Then pointed at the man in the head wrap. "Do you guys know each other?"

It was Stevie Vaughan.

Perry Patterson had married a gal named Patty. Her name alliterated and Perry knew he was lucky to have found her. Turned out, Stevie was living temporarily with the happy couple.

Stevie told me his Triple Threat Review with blues singer Lou Ann Barton had been renamed Double Trouble and now featured sax master Johnny Reno.

Perry said that Stevie had the most distinctive blues-rock guitar sound he ever heard. Played better than Billy Gibbons. He and his wife had put together a modest in-home recording studio. Stevie was staying with them and was recording and listening and re-recording to refine his approach. Perry was hoping soon to open a professional studio, eight-track. "I'll record Stevie free of charge."

It didn't take long to see that Perry Patterson was totally certain of the guitar player's future stardom. That kind of extreme passion took me back to early spring of '76 and a small table in Antone's on 6th Street.

* * *

IT'S MIDNIGHT. Paul Ray and the Cobras are playing "Hideaway" with Stevie and Denny Freeman trading leads. I'm sitting at a table in a half-empty Antone's with Dallas filmmaker Danny Brown and musician Marc Benno. Benno is held in reverence for his *Look Inside the Asylum Choir* album with Leon Russell.

Some music industry folks say Leon Russell—a musical genius known for great session work on hits by Jan and Dean, the Beach Boys, Herb Alpert, the Byrds, and Glen Campbell—modified his distinctive singing style to a more soulful approach while recording *Asylum Choir* with Benno.

Others say Leon's style fully developed while he was bandleader for Joe Cocker's notorious 48-city *Mad Dogs and Englishmen* tour. Two of Leon's songs were featured on that famous tour: "Delta Lady" sung by Cocker and "Superstar" by Rita Coolidge.

When it became obvious that Cocker would have to drop out for a rehab detox, Leon seized the moment. Using several musicians from Joe Cocker's blues-rock band, the album, *Leon Russell and the Shelter People*, targeted the English hit-maker's built-in audience for that particular sound and got FM radio play.

Then in 1972, the hit, "Tight Rope," broke out from his top-selling masterwork, *Carney*. Leon himself became the "Superstar" he and Bonnie Bramlett had written about four years previously.

* * *

MARC BENNO and Stevie Vaughan had long been friends. Along with his drum-playing Dallas mentor,

Doyle Bramhall, Stevie had been in Benno's quintet, the Nightcrawlers.

The Cobras take a break and Stevie joins us at the table. We had once been introduced as part of an after-hours crowd at the One Knite and had met again at Soap Creek. I listen as two old friends trade war stories. I'm greatly taken aback by Stevie's certainty that he will be a big star.

I can still see Stevie leaning intently across the table toward Benno, their eyes locked.

"Marc, I'm going to make it." He says it with the kind of passion expressed by champion prizefighters. "I'm going to be a star. I know I am. I can feel it."

Stevie Vaughan was a true believer.

I don't say anything. His burning proclamation makes me a bit sad. I know Stevie's chances are a million to one.

The star-making ignition spark is an elusive and unpredictable phenomenon. It takes more than an exceptional and unique talent to be a top-grossing and lasting performer.

I list three requirements other than Music and they all start with M:

Management, dedicated and tireless, to build and guide the stardom.

Money—capital investment—to finance tours and buy staying power for the long haul.

Magic - often a talent plays excellent music, has top management, and the money gets spent to keep it going. But you can't administrate or buy the magic, it just happens, or not—most often not.

12

Stevie at Pappy's

On a cold Wednesday night in February 1983, Stevie Ray Vaughan and Double Trouble were in San Antonio at Pappy's.

Driving to the club, I thought about Stevie's career and its progress since hiring, or being selected by, Chesley Millikin. The guitarist had already made significant changes to his sound and image, like adding Tommy Shannon and using a middle name.

Greg Geller at Epic Records said he liked it because of Jerry Lee Lewis, but I liked it because it sounded like Stevie, Rave-on.

He also had evolved into a hat act, a showbiz term used for musicians who perform wearing hats. It's fashionable with country stars and 1970s musicians. Cat Stevens and Chuck Mangione were famous hat acts. George Strait wore a white hat and Clint Black wore a black hat. To the chagrin of photographers, filmmakers and stage lighting teams, hat acts create a shadow cast on their face.

I first saw Stevie playing without a hat. Then one night he wore a beret. Through the years, I saw beret, porkpie, fedora, and eventually he settled on a colorful headscarf, like a biker.

Then in early 1982, Little Steven Van Zandt, lead guitar for Bruce Springsteen's E Street Band, formed his own band. This was a time when nightclub regulars around Austin still used the term "Little Stevie" when referring to Jimmie Vaughan's younger brother. That year Little Steven and the Disciples of Soul released a pretty good album on Capitol Records, *Men Without Women*.

Playing hot licks on a Springsteen album was as hip as playing on a Bowie album. Chesley was relieved when Van Zandt didn't get much radio play or generate any retail sales. But the album's cover showed the Yankee guitar ace wearing a headscarf!

Stevie Vaughan immediately quit wearing one and permanently went to a black, flat-brimmed, Zorro-style hat. Good move for his showbiz image.

Thirty years later, Steven Van Zandt still performed wearing a colorful headscarf.

In the getting-acquainted stage of the Chesley and Stevie relationship, they drove to Corpus Christi to visit C-101 and spend the afternoon with Bruce Baxter, Bill Seale, and me in Bruce's office. Stevie liked the looseness of Frances Carr's big brother, appreciated his knowledge of Texas blues, and was wholly mesmerized by the office's exotic fish tank.

Chesley used the speakerphone that day to call Ronnie Lane and the six of us chatted. Then he tried to reach Rod Stewart but no luck. Chesley wanted to convince Rod to do a benefit for Lane. The man was Rod's bass-playing bandmate in Faces and he suffered from MS. Never happened.

From the first, Chesley searched for a female to share vocals with Stevie. I figured the ideal was a resurrected Janis Joplin playing keyboards. I encouraged a couple of San Antonio women to send audition tapes, but their voices lacked the grit.

In a few months, Chesley gave up and instead encouraged Stevie to experiment with his vocal range and take a few basic singing lessons.

Arriving at Pappy's, I paid my $2 and got a purple smudge on the back of my hand. I went to the bar and ordered a draft Shiner Bock. On the far side of the room, the band played "Rude Mood" to an empty dance floor. I counted 36 seated customers, mostly guys. Ecstatic word of mouth had made Stevie Vaughan a hot property for Austin clubs. Not in San Antonio.

When Double Trouble took a break, Stevie came over to the bar for a visit. I could tell the lack of customers had the musician bummed out. The guitarist looked about the room, shrugged and shook his head. He asked me about Bruce Baxter, who had died in 1981 of liver failure. Did his will really give ten thousand dollars to the Hells Angels for a wake? Yes.

Then I announced, "I'm closing my San Antonio office and going to work out of Manor Downs with Frances and Chesley."

"Hey, that's great." He grinned. "They're good people. Frances is so cool. Did you know Chesley got me with John Hammond? My album will be on Epic."

"Congratulations."

"You oughta see it." He laughed. "My name on the cover in big letters... and there is a painting of me. Like a star."

"If Chesley plays it right, you may be a star."

"I'm getting close. I think it's going to happen."

Band break was over.

Stevie Ray Vaughan and Double Trouble began their midnight set with "Love Struck Baby." Now there were only 27 customers.

Departing, I looked back to see a lone couple on the otherwise vacant dance floor. They were doing the dirty bop.

13

I Meet the Catalyst for the Magic

Greg Geller, the VP of A&R (artist and recording) at Epic Records signed Stevie Ray Vaughan. Chesley himself once had been European promotion director for Epic so he knew how to work the label to the max.

It took me back a dozen years and reminded me of how Bill Ham placed ZZ on a label he had promoted, London Records. Ham, too, had associated his band with the Rolling Stones to further their image. It all fit neatly with my belief that Stevie was next in line for Texas blues-rock stardom. I started going to Manor Downs and staying in Frances' guest room.

My life at Manor Downs went by in a flash, packed with a thousand great memories. Plus a couple of weird ones.

When I first came to the Downs, Frances took me to St. David's Hospital where Chesley was bedridden with asthma. Even while using a breathalyzer, the man was weak but still full of fire.

After we returned to her home, we walked across Hill Lane to the Downs' office, where she picked up her mail and introduced me to the bookkeeper, Edi Johnson. She was a hefty woman standing by a chattering TELEX.

Office fax machines were not yet on the market so all of Classic Management's out of town agreements were verified with a TELEX unit—built like a newsroom tele-type with a keyboard.

We shook hands.

Frances took her mail back home and I had my first visit with the bookkeeper. She motioned me to sit down and pointed to an old wooden chair with high armrests... and a seatbelt?

I laughed and sat down.

Edi leaned forward and, with all seriousness, said, "If I had a dick, I'd be running this place."

Hmm?

From there she explained that horse racing was a man's world and Frances had to have men running the Downs. Fistfights happen, she told me, and collecting back rent on stalls could get rough. Texas horse racing was a man's world.

Until now, I had not heard mention of Edi Johnson from either Chesley or Frances. I learned that she had been the catalyst for the "magic" in my four-M formula to success: Music, Management, Money, and Magic.

Edi had once worked at the Rome Inn and met Stevie through his band's regular gigs at the club. Often the credit for Stevie's career is given to Antone's or Steamboat. But Rome Inn was where his band first became a serious local draw.

It is also where Stevie married his wife, Lenny.

Rome Inn opened in 1978 and for two years took up

where the original Soap Creek Saloon left off. Three nights a week it was a blues-rock party scene: Stevie with his Triple Threat Revue on Sunday, Jimmie Vaughan and the Fabulous Thunderbirds on Monday, then Paul Ray and the Cobras on Tuesday.

C-Boy Parks booked the bands and held court each night after the joint closed. Billy Gibbons was a fan of the scene and on *Degüello*, their first ZZ album for Warner Bros., he paid tribute with a hat tip, "Lowdown in the Street"… "So *roam* on in, it ain't no sin to get low down in the street."

Employed at Manor Downs, Edi knew Chesley was looking for talent and she thought of Stevie. Had Stevie not met Edi Johnson, most likely his astounding career would have never happened.

Then a momentary flash of three-person synchronicity lit a magic spark: the goals of Frances and Chesley… coupled with Stevie's desperate need to be a star. And likely the luck of the Irish played its part in jumpstarting that spark into a roaring blaze.

The initial change in fortunes began one night at the Steamboat 1874 club operated by the beloved Danny Crooks and his sidekick helper, David Cotton. In that 6th Street venue, Edi introduced Stevie and Chesley. It was at the 'Boat where Chesley and Frances first saw Stevie perform, where Chesley and Stevie shook hands, and the guitarist's phenomenal rise to stardom began.

Once Edi said to me, "Frances and Chesley are lucky they got Stevie. He's one of a kind."

"It's equally the other way around. Stevie is the lucky one. Takes more than talent and showmanship. There are a lot of great guitar players in Texas."

"Yeah? Like who?"

"Well, like Chris Holzhous or Jumbo Jimmy Madera in San Antonio. Austin has old-timers whose day has past, like Charlie Prichard and Bill Campbell. Van Wilks is a master. And have you heard Little Charlie Sexton? He is supposed to record some demos with Dylan. Fact is, Little Stevie is really, really lucky you brought him to Frances and Chesley."

It took a few years before Edi agreed with me.

Just as a hit record can die without national promotion, a great musician can die in their hometown without industry connections. Classic Management got SRV in front of the Stones, and Keith Richards, and Bowie. It was Chesley's friend, Jackson Browne, who offered studio time in L.A. He brought John Hammond on board.

Looking back, I have often thought if only Charlie Sexton had been five years older, and if Classic had managed him instead, Sexton would have become an even bigger star than Stevie.

My introduction to the guitar of Little Charlie came on that night when an astounded Doug Sahm and I bar sat at the Austex Lounge on South Congress Avenue. The twelve-year-old guitarist was playing an intermission set and caught our ears. Club owner and under-recognized Austin blues champion Steve Dean served up the cold beer, saying, "This kid's special."

Doug and I agreed.

When I say Charlie Sexton could have been a superstar, it was not because he was a better musician, but one marketable to a broader audience. Here was an excellent guitarist and singer with the showbiz benefits of sexy looks and a sexy name. And he was not heavily into drugs. In time, both Dylan and Bowie recognized his talent, and hired the guitarist to play in their touring bands.

Sadly, the promising teenage Charlie Sexton ended up with the wrong record producer. His 1986 pretty boy, pop-rock album, *Pictures for Pleasure*, for MCA Records was a soulless and over-processed image killer. Its MTV targeted single "Beats so Lonely" made it to #17 and pushed his album to #15 on the *Billboard* charts.

However, national reviewers didn't notice that this sixteen-year-old singer was an exceptional musician. His budding recording career was pinned to Top 40 radio singles and not FM rock. The record company was trying to make the good-looking Charlie Sexton into another Billy Idol. His next and last MCA album tanked.

14

My Office at a Quarter Horse Track

The Manor Downs revenue streams were varied and volatile. Edi Johnson was in charge of monitoring the money. She had a ledger, a pencil, and a crank-handled tabulating machine to record the incomes and expenses of four different companies and issue their payrolls. The woman oversaw event-related contract wages, such as stagehands, jockeys, talent, and security.

There were stall rentals, race entry fees, winning payouts, and audience ticket sales to collect. Beverage and food sales to collect. Facility rentals. It could be terribly confusing, but Edi and her young female assistants kept it under control.

This was quite unlike operating a radio station or even the Armadillo World Headquarters. Logistics were more like managing the early South by Southwest events. Layout was spread wide; we used golf carts to get from one distant location to another. Going from the main office to Classic Management to the stall rental office to the racing office to the box office was quite a trek.

With over one hundred stalls, affable Jim Rix worked

directly with horse owners, trainers, jockeys, and groomsmen; plus he managed the equine aquatherapy pool. Downs foreman Gary Harover was in charge of maintenance. The expensive oval dirt track had to be smoothed daily and watered down during races.

There were trucks and tractors and golf carts that his crew had to keep running. Something always needed repair, for example, the starting gate. One winter a hard, hard freeze burst all water pipes and the essential liquid had to be trucked in for the horses.

Fridays would often find Harover firing up a BBQ pit in the tool barn for an end-of-the-week get-together with beef brisket, pork ribs, six-packs of Lone Star Beer, and a fifth of Crown Royal. I always had my fill and lots of fun.

The racing office housed a track manager and racing secretary with an assistant and staff in charge of writing and filling the various races. They set the distances, the qualifications, and the size of a winner's cash purse.

A video crew recorded every horse race from a high tower. A bar team operated the clubhouse and separate VIP room. A catering food truck would roll in for customers and start cooking. Security moved into position. Box office opened for tickets.

Edi brought in her teenaged daughter and extra office help to process the enormous amount of noncomputerized racing association paperwork along with check writing and the handling of sacks of cash. That was just to run horse races, but didn't cover day-to-day operations or the preparations needed for rodeos, community bake sales, dog shows, live concerts, and especially not for managing a rock star.

The ongoing success of Stevie meant the bookkeeping

for Classic Management grew exponentially. The overload kept Edi working late hours on a regular basis. Now she was on the phone getting equipment rental bids or lining up tour buses and making hotel reservations.

She even arranged for shipping pounds of dry ice with Sam's Bar-B-Que ribs to the guitarist on tour. Then I learned she also helped with his bank account. Edi worked directly with Stevie and his wife, Lenny. It seemed Lenny was *always* running short on cash and Stevie calling from the road asking for help.

Edi did much hand-holding for Classic, going far out of her way to accommodate the increasingly eccentric Vaughan couple's often spontaneous needs. This often necessitated long distance telephone counseling. Edi also helped Frances' younger brother, F. William "Billy" Carr, balance his checkbook. She was a busy woman.

I spent my first week at the Downs sitting behind a desk in Chesley's office and learning about the operations of this combination racetrack, talent management company, concert facility, and community event center. One morning, in talking with Frances while sitting at her round glass kitchen table that served for both casual meals and business discussions, I said, "You need a professional CPA firm handling Stevie's bookkeeping."

Processing my recommendation, Frances raised her coffee cup, took a sip. "What makes you say that, Woody?"

"First, this has nothing to do with the quality of Edi's bookkeeping. I have no way to judge that. This has only to do with rock bands and their managers. Of all the musicians I've known these past twenty-five years, only two stayed with the managers who launched their careers. Elvis Presley and ZZ Top."

I had her attention.

"Look, you and Chesley have seen the breakups. What usually happens?"

Frances smiled. "You tell me."

"Sure. The artist decides management owes them money. They end up in litigation. Management fraud. Band managers accused of stealing from their musicians is a cliché. Even the Grateful Dead went through it, more than once. You need to neutralize that part of the ritual."

"I don't know, Woody. The band likes Edi, and Stevie is our friend. I don't expect to part ways."

"I'm not talking about tomorrow, Frances. I am talking years from now. Having a respected CPA in the courtroom to explain specific ledger entries on your behalf is invaluable."

"I don't know who would do it."

"Peat, Marwick, and Mitchell. They already work for you."

"They don't do that kind of work."

"Last year, Cebe Musgrave and I met with them to discuss movie investments. Their Austin office told us they have started actively looking at film and music opportunities."

To follow up our conversation, I later phoned my acquaintance at Peat, Marwick and explained the SRV project. He was interested. I said nothing is definite, just exploratory and keep it confidential.

He did not. Lesson learned.

The next morning, Edi exploded!

I had gone around her to Peat, Marwick and Mitchell!

My contact had talked with Edi's contact, who handled work for Manor Downs and Frances. My relationship with Edi never recovered. There was no way I could repair the damage.

I told Chesley it might be best if I stayed in San Antonio.

"Listen, Woody, I want you here. Frances wants you here. Don't worry about the Sergeant Major. Just don't tell her anything, nothing, communicate with me."

Bill Seale said, "Hey, there's lots of pressure on the majordomo. Remember, Edi has kids to raise and put through school."

I hadn't known that, but nodded my understanding.

A few months later, the Classic contract with Stevie expired and everyone continued with just a handshake. After all, they were good friends and it was the Austin way of displaying trust and camaraderie.

The resignation of Cutter Brandenberg, the person in charge of road management and getting the band to and from gigs, however, caused me to become concerned.

Why? Because the man had been close to the guitar wizard since the mid-1970s. He'd been down a lot of roads with Stevie.

Not a good sign, especially since everything else seemed to be putting Stevie on the verge of stardom and big money.

15

Inside the Downs

My drive from a wooded home in rural East Austin to my Downs office passed Decker Lake on FM 973. On both sides of the highway approaching the town of Manor, I'd see cotton fields. That impressed this city boy. I stopped to pick some fluffy bolls, which I still have, but those old fields today are neighborhoods.

Sam Cutler built Manor Downs on a modest budget and he created a rustic western setting of cedar planks with buildings painted green and trimmed in white. Texana picturesque. Bill Seale claimed that since Cutler was an Englishman, the rodeo arena and the racetrack turned out a bit too small. I think he was right.

Tracks are complex, with layers of clays and sands of various densities. They are crafted like a work of fine art. The base layer here was excavated from a quarry next to where I lived on Gilbert Road. When Cutler found Indian spear points and choppers in the clay, he flew in Chief Rolling Thunder to exorcise and bless the track.

Took me a while to understand the strange pecking order that had evolved from the era of Sam Cutler at Manor Downs. My first day in the office, Gary Harover, the lumbering foreman who formerly road managed the New Riders of the Purple Sage, sneered, "Chesley's assistant. Ha!"

What is that about? I wondered.

The Downs' receptionist, Sheri Carroll, lived with Harover. She greeted everyone, distributed the daily mail, answered the telephone switchboard, and checked the Code-A-Phone for messages. A wide smile made her the favorite with all the guys. I had met Sheri years before at Rod Kennedy's Kerrville Folk Festival. She was then with her singer-songwriter husband, Milton Carroll, who next married country gospel singer Barbara Fairchild.

The working atmosphere at the track was different from anything I'd been around. Everyone belittled everyone else.

It happens at many companies, yet I had been fortunate to miss that experience.

Gary and Sheri lived at the downs and often invited me to dinner. I soon realized the bickering was a pressure releaser and everyone knew everyone did it to everyone else. There weren't any real tensions, and so the staff had to create them.

Make no mistake; we all were having fun. No one quit. No one got fired. Everyone at the Downs had the chance to display their own eccentricities a safe distance from civilization and insulated by hundreds of acres of open prairie. Highway 290 was our boundary with the real world.

A good screenwriter could use this rural track with its horsemen, jockeys, rowdy foreman, gruff female bookkeeper, drugged-out rock star, wild Irishman, and young oil heiress boss as the stuff of a top-rated sitcom. Firesign Theater best described our situation when they proclaimed: "We're all bozos on this bus."

During special events, staff infighting vanished. This pseudo-dysfunctional team of professionals immediately pulled together and strove for quality and success. And we stood up for each other in disputes with outsiders.

By 1984 it was obvious the diverse set of events produced by this weird Manor Downs chemistry excelled in comparison with all other Texas entertainment venues. Manor Downs brought acclaim to Austin. This bucolic track in Manor, Texas, had become a world-class quarter horse training facility producing million-dollar champions. Accredited horse races ran both spring and fall. There were annual rodeos.

The staff produced outdoor concerts with artists such as the Allman Brothers, The Kinks, The Chieftains, Charlie Daniels and Cheap Trick. In the clubhouse you might hear Doug Sahm or Gary P. Nunn with his band Sons of the Bunkhouse.

Meanwhile, these racetrack folks lifted Stevie Ray Vaughan into stardom. You could say about Manor Downs what Bill Graham once ballyhooed about the Grateful Dead: "They're not the *best* at what they do; they're the *only* ones who do what they do."

Frances Carr bucked a good ol' boy, time-honored tradition when she mixed, as Chesley put it, "horse racing and rock 'n' roll."

It worked.

To reach Chesley's office, I climbed a steep twisted metal stairway. Watching him work the phones from morning to evening on behalf of Stevie gave me perspective. I liked that Chesley repeated, over and over, he and Frances wanted a class act, not a pop flash. "I'm building an international reputation for a virtuoso guitarist."

Epic was getting exceptional FM rock attention for *Texas Flood*. It was the fourth nationally released blues-rock album out of Austin, following Johnny Winter, the Fabulous Thunderbirds, and Lou Ann Barton.

Lou Ann, Stevie's former bandmate in Triple Threat Review and a founder of Double Trouble, had beaten him to the punch. In 1982 Jerry Wexler and Glenn Frey, whose group, the Eagles, had broken up the previous year, produced *Old Enough* for Asylum Records. Blues aficionados gave Lou Ann Barton great reviews, but no radio play or sales followed.

Texas Flood was a rock album with a pure blues core that let Stevie's playing stand out from the other rock guitar stars heard on FM radio: Page, Beck, Clapton, et al.

It was more than good. It was special.

"Chesley, if you're image-building, we still have time to see if Epic can get a Grammy nomination for Stevie."

"I'll call Greg Geller."

Didn't win a Grammy, but his first album was nominated Best Traditional Blues Recording for its title song "Texas Flood" and Best Rock Instrumental Performance for "Rude Mood," a jazzy shuffle noted for its difficult 264 beats per minute.

I tried to convince Chesley and Stevie that we could get Adult Contemporary radio play off the song "Lenny," a haunting, slow instrumental. Yes, it's five minutes long but you can take a couple minutes out for a short version.

Stevie told me he had written the lovely melody for his wife and named a favorite guitar after her. It seems Lenny had once passed the hat and raised enough cash to buy her man, for his 26th birthday, a 1965 maple-neck Fender Stratocaster with a rosewood fingerboard. Stevie played her special gift for her special tune.

The man was quite the collector of old guitars. Another favorite was a 1963 alder body Stratocaster that once belonged to Christopher Cross. And he liked to show off his customized Charvel maple neck gifted by Billy Gibbons.

"You want to release 'Lenny' for radio stations? A slow instrumental?"

No one believed.

John Hammond was producing the second album, *Couldn't Stand the Weather*. After the band recorded their version of "Tin Pan Alley," he phoned Chesley. "Stevie's just recorded a masterpiece!"

Indeed so, but that masterpiece didn't get the deejays' attention when radio play started. My friends in radio told me their listeners phoned in their stunned reactions after they heard Stevie Ray Vaughan daring to perform Jimi Hendrix's "Voodoo Child (Slight Return)." Right away people compared the original Hendrix track to his track.

My 2-cents worth? Stevie's recording of "Voodoo Child" is brilliant. He played it magnificently, but I had three times seen Jimi Hendrix perform live and once up close. Hendrix's tones were fatter and rounder and deeper. Stevie gave his Texas strings a touch of twang.

Thing is, Stevie Ray Vaughan should not be compared

to anyone, but only taken for himself as a most exceptional talent.

Nevertheless, if I were to compare Stevie's technique, it wouldn't be with Buddy Guy or Albert Collins, but rather with Jimi Hendrix and Freddie King—not only Freddie's interpretive approaches to melody but also his intensity of performance, even down to his facial expressions when the artist was concentrating and lost in musical ecstasy.

Freddie was also a son of Texas. He was born in the charmed town of Gilmer, as were Johnny Mathis and Don Henley of the Eagles. You could always count on finding young Stevie at the Armadillo in time to hear Jim Franklin call out to a packed house, "Are you ready... for Freddie!"

I believe Freddie's 1961 signature tune, "Hide Away," and his 1971 rock anthem, "Going Down," influenced a young Stevie Vaughan's guitar style as much as "Purple Haze." Even Stevie's on-stage costume and persona evoked Hendrix and Freddie, except when he got chatty and talked. But Stevie created a personal and distinctive sound that could hold its own with both guitar masters.

* * *

FINDING SPONSORS to underwrite non-pari-mutuel quarter horse races is next to impossible. I had an idea about bundling all the Texas tracks for a single major client and flew off to an International Events Conference in St. Louis. While there, I introduced myself to writer and polymorphic impresario George Plimpton. His most recent major accomplishment was the spectacular closing night fireworks display for the 1983 Brooklyn

Bridge Centennial.

As we chatted, a man I recognized as Steve Corey approached. Corey was a famous marketer of sports personalities to corporate advertisers and had set up distribution channels for their related merchandise. The man represented tennis megastar John McEnroe.

He looked at George Plimpton. "Today I must have told 30 people I can't handle their client."

An exasperated Corey shaking his head turned a light bulb on in mine. Chesley wanted corporate money for Stevie... maybe this fellow could cross over from sports. Plimpton introduced us.

I said, "Steve, there's another Steve you need to know about."

We talked in his hotel room and I could sense his interest.

He frowned in concentration. "McEnroe is really strong on your boy. Says he's a great talent. I'm interested. Let me think."

I put Corey and Chesley on the phone. Corey flew to Austin and cut a marketing deal.

Stevie was flattered that McEnroe liked him and was excited about meeting the sports superstar, then living with Academy Award-winning actress Tatum O'Neal. The guitarist also wanted to meet the athlete's prestigious circle of Dallas friends. I noticed it was not long before Stevie Ray Vaughan spent a share of his off-the-road time in his hometown.

16

Connally and the Sesquicentennial

Ihad a grand idea for a Texas Sesquicentennial event at Manor Downs. Richest horse race ever held, uplinked by satellite to the world. I had mused about it with George Plimpton in St. Louis and he liked the idea.

"If you pull it together, give me a call. We'll do something spectacular." He gave me his card.

The All-American Futurity at Ruidoso Downs, New Mexico, with its annual purse of $1 million, was the richest in the U.S., and two Manor Downs-trained horses had won it. I came to know former Texas governor and horse owner John Connally, who often showed up for the races with his wife Nelly. I reminded Connally that in 1965 he awarded me with an "Honorary Texan" certificate for raising money to help homeless boys. This was before the Democratic governor changed horses midstream and became a Republican.

It's amazing he served as Secretary of the Navy for John F. Kennedy and then served as U.S. Treasury Secretary for Richard Nixon. He was in the front seat of the limo when Kennedy was assassinated. And he saved the political career of George H. W. Bush. Quite a résumé!

Because of his exceptional background, Connally attracted high-profile investors to finance his partnership with former Texas Lieutenant Governor Ben Barnes. They had commissioned a brand new building to house their venture. I was invited to meet with the former governor in his office.

The plush carpeting in the Barnes-Connally office suites was a peaceful blue. The quiet surroundings made me glad I wore my charcoal-gray pinstripe suit, white shirt, and best silk tie. A beautiful and well-dressed receptionist announced my presence. Soon an equally attractive personal secretary arrived to escort me down a hallway.

What surprised me was how comfortable this posh scene felt. I was as much at ease meeting with John Connally as with Willie Nelson.

The famous politician sat behind his polished oak desk in shirtsleeves and puffed on a long cigar. He was trim and healthy. Photos of Connally with LBJ, JFK, Nixon, Neil Armstrong, Henry Kissinger, George H. W. Bush, and others hung on the walls.

Connally was much interested in the idea of a Great Texas Quarter Horse Race to celebrate the Texas Sesquicentennial. He was one of the movers and shakers who had brought a World's Fair to San Antonio for the city's 250th anniversary.

If we have the budget, we might get George Strait to host, ZZ Top to perform. I imagined Strait and Willie singing a duet, Stevie Ray and Billy Gibbons jamming. Dream big, you never know... Strait and Connally had boarded horses for training in Manor Downs stalls. If we procured an exemption to allow people from around the nation to bet on these races we could donate millions to a worthy cause. Some heavy political wrangling could get the job done. George Plimpton might help.

We stayed in touch, and because of Connally and the fine reputation of Manor Downs, others became interested. Progress was being made.

Then it happened.

After several conversations and helping develop a fund-raising plan, John Connally bowed out. "Woody, believe me, I really like this idea and wanted to help make it happen. But right now, I'm up to my ass in alligators."

I felt downtrodden. Driving back to the office, I was convinced the man had just blown me off in a kindly way. The mega-event was twenty months off, but it was dead. No one else with the influence and connections of the former governor could bring home this ambitious celebration.

John Connally, with his wife Nelly, continued to attend races at Manor Downs. But now he looked like a man carrying a great weight. Texas oil investments were in trouble. It was in the Sesquicentennial year when his bankruptcy hit the front page. Not the kind of event we had been planning.

Then I knew John Connally had not politely brushed me off. The former governor was honest about those alligators.

17

A Homeless Wagon Train

The state was celebrating 150 years of becoming a state. In 1836 Texas won its battle for independence from the new revolutionary government in Mexico. Texian leaders had made their initial land arrangements with Spain and not the rebels who had formed a new government fifteen years earlier. They decided to follow suit and form their own republic.

From Gonzales came the first shout: "Come and Take It!" Then a cry from San Antonio: "Remember the Alamo!"

Texians won their war and the freedom to govern themselves. Nine years later, many who had fought for independence felt betrayed when their government in Houston signed the Republic of Texas over to the government in Washington, D.C.

Oh well, no point crying over spilled beer. Now it was time for a giant 150th birthday party!

On a cold January 2nd, the official 1986 Sesquicentennial wagon train pulled out of Sulphur Springs, just a few miles north of Dallas, on a 3,000-mile journey around the Lone Star State. The send-off for this long train was the largest of the year's many scheduled events. As they plodded south toward Austin, these hardy folks found themselves driving their horse-drawn wagons through an endless series of frigid winter downpours. The rain was heavy and relentless.

When these beat-up wagoneers finally approached the Texas capital, their advance team got caught up in a last-minute dispute over concession rights with the Travis County Exposition Center. The giant wagon train found itself inching west on Highway 290 with no place to stay. The group had traveled 275 miles in the cold and wet to learn they were homeless.

Someone at Café 290 told them about Manor Downs. In desperation they phoned, and I invited them to camp in the field across from the track. Unfortunately, another driving thunderstorm exploded as they approached the city limits of Manor, so the wagons arrived at the Downs to find a 20-acre bog that in normal weather we called a parking lot.

Bravely they rolled into the mud and set up camp like true pioneers. Friendly bunch of folks gratified to find a place to rest. They numbered about 40 or 50 covered wagons, stagecoaches, buckboards, and trail riders.

That Sunday of wagon train weekend, with George Jones' recording of "The Race Is On" playing through the sound system, Manor Downs ran quarter horses. Noted sports announcer Wally Pryor, known at UT as The Voice of the Longhorns, was calling the day's races. Meanwhile, next door in the arena, bull riders and bronc riders competed in the Sherriff's Posse Rodeo. Racing and rodeo winners received cash prizes.

Quarter horses are very Texas. The first registered American Quarter Horse came off the King Ranch and they represent the heart of western lifestyles. The breed, used in a million cowboy movies, was featured in all three events that day at the Downs.

Roping and barrel racing quarter horses are most like the original ranch horse. Same goes for trail riders' horses. But the racehorses are crossbred with thoroughbreds, to where the offspring barely resemble a registered quarter horse. Nevertheless, it does qualify for Quarter Horse Association sanctioned racing.

Three great western lifestyle events happened next to each other. It was a three-ring circus. I expected a big day for concessions and a spiked increase to overall facility gross from the extra tickets sold to folks attending both the races and rodeo.

To my great surprise, the racing people weren't interested in the rodeo. The rodeo people didn't care about the races. Wagon train folks stayed in their camp while people from the racetrack and rodeo didn't visit the historic wagon train. Weird. All those quarter-horse-loving people dressed western style and listened to country hits on KASE 101.7-FM, but they didn't mingle.

Only food attracted all three of the cowboy tribes. They stood in a queue with each other, waiting to order their chicken breast sandwiches, burgers, and BBQ with potato salad, iced tea or lemonade from the Le Beast food trailer. It belonged to big Joe Aronson, the affable tour cook for Willie Nelson and other music notables.

Although shaded picnic tables were nearby, everyone carried the food back to their own event areas. Here was a perfect example of the difference between demographics and psychographics and lifestyles. It showed me the western lifestyle was not just traditional or urban but splintered into subgroups. Not unlike the quarter horses they used for cattle herding, transportation, and racing.

18

A Homeless Farm Aid II

Willie Nelson had reserved UT's Texas Memorial Stadium to use on the Fourth of July, 1986. Not for his now famous Picnic, but for Farm Aid II. It would be the first concert allowed there since the ZZ Top Barndance disaster twelve years before.

Fears of a repeat performance crept into the negotiations and caused arrangements between Farm Aid and UT to break down over insurance and deposits. Then too, no beer could be sold in the stadium.

When I heard top-rated KLBJ 93.7-FM rock jock Jeff Carroll announce that Farm Aid had lost the stadium, right away I called Larry Trader at the Pedernales Golf Club to let Willie know Manor Downs was available. At his recommendation, I phoned event producer Tim O'Connor at the Texas Opry House and said he could bring the show to the Downs.

Tim confirmed Farm Aid II was homeless and in crisis mode. They had already started a frantic search for another location. Trucks full of equipment were heading toward Austin. VH1 was preparing a live national telecast.

In a few hours, Tim called Frances and set up a meeting for Willie. Chesley, who was out of town, flipped out.

Over the phone, he shouted, in his loudest Irish brogue, "Willie's Picnic will *destroy* Manor Downs!"

However, I read from his left-field reaction that Chesley was trying to satisfy his ego's drive to maintain authority. The outdoor event team for the Downs gathered with Willie's team around Frances' dinner table to finalize rental arrangements. The megaconcert was only a few days away.

Next morning, much like the homeless wagon train a few months before, people arrived to appraise the site. We did not have anything like the power grid at UT Stadium and so power had to come from diesel generators.

By afternoon, eighteen-wheelers towing monster generators rolled into the Downs' parking field. Fortunately, it was dry. Two giant Diamond Vision video screens arrived for placement on each side of a massive stage growing in the center of the track. These power-gulping Mitsubishi screens were groundbreaking as visual enhancements for large events years before Sony introduced its competitive Jumbotron.

Soon, endless chugging from dozens of large diesel- and small gasoline-powered generators broke the peaceful rural silence of the Downs. The loud chugging penetrated our wooden office walls so that we found ourselves shouting to communicate.

Stage crews worked feverishly through the night and with sunrise, the VH1 TV trucks ambled down the narrow bumpy road to set up their satellite uplink for live music from Manor, Texas.

And the news media arrived. The Downs was not quite what they expected. No air-conditioned dressing rooms or press box with telephones, no water fountains.

Port-a-cans for toilets. And their booked hotel rooms were miles away in downtown Austin.

Statewide media had picked up on the UT stadium dilemma and were closely following Farm Aid II through its many trials and tribulations. That's when I made a press mistake.

A reporter asked me if we would sell beer at Manor Downs. Alcohol had been an issue during the failed UT stadium negotiations. I said, of course we'll sell beer. Manor Downs will open the biggest bar in Texas.

Oops. Willie had decided not to sell beer.

I was dumbfounded. No beer? Getting a percentage of alcohol sales was a big part of my motivation to have his event at the Downs. It had never entered my mind the Whiskey River man would not allow cold beer on a blazing hot Independence Day. To me this ancient beverage is ultimately a farm product! Why, I count beer as a grain on my food pyramid. Wine is a fruit.

To this day, what stands out as the most incredible part of Farm Aid II was seeing 40,000 Texans enduring hours of blazing shade-free 101-degree heat... with no cold beer.

The diversity in the Farm Aid II artist lineup was spectacular: George Jones shared the stage with Bon Jovi, Julio Iglesias, the Beach Boys, Bonnie Raitt, and Alabama. Of course, Willie's friends John Mellencamp and the forever-young Neil Young were there. Stevie Ray played and that had its awkward moments as his painful break with Classic Management happened just a month before; old friends trying to avoid each other. There would be a rare performance by the Highwaymen, aka Willie, Kristofferson, Waylon, and Johnny Cash.

Backstage was the place to be. That was where the cold beer could be found. But I spent much of my Farm Aid time in the press tent, and with the VH1 staff. They also had beer.

The year before, sister channel MTV had come to town and taped a special: *Austin Avalanche of Rock 'n' Roll*. They returned in 1986 to film *The Cutting Edge* from which IRS Records discovered Timbuk3. Both specials featured Austin's punk, new sincerity, and new wave groups.

Lee Cook's team negotiated the initial MTV arrangements and got local businesses to pitch in and help bring their crews to town. These shows were normally taped in L.A., so going on the road added unbudgeted expenses. Richard Kooris at Third Coast Video donated cameras; the Driskill Hotel and American Airlines offered heavy discounts; Threadgill's and other restaurants donated free food. The shows were a huge success and Austin generated national press as a music center.

Adding to this mid-'80s rush of media attention to our music community, Farm Aid II would be televised via a twelve-hour live special from Manor Downs. That meant VH1 would introduce a dozen Austin bands to its national TV audience.

Farm Aid II backstage security temporarily cleared out the gawkers when a black stretch limo with darkened windows arrived, carrying Jesse Jackson. His bodyguards were dressed like the alien-fighting *Men in*

Black, complete with the shades. Impressive.

Texas Agriculture Commissioner Jim Hightower introduced Jackson to the crowd. A decade later, I consulted Hightower's nationally syndicated talk radio show live from Threadgill's World Headquarters. It was the only talk show with live bumper music, thanks to Grammy-winning pianist Floyd Domino.

Jesse Jackson, a born preacher, took the mic and gave a passionate and eloquent "Save the Small Farmer" speech that brought tears to my eyes. Jesse asserted it was fitting that Farm Aid, a populist farmers' movement, had been started by a Texan. The original National Farmers' Alliance political party grew from a Texas seed planted during the 1876 U.S.A. Centennial. Then in 1892, it took the name United States Populist Party. Jesse Jackson commented on the racial conflict in the U.S. by pointing out that those heartless bankers repossessing family-owned farms were *not* black.

In closing, the former presidential candidate invited the Farm Aid audience to join him in a populist Rainbow Collation of all races and creeds in pursuit of social justice.

Next, it was time for the Grateful Dead. The guys were playing a large outdoor concert in Buffalo, New York, and they would be satellite downlinked to the Diamond Vision screens looming on each side of the revolving stage. The band's audio would be pumped through Farm Aid's two massive speaker stacks. All this was the pinnacle of high tech in 1986.

I went to the track's five-story video control tower we used for recording the races. Six of us passed joints and observed the distant stage from its small balcony. The huge Diamond screens flashed to life.

In Buffalo, Jerry Garcia smiled into the camera, and he actually spoke: "Howdy to our friends at the Downs in Texas."

The crowd whooped out a loud cheer. Everyone was thrilled. Jerry, like Bob Dylan in those days, never spoke between songs.

Though none of us knew it, this would be the last time the Grateful Dead played at Manor Downs.

This Sesquicentennial year was a national turning point for Austin musicians. Everyone in the music community basked in the glow of their newfound notoriety. Stevie Ray Vaughan was a bona fide rock star, and his brother, along with the Fabulous Thunderbirds, surprised everyone with a Top 10 hit. Timbuk3 scored with their Top 20 hit. MTV music television and its spinoff VH1 ran specials that promoted our local scene nationally, and Willie's album, *Red Headed Stranger*, was turned into a movie.

The success of these blues-rock, punkish new wave, and older progressive country artists showed the record companies that Austin's music scene was not a one-trick pony. The following year came the first SXSW festival and conference that would firmly cement the city's reputation for musical diversity.

19

Critically Acclaimed Money-Losing Shows

Not every live music event at the Downs was a financial success, but all were artistically successful productions. Rod Kennedy lost money promoting "Celebrate Austin," which featured the best eclectic local performers. It was the last time I saw Dan Del Santo perform with his World Beat Orchestra, musicians dressed in flowing Africana robes swaying with the beat. Big voice Dan had coined the phrase, "World Beat," on his KUT radio show, but he disappeared into Mexico after a marijuana bust.

And one of the most memorable performances I've ever seen was the renowned Sippie Wallace, then eighty-seven years old, backed by cornet maestro Jim Cullem, Jr., and his Dixieland Jazz Band. Cullem's *Riverwalk Jazz* show out of San Antonio later became a weekly staple for public radio audiences.

Having a top-notch Dixieland band playing behind her meant Sippie never sounded better. Adding to her bluesy performance, a misty drizzle fell as she began her set with Noel Coward's 1925 classic, "Poor Little Rich Girl."

As I stood in that drizzle out front of the paddock stage with Frances, I had to wonder if The Texas

Nightingale was sending a message. A year later Sippie Wallace passed on to a heavenly meetup with her sisters in blues, Ma Rainey and Bessie Smith.

Another phenomenal event that did not pull a crowd was Cowboys for Indians II. It was an acoustic show produced by Wavy Gravy to benefit the Seva Foundation. The famous clown was also raising money for his fabulous nonprofit children's project, Camp Winnarainbow. He arrived two days early and directed the setup of a temporary hogan under the hot Texas sun. As is traditional, its entrance faced east.

Chesley grabbed my shoulder. "Woody, you have to go in with me."

Gary Harover joined us and we crawled inside the sweat lodge to sit in a circle within a dim room where the aroma of sage incense hung thick in the air. I knew Chesley had asthma, and he shouldn't be there. But the man did not want to miss this special ceremony or disappoint his friend Wavy.

They didn't have any ceremonial peyote but a small bowl of magic mushrooms had been set out. We each ate a couple and took draws off the long clay pipe passed around. It held a heady blend of tobacco, marijuana, shredded red willow bark, and shredded arrowroot. Next came rattle-shaking and low chanting in a language I didn't understand.

Crawling out an hour later, we found ourselves covered in sweat and blinded by the sunlight. But everyone felt rejuvenated and glad we'd done it.

Check out Wavy Gravy's talent roster, so fine: David Crosby, Sandy Bull, Ramblin' Jack Elliot, Kris Kristofferson, Max Gail, Ronnie Lane, Timbuk 3, David Lindley, Jerry Jeff Walker, Jimmy Dale Gilmore, Butch Hancock, Peter Rowan, Stephen Stills, and Floyd Westerman.

Austin missed a truly great concert.

20

A Merry Prankster Moves in to Stay

One afternoon at Manor Downs, I was introduced to Ray Donavan Slade. Through the years, I had heard Bruce Baxter, Bill Seale, Sam Cutler, and Chesley mention the name. Slade.

He had returned from prison for a drug infraction and was going to handle beverage sales at the Downs.

In his gruff Irish voice, Chesley said, "Now that Slade's here, he'll never leave."

He was right. Twenty-five years later, Slade still lived in the Orchard House that had once been Chesley's office. And that's where he died, surrounded by loved ones and the music of the Grateful Dead.

Slade was great fun. He always had a smile and bounced in his chair when he told a good story. His thick white mustache made him look distinguished. Like Baxter, Seale, Cutler, and Chesley, he sported a gold skull ring cast by Owsley Stanley III.

I knew Slade had been one of the Grateful Dead's notorious Pleasure Crew but had to ask, "Were you really a Merry Prankster?"

He grinned and opened his wallet. "I still carry my card."

I looked. Sure enough, it was a worn but readable Prankster ID with their slogan "Never Trust A Prankster." That was enough to put me slightly in awe. Tom Wolfe in his *Electric Kool Aid Acid Test* had made Ken Kesey's fun-loving Pranksters an integral part of counterculture lore.

This Prankster always had a twinkle in his eye. High up on the office wall, he thumbtacked a giant poster of the *Saturday Night Live* Coneheads wearing Grateful Dead T-shirts. We laughed a lot.

* * *

MUSICIANS OFTEN dropped by Manor Downs just to say hi or leave a demo. Ramblin' Jack Elliot would park his Winnebago next to the offices. Jack liked to visit Frances, who in her Marin County days had booked his tours.

Ronnie Lane of Small Faces moved to Austin and first stayed with Chesley, and then, until he found a permanent address, he moved to the Downs and lived in a brick ranch-style guest house dubbed the Gatehouse. Doug Sahm stopped and visited with us when motoring by on Highway 290.

I was always glad to see jazz singer-pianist Julie Burrell, born and raised in Manor, and it was a guaranteed hoot when country songwriter, singer, and bandleader Tex Thomas dropped by to share a few jokes. Soul man Junior Medlow and teenage Will Sexton came around to hang in the office.

A couple of years later, MCA released Will's first album, *Will and the Kill*. Joe Ely at Lucky Tomblin's Fire Station Studios in San Marcos produced this classic, which features guest licks by big brother Charlie Sexton and Jimmie Vaughan.

Another office regular was superstar saxophone master Bobby Keys, who grew up playing music with rock royalty. He moved into a secluded house in the center of a pecan grove at the Downs. A house with good vibes.

The home was originally was built for Frances' younger brother, Billy Carr. In crazier party days, we called it the O.D. Corral. Billy moved into the city and ran the kind of open house where you might find Jim Franklin or Townes Van Zandt or Blaze Foley having a smoke by the winter fireplace or enjoying a summer afternoon beer by the pool.

Bobby Keys was born at Lubbock Air Force Base. Age fourteen, the boy played behind Buddy Holly and years later became the sax man for the Rolling Stones.

By coincidence, the Stones' first U.S. charting single was Buddy Holly's "Not Fade Away," a song written in Lubbock for the Crickets. The song forever tied the guys to Texas, as were the Beatles, who chose their name to acknowledge the Crickets. The Beatles, aka the Quarrymen, chose the Crickets' first single, "That'll Be the Day," for their first demo recording.

About that same time, Allan Clark and Graham Nash formed a band they named the Hollies after Buddy. They charted several Top 40 hits, such as "Look Through any Window" and "Bus Stop."

Little ol' Lubbock from West Texas played a seminal role in the birth of rock music.

The rockin' saxophonist first met the Stones in 1964 in San Antonio, during their second-ever U.S. performance when the five guys toured on the strength of a single that had only managed to inch its way into the Top 50 records. The band played an event called "Teen Fair" and I was the program director at KONO so I got a backstage pass.

One afternoon following their poorly attended

concert, the guys in the Joe Freeman Coliseum parking lot had to push their car to get it started! Wish I had taken a photo.

The Stones booked rooms at the El Tropicano Riverwalk not far from the KONO studio. Along with others, I hung out there. Brian Jones was still the bandleader.

Feeling high and very tipsy, I took him at 3 AM to the members-only Navy Club, where Brian was introduced to margaritas and blown away by Latino singer Jimmy Edward. He danced to an extended 1950s oldies-but-goodies medley with a lovely young Latina named Rose. The next day Mick bought John Lennon a two-gun holster set, black leather with silver studs, Lash LaRue style.

After he met the Stones, it was discovered fate had assigned Bobby Keys and Keith Richards the same birthday in the same year, so the guys developed a deep friendship. Check out Keys' outstanding sax solo in the Stones' 1971 smash "Brown Sugar," and three years later for John Lennon's chart-topper, "Whatever Gets You through the Night."

Bobby was part of the Plastic Ono Nuclear Band on that *Walls and Bridges* album. And toured with Joe Cocker. He even played that great honking sax you can hear in Elvis Presley's 1962 hit, "Return to Sender." Bobby Keys had seen it all.

And Wavy Gravy was always a welcome sight in the office. He could be a philosopher or a clown. A week after his Cowboys for Indians fundraiser, I walked past Ray Slade's desk and he pointed. "Have you checked out that cabinet?"

I opened it to find a large brown paper grocery bag. It was full of magic mushrooms!

He grinned, a Merry Prankster grin. "Take as many as you want."

21

Fame Rubs Off

Being associated with Stevie's rise to fame in the Austin music scene of the '80s meant folks from Manor Downs got treated a bit special at local music events, much like the people from Armadillo in its day. Stevie's success, like Willie's success a decade before, benefitted other local musicians by lending credibility to the Austin music scene.

For an obvious example, because Chesley Millikin's connections at CBS had brought Stevie and Epic Records together, his brother's band, The Fabulous Thunderbirds, was also signed to Epic. The band even hired Chesley's old pal, Charles Comer, to be their publicist.

While at Epic, the four guys recorded their only hit. It was harmonica player Kim Wilson's Top 10 song, "Tuff Enuff." Stevie had returned Jimmy's favor. Back when the T-Birds were recording their *Girls Gone Wild* album for Tacoma Records, the label had offered Stevie a deal.

Because Chesley brought CBS a successful blues-rocker from Austin, their doors opened in 1987 for manager Kevin Wommack. Epic's sister label, Columbia, signed his Austin blues-rock trio, Omar and the Howlers, to a contract. Their album, *Hard Times in the Land of Plenty*, struck gold and sold 500,000 copies.

Twenty years later, Wommack managed Los Lonely Boys and signed that Texas blues-influenced trio to a contract with Epic Records. Wommack had lured these San Angelo-raised boys from their homes in Nashville to Austin and recorded the band at Willie Nelson's Pedernales Country Club. He even hired the former organist with Stevie's band, Reese Wynans, to augment their session.

Right out of the box, *Los Lonely Boys* scored double-platinum! It held a sweet tune called "Heaven" that bounced up to #16 on the coveted *Billboard* chart. That record won the Garza brothers a Grammy Award: Best Pop Performance by a Duo or Group with Vocal.

I first met Kevin Wommack in the Armadillo kitchen where he and his twin brother Keith worked. They both sported longer-than-shoulder-length, straight brown hair and really did look alike, especially wearing their white chef's aprons.

Like many 'Dillo employees, they were musicians. The twins would often hang up their aprons and take to the 'Dillo stage as the Wommack Brothers Band. They opened for major touring acts such as Journey and Elvis Costello. Without a doubt, one of Armadillo World Headquarters' greatest contributions to Austin's musicians was its policy of putting local artists on the bill with nationally recognized talent.

Los Lonely Boys aside, it says much good about the character of Kevin Wommack that, decades after his first CBS deal, he was still managing Omar and the Howlers.

22

Storm Warning

There was a peak of elation when Stevie played the prestigious Carnegie Hall. It was a milestone for our down-home Texas guitar player. Austin was proud of their newest star. Local music club goers had watched him mature and blossom. Now they had someone besides Willie to brag about.

The management company had scrambled around for charro outfits, because Stevie wanted Roomful of Blues from Rhode Island, his backup horn section, to wear them. To me, it made the guys look like Mariachis.

For the event, he also booked singer Angela Strehli from San Francisco, pianist Dr. John from New Orleans, second drummer George Rains from Dallas, and big brother Jimmie. Expensive.

Days of rehearsals were scheduled in Austin. One afternoon in Clifford Antone's office, a back room of his Record Shop, I told Stevie he should think about emulating the early Dylan and James Brown concerts, do his first set with the trio, and then with the second set bring out the full-tilt blues band.

Said he'd think about it.

Benny Goodman, aka the "King of Swing," was the first pop recording star to bring a band into the hallowed hall. Critic Bruce Elder said of his 1938 Carnegie Hall concert, "The single most important jazz or popular music concert in history: jazz's coming out party to the world of 'respectable' music."

As he did with Stevie, John Hammond had brought Goodman to CBS. The famed clarinetist later married Hammond's sister, and it was Hammond who encouraged Benny Goodman to hire Austin pianist Teddy Wilson.

With the Carnegie show a few days off, the band held a dress rehearsal in Fort Worth at the Caravan of Dreams. The reviews were raves.

Then came Stevie's big night in the Big Apple. He opened the night with his trio to standing applause, and for the second set brought out the big band. Reviewers said he rocked the joint.

However, some New York friends told me his show was good but much too loud for Carnegie Hall. Amps were jacked up for an arena. Those who attended both events said the Caravan of Dreams was musically the better of his two shows.

Soon the Carnegie elation dissipated. I sensed things had reached a point where something had changed between Classic Management and Stevie Ray Vaughan. Chesley still called him Junior, but now he was saying things like: "Why do I do this? What am I getting out of this?"

I often heard major drug abuse reports from Chesley, and even Edi. One late morning I saw Stevie's classic white tailfin Cadillac parked in Frances' driveway. The band had just completed the Scandinavian tour and she had road managed.

I stopped in and found Stevie bumbling around. He didn't recognize me at first. He had gone almost 24 hours without sleep. Frances was trying to get him to rest in the guest room and not drive while he was incoherent. His face was pale and washed out.

That's when it was apparent to me Stevie would end up in rehab or destroy his health. This musician needed to detox before going back on the road.

Like many great talents before him, Stevie Ray Vaughan became a serious cocaine abuser. He wasn't alone. Lots of media stars and Wall Street brokers have gotten lost in that blizzard. Springsteen, Zappa, and Todd Rundgren finally had to enforce "no coke" rules on tours. The Bolivian Marching Powder had felled many before it ravaged Stevie Vaughan.

Even Willie Nelson once wrestled in the snow. It had infiltrated his crew. By the late '70s, he was known by some in Austin as "Cocaine Willie." He finally added a "no coke" rule and it cost him a couple of roadies.

To my thinking, we Baby Boomers were the crash test dummies for recreational drugs. We matured in an experimental moment of free love and groupies before AIDS, and drug use before crack, Fentanyl, and opioid pills. During that period I saw more lives ruined by the drug police than the drugs.

Some who knew him in the late '70s talk about Stevie messing with heroin. The music business has a history of jazz and blues greats who found themselves addicted.

Austin music circles credited Stevie Vaughan's bride-to-be, Lenora Bailey, with getting him away from the needle, itself addictive. But I doubt Stevie ever used heroin, as then even Lenny could not have stopped him. Stevie's preference was a mix of Crown Royal and nose candy. He could never solve his coke problem without quitting the booze he also craved.

And it was killing him.

In the 1990s, the notorious industrial metal band, Ministry, had a ranch near Austin at Marble Falls. It seemed to me heroin was more present in local music circles at that time and not because there was more of it. I recall alt-rock pop band, Sixteen Deluxe, having to take a break while lead singer, Carrie Clark, dealt with her addiction. It happened during the national promotion for their 1998 Warner Bros. album, *Emits Showers of Sparks*.

You may question why I refer to drug usage in my cultural recounting of Austin's music scene. Well, describing a live music scene without mentioning drugs is like trying to describe Tex-Mex food without mentioning jalapeños.

Al Jourgensen and Ministry in the '90s were uber popular among the cognoscenti, as Lou Reed and the Velvet Underground had been in the late '60s. Ministry's infamous ties to gentleman junkie William S. Burroughs influenced local rock musicians and many rich kids who on their walkabouts decided to check out the H as their path to instant hipness.

Timothy Leary stayed at the ranch with Jourgensen when he made his final Austin trip and spoke to a packed Austin Opera House. During this Austin visit, Dr. Leary made a dark-humor point about drug laws by letting himself get busted at the airport for smoking a Marlboro.

* * *

ONE DAY in early '86, Stevie dropped by when I was visiting Clifford Antone in his office across the street from his nightclub. That venue on Guadalupe remains my favorite Antone's; the perfect listening room for blues; not too big, not too small, not too fancy. It was open sixteen years.

"I'm moving to Dallas," Stevie said.

Dallas? Stevie going back to Dallas would be like Willie returning to Nashville.

With my brain reeling, I mumbled something like, "Lenny will like Dallas."

"Not with Lenny, just me."

That bombshell silenced me.

Then Clifford said, "You have a lot of friends in Austin."

"I won't be that far away," Stevie said. "Maybe I'll keep a place here. But I need my privacy."

Stevie didn't allude to any problems with Classic Management. He seemed rested and lighthearted. The band was getting ready to go back on the road and Chesley was scheduling New Zealand and Australia.

I also knew Stevie did not want to go on an international tour. Fact is, had that Down Under tour not happened Classic Management and SRV might not have parted ways... and Stevie would never have met sixteen-year-old Janna Lapidus.

As talent managers, Frances and Chesley were closer to the personal style of Elvis Presley's Colonel Tom Parker, the Beatles' Brian Epstein, Springsteen's Jon Landau, or ZZ Top's Bill Ham than a corporate approach like the William Morris Agency. Classic Management's style, as I witnessed it, perfectly matched to the initial needs of then-undiscovered-and-broke Stevie.

Chesley used to laugh and say his first job as manager was to bail Junior out of jail from a coke bust, and his first accomplishment was getting permission for the guitarist to perform out of state. Frank Cooksey, future mayor of Austin, achieved both. None of this was cheap, and so his legal bills went on the ledger as a loan to be repaid eventually.

It's a fact: the management team worked every bit as hard as Stevie to launch his career. Those were the days before highly automated ticket sales. They predated cell phones with texting and unlimited calling, before email, social media, search engines, and convenient music file downloads. All business documents were still being keyboarded into IBM Selectric typewriters. Copies were runoff on a Xerox. A Rolodex card file was on every desk. As a matter of fact, when I arrived Manor Downs did not even have an office computer.

Managing a band was an extraordinarily physical endeavor. I witnessed the daily energy that went into maintaining the guitarist's upward momentum while at the same time keeping Manor Downs running. Edi Johnson worked hardest.

Safe to say, at the beginning of Stevie's international recognition, it was the Manor Downs' racing fees and stall rents that provided much of the capital to finance his budding career. An outsider might imagine Chesley simply made a few phone calls and everything fell into place.

Not so. It took expensive years filled with 12-hour days to launch the starship called Stevie Ray Vaughan.

23

Going Down Down Under

The end of Classic Management was abrupt. It was March 1986 and Stevie did not want to tour Australia. Travel would be expensive and the band didn't make as much money on foreign soil. Not to mention, it was a lot harder to score drugs.

Chesley, however, was building a world-class image and he knew the importance of foreign tours. "Remember, we launched your career from Switzerland."

In reality, it was two British superstars who first turned an international spotlight on this unknown Austin guitarist. Jagger and Bowie. Heck, Stevie's manager and his publicist were accent-laden Europeans.

To keep everything smooth on the road, Chesley decided he would travel with the band. He didn't want to be a chaperone, but he was afraid to leave the group unmonitored in Australia.

Big mistake.

The guys all flew off together. Stevie was still negative about the foreign tour, but all in all, their spirits were high. Chesley phoned in reports of great performances... and heavy drinking. There were reports that Chesley, too, was drinking. And of Stevie having long-distance marriage arguments with Lenny.

But the audiences were enthusiastic, and Stevie was headlining a show in Perth.

It was a lovely morning as I walked over from my Downs office to see Frances. She was sitting at her kitchen table with a cup of coffee and when I entered she went to the stove to heat another kettle of water. Her phone rang.

Frances answered brightly. "Hello. Hi, Chesley. What's up?"

In a moment, her mood changed to somber. Her tone lowered as if she was trying to reaffirm bad news. "Are... you sure, Chesley?"

Long pause.

"We'll talk when you get back." Frances hung up and looked at me. "Chesley has just quit Stevie." She lit a Camel.

"After all this work? That's crazy."

"He said he already told Stevie and it is irrevocable. Says he doesn't want to be the manager when Stevie kills himself."

"Oh, my God."

I paused to think.

"Sounds like more of an excuse than a reason. Too much booze down under, not enough pot. Bet in a day or two things will mellow out and he and Stevie will come to their senses, patch it up."

I lost that bet.

* * *

I WAS MIFFED Chesley had quit Stevie without consulting Frances. He didn't have the right to do that.

After all, the incredible effort Frances had contributed to the guitarist's success deserved consideration. She might have wanted to hire another manager. But what was done was done.

Within the week, Chesley and I were in his Orchard House office. He looked at me with tired eyes. "Woody, I had no choice. It had gotten entirely out of hand. Entirely. The cocaine and alcohol are killing him."

"Chesley, lots of people snort cocaine. You do it. Lots of people drink. You've done it."

"I'm telling you, it's out of control! You haven't seen it up close. Look, I watched it happen to Keith Richards and Jerry Garcia. I know when someone is heading for an overdose."

I nodded.

"Plus, the sound of his band is changing."

That I had heard for myself. You could hear it on *Soul to Soul*. When compared to Stevie's first two albums, the record was met with tepid reviews and sales. Fans and industry insiders seemed to share the opinion that it was a drugged-out session and that Stevie played subpar.

I didn't agree. The music was overworked, too much time in the studio, yes. But it was the sound of the band. People wanted more of that clean, sharp trio.

Here was Reese Wynans thickening their sound and clouding Stevie's clean blues licks with a big Hammond organ. Adding a fourth musician was inevitable. But if you listen to Stevie's guitar after Wynans joined, you can hear the change in technique because he no longer had to fill out the rhythm while playing lead.

SRV at heart played his Texas blues authentic Delta-blues-style rhythm guitar while singing; peppered with fill lines and turnarounds and a solo on the bridge...

strumming intermixed with fingerstyle accompaniment. It was integral to the band's clean and distinctive blues-rock niche. But now he could lay back.

I felt Stevie should have waited another year before altering the band's signature sound. Wynans in time lived down to his name and turned out to be a whiner, always complaining about management.

With a sad expression, Chesley looked at me from across his desk, hands folded as a man resigned. "Woody, you know I mean Junior no harm, no ill will. I'm going to suggest Al DeMarino or Alex Hodges manage him. Both have good qualifications, they each helped build him."

Al was in charge of A&R—artists and repertoire—for Epic Records; he guided the process before each album's release. Alex booked Stevie's tours.

"Both sound good," I said. "Al would be more hands-on, more personal. He knows the record business."

"Alex knows the blues-rock market and has ICM behind him with their top entertainment connections. I remember him from the Phil Walden scene in Athens, Georgia; back when Southern rock was hot: Allman Brothers, Wet Willie, Grinderswitch, Marshall Tucker..."

"Yes, yes. But first, I want to get Comer's opinion and make sure he continues with Stevie."

I nodded. Charles Comer had phoned me two days before and wanted to know what the hell was happening? Did Chesley really leave Stevie?

The publicist was a key player and, like Chesley Millikin, a no-nonsense kind of man when it came to business. In a way, he and Alex Hodges were part of Classic Management. From day one, Chesley had called on Comer to guide the SRV press image. He was a rock music publicity veteran who arrived in the New York

City of 1964 as the advance contact on the first U.S.A. tour of the Beatles.

It was a genuine treat hearing these two men scheming on the phone: Chesley putting on his best Irish brogue and Comer emphasizing his newly acquired British-Irish accent. Lots of laughter.

One artist quality this press wizard insisted on was prompt and sober compliance with media assignments. Many times Charles Comer had expressed concern over Stevie's behavior, so I knew it would take some convincing to have him stay on board this drug-laden ship. I doubt that he would have continued without the urging of his old friend Chesley.

Then the other shoe fell.

I felt like a prophet but never said *I told you so.* Stevie and band decided that Classic Management's accounting was faulty. He didn't owe money. They had shortchanged him.

Double Trouble drummer, Chris Layton, in *Rolling Stone* said, in effect, that Frances and Chesley had stolen from the band. None of us at the Downs ever felt right about Whipper after his asinine remark. Classic Management was having the *classic* rock star breakup.

People wondered, how could a talent like Stevie Ray Vaughan be that far in debt? Good question. That he didn't understand his debt astounded me. A thirty-two-year-old man who doesn't know how to read a checkbook? Guess it's possible... after all, Stevie was a high school dropout.

Edi often had several daylong meetings with him. She showed him the red ink indicating he was borrowing to build his career. There would have been several warning flags. Maybe he was too drugged out to see them. Perhaps the musician only cared about his bills after the relationship ended...

Chesley Millikin was accused of wasting money in swanky hotels and expensive restaurants. Crap. The manager of an international star has to stay in the best hotels and take clients to fancy restaurants. Just as Stevie had to tuck a couple of long red feathered plumes in his black hat for the stage act.

After all, show business is an illusionary industry. Everyone puts on the airs. The former manager just bowed his head and muttered, "Junior, Junior, Junior, what are you doing?"

Stevie's wild accusations hurt Frances. This clash between Stevie and Frances signaling the end of their friendship changed the woman. Classic Management no longer seemed worth the effort.

She had worked 16 years in the music business and what a long strange trip it had been. No more artist management for her. No more producing concerts. Parimutuel betting was again coming up for a vote and had a chance of passing.

* * *

IT TOOK a few months for Chesley Millikin to realize Classic Management was forever gone, as was Furlong Productions. He brought two other excellent musicians to Frances but she wasn't interested. Without her enthusiastic partnership, Chesley would not be able to resurrect the energy that had made an international star out of Stevie Vaughan.

Moreover, because of his personal, almost fatherly, management style and the friendship he once shared with "Junior," their breakup had been emotionally damaging. He wouldn't admit it, of course. Too proud for that.

One day, unannounced, Chesley got in his Buick and like Sam Cutler before him, rode off into the sunset. He phoned me from outside El Paso and said he couldn't take being snubbed by Frances anymore. He was moving to California.

We spoke at length and I came to realize he was not coming back. Closing our conversation, I heard his Irish brogue command: "Carry on."

* * *

IT WAS 1987 when Texas finally legalized pari-mutuel horse race betting. The following year I wrote the marketing section of the track's license application and in 1989 Manor Downs became the first horse track in Texas to secure the highly coveted gambling permit. This signaled closure.

Many of us felt a great sadness when the paddock's concert stage was torn down. We knew it was over. Austin's splendid era of Horse Racing and Rock 'n' Roll was now but a memory and, like the Armadillo World Headquarters, was crystallizing into its own special category of pop culture legend.

24

A Manor Downs Eulogy

The Manor Downs racetrack closed in 2010. I was always mystified that Frances Carr didn't get the recognition she deserved. From scratch, Frances created a nationally commended Texas quarter horse racetrack and took it into the world of pari-mutuel thoroughbreds. She held rodeos. Produced major concerts. Managed the rise of a rock star praised worldwide.

But is Frances Carr in the Texas Horse Racing Hall of Fame or embraced by feminists for breaking glass ceilings? Is she in the Rock 'n' Roll Hall of Fame? How about the Austin Music Hall of Fame?

No.

Why?

For one thing, she is modest and never sought recognition. Her management style was so laid back, I never heard the woman raise her voice in anger. Or issue a sharp order... and she managed some of the most difficult-to-handle people in Texas. A cat herder extraordinaire.

That's my salute to Frances Carr Tapp and her dreams for Manor Downs.

25

Starry, Starry Night

Strange how the aging mind associates disparate events. Reading over the memoir I have just written flashed me back to a hot and starry night.

It is August of 1990 and I'm with thousands of people in Zilker Park, the acknowledged heart of Austin. In the blink of an eye, a decade had passed since Frances Carr and Chesley Millikin from out of Manor Downs launched the acclaimed career of Stevie Ray Vaughan. That night, the park is quiet aside from occasional whisperers and sobs of people crying.

The guitar hero is dead.

A thousand candles glow while cigarette lighters flicker and penlight laser beams crisscross the darkness. Mayor Lee Cook said the evening made him mindful of another wake held ten years before in Zilker Park following the death John Lennon—when Stevie himself had come to heal and mourn a fellow musician. Now, unexpectedly, Stevie, too, has left the building... and there will be no encore.

In Closing

Thanks for the memories, everybody. I've been privileged to meet and work alongside dozens of highly unique talented people. Most of us shared the same dream. We thought we could change the world for the better. In the end, at best, maybe we helped change Austin.

Woody

January 2022, Austin, Texas

No Book Is An Island

Robert Stikmanz - asked if I would consider writing an Austin cultural arts memoir. This book is his idea and it was his encouragement that got me started.

Dev Green - the developmental editor who patiently steered me to completion of the first version of the manuscript. Her voice is throughout and she created the excellent subtitle.

Rick Williams - gave me direction before I started writing, and later he did the initial line edit and revision.

Dr. Arron Benfield - read parts of the manuscript while flying cross-country and offered useful suggestions.

Dr. Robert Weisbuch - guided me through multiple revisions of the manuscript and suggested its form as a collection of four short books.

Michael Ambrose - proofreading and suggestions

Dr. Jason Mellard - final proofread

Cynthia J. Stone - provided the final line edit and directed the book's production through publication.

9 781943 658404